Modernity and Subjectivity:

Body, Soul, Spirit

Richard Lectures for 1996

Harvie Ferguson

Modernity and Subjectivity

Body, Soul,

Spirit

University Press of Virginia

Charlottesville

& London

.

THE UNIVERSITY PRESS OF VIRGINIA

© 2000 by the Rector and Visitors of the University of Virginia

All rights reserved

Printed in the United States of America

First published in 2000

∞ The paper used in this publication meets the minimum
requirements of the American National Standard for Information
Sciences—Permanence of Paper for Printed Library Materials,
ANSI Z39.48-1984.

Library of Congress Cataloging-in-Publication Data

Ferguson, Harvie.

Modernity and subjectivity : body, soul, spirit / Harvie Ferguson.

p. cm. — (Richard lectures for 1996)

Includes bibliographical references (p.) and index.

ISBN 0-8139-1965-7 (cloth : acid-free paper) — ISBN 0-8139-1966-5
(paper : acid-free paper)

1. Subjectivity—History. 2. Body, Human (Philosophy)—History.
3. Spirit—History. 4. Soul—History. 5. Philosophy, Modern. I. Title.
II. Richard lectures ; 1996.

B841.6 .F47 2000

190—dc21   99-05551

Contents

Acknowledgments   ix

INTRODUCTION
*The Dynamics of
Modernity*   1

1 · Body   20

2 · Soul   80

3 · Spirit   136

CONCLUSION
*Toward a History of
Modernity*   189

Bibliography   201

Index   215

Acknowledgments

THIS BOOK began life as the Richard Lectures delivered at the University of Virginia in the fall of 1996. It is a pleasure to be able now to acknowledge in a more public way my indebtedness to the members of the Page-Barbour and Richard Lectures Committee for the opportunity and challenge of their kind invitation.

Years of adjustment, sometimes painful, to living and working in Glasgow has made me—when I am there—fiercely critical of its limitations as a city and, more particularly, disillusioned by the shortcomings of its university but—when I am elsewhere—just as fiercely partisan in defense of its urbane sophistication and venerable seat of learning. I have, in other words, become a fan of my adopted home. That is, no doubt, why I approached my visit to Charlottesville with a certain skepticism; universities, I thought, should be located in large cities and their members afforded the protection of anonymity and indifference. Jefferson's idea of an "academical village" struck me as a quaint anachronism. During an exhilarating, and too brief, visit, however, I came to recognize my prejudice for what it was; and I have carried back to Glasgow the inspiring memory of a genuine community of scholars.

I would like to thank all those who participated in the lively discussions that followed and, certainly for me, enhanced the lectures. I would like particularly to thank Jamie Ferreira, Alan Megill, Murray Milner, and Krishan Kumar for their many insightful comments, difficult questions, and, above all, for their warmth and generosity in making my visit so pleasant as well as stimulating. Their response to my lectures was altogether more than I could have hoped for and has resulted in a considerable period of further reflection and revision before presenting them in published form. Though I remain, of course, wholly responsible for both the content and form of the present book, I hope they will find at least some of their ideas, however inadequately, reflected in the following pages.

I would like also to record (if it were possible) my continuing and immeasurable gratitude to Sandra, who, in addition to everything else, bore my nervousness without complaint.

Modernity and Subjectivity:
Body, Soul, Spirit

Introduction

The Dynamics
of Modernity

WHAT IS MODERNITY?

Few concepts have so come to dominate the human sciences, in all the variety of their historical, literary, and cultural offspring, as has that of Modernity. We are invited to regard any aspect of contemporary human reality as a specific aspect of its distinctive and all-embracing presence. *Modern* society, *modern* life, *modern* times, the *modern* world, *modern* science, *modern* art, *modern* music, and so on, are all more or less arbitrary differentiations of the defining common term through which each takes form and becomes meaningful. Yet there is little agreement over the formal definition of this common term, and far less about the presumed reality to which it refers. How can such a promiscuous concept engender the clarity and analytic precision required of a genuine understanding of our experience? Does it not, rather, serve only further to obscure and confuse matters already fertile of bewildering complexity?

There are, certainly, many competing definitions and conceptualizations of "Modernity," "Modernism," and a host of cognate terms. Modernity refers both to the ostensibly neutral discourse that seeks to describe all that is characteristic and distinctive in the human experience of the world that has been formed through a continuous process of development and expansion out of Western Europe since the Renaissance, and to a series of partisan discourses—literary, scientific, and spiritual as well as openly political—through which these distinctive characteristics have been articulated, criticized, defended, and legitimated. Modernity is at once philosophy, history, and ideology. Ironically, the richly polyvalent texture of the term "Modernity" is itself atypical of Modernity as a process of social and cultural differentiation and of the specific discourses that reflect upon this process, both of which tend toward specific, limited, and precise meanings. And it is just this overlooked and paradoxically nonmodern generality that makes the idea of Modernity so significant and controversial. Generously accommodating ambiguities and contradictions, the most general notion of Modernity has been spared the ruthless clarification of scientific conceptualization and, as a result, has remained at the center of contemporary intellectual and political life.

This is not to say that the idea of Modernity is wholly arbitrary or incoherent. Modernity is the culture of modern society (perhaps we should now say specifically of modern Western society) and in its broadest sense refers to the unprecedented forms of human self-understanding that have developed along with, and as aspects of, modern society. And modern society, reflected with subtle variations through explicit and implicit comparison with archaic, ancient, primitive, or premodern society, is traced through these acts of self-conscious reflection to a decisive rupture (variously identified as the discovery of the New World, the Reformation, the Renaissance, the Scientific Revolution, the Enlightenment, industrialization, urbanization . . .), in which were born all its unique characteristics. Modernity, that is to say, defines itself, and does so by self-consciously detaching itself both from nature and from its own prehistory. These quite general characteristics of Modernity, which were already present in the writings of the Italian humanists and came to maturity in the philosophy of Hegel, are expressed in an appropriate way in every discourse that calls itself modern (Habermas 1987). It is, therefore, plausible to suggest that Modernity should be grasped through forms of understanding that are themselves uniquely modern (Blumenberg 1983).

Modernity, thus, has frequently been considered to be the consciousness of the human world as a self-generated and autonomous realm of meaningful experience. Indeed, more than being a specific form of experience, Modernity makes central to its reality the category of experience itself and might justifiably be thought of as the sovereignty of experience. For the modern world there is no higher authority than experience; all issues, ultimately, are referred to its arbitration. Whether it is understood in terms of the senses or of reason, the appeal to experience is the most common expression of the postulate of human autonomy that is foundational to every aspect of Modernity. Equally, that which lies beyond experience ceases to have significance other than as the surviving "illusions" of an earlier epoch.

A fundamental shift has occurred. Where, for the premodern world, human experience was always defined as subordinate to, and dependent upon, a greater, extraempirical reality which it symbolized, Modernity, in its most general form, reverses this relation and identifies the real with the experienced.

For Modernity the human world continually creates itself from itself; it does not rest on some mysterious natural substratum or emanate from some equally mysterious divine principle. Freed from all earlier forms of subjugation, Modernity comes to itself in perpetual inner motion, as a continuous process of restless self-production. Modern reality, in contrast to premodern Western conceptions of the world as a changeless essence of things distributed in a fixed spatial order, reveals itself through continuous movement. Human autonomy, that is to say, is actualized in dynamic self-transformation rather than in the creation of a fixed structure. Modernity is an endless project of human self-realization, and dynamic concepts, therefore, have become central to those intellectual traditions which have sought to understand its world.

Nor, in spite of its variety, is the notion of Modernity necessarily vague. Running through the initially confusing variety of its uses and references is a series of interrelated discourses in which Modernity comes to fullness in terms of characteristic postulates. These distinctive perspectives of, and on, Modernity might be characterized briefly as: first, the postulate of human autonomy linked to a categorical separation of Subject and Object; second, the postulate of creativity grasped in relation to the differentiation of Self and Other; and, third, the postulate of freedom understood in the context of a dialectic of Ego and World. Each discourse finds in modern society a specific defining feature which is taken to be its essence (again atypically so, as Modernity is generally viewed philosophically as a radical rejection of all forms of essentialism) and, consequently, locates the origins of Modernity in a specific rupture from the past in which this defining feature first came to prominence.

Just as significantly, each discourse is organized in terms of a logic of duality. Modernity is stretched between a series of polarities, and many of its peculiarities may be understood at a formal level as aspects of dichotomous classification. The modern, indeed, is characteristically "primitive" in this sense (Lévi-Strauss 1966).

Subject/Object

General characterizations of Modernity as a radical break from the past—implying human autonomy, novelty, and self-movement—have been immensely influential in shaping every field of contemporary human action as well as every aspect of contemporary human thought. Such characterizations, however, gain their meaning only in relation to nonmodern societies and cultures, so that any understanding of experience in terms of Modernity is always liable to provoke a contrary perspective. Do not novelty and autonomy only come into being against a background of continuity with, and dependence upon, the past and its traditions? The notion of Modernity all too easily calls up images of the premodern and reinstates (albeit as an ideal possibility) the very reality it was designed to replace. The most decisive attempts to clarify the character of Modernity, therefore, rather than rely upon general contrasts with nonmodern social and cultural forms, define its reality implicitly through sets of relational terms each of which is uniquely modern. The dynamics of Modernity can then be analyzed internally in terms of the relations among elements that belong exclusively to its world.

The boldest attempt to do this is to be found in the philosophy of René Descartes. His method of universal doubt—an immanent principle of self-movement—might itself be regarded as a specific form of the self-consciousness of Modernity. Doubt is the radical starting point that will found a wholly modern philosophy. And the rigorous practice of doubt reveals, uniquely to be certain, the persistence of the self-awareness upon which the continuous flux of (doubtful) experience is registered. In this certainty the distinction between Subject and Object is established. Subject and Object, thus, are categorical novelties, and their differentiation has remained central to the elaboration of every subsequent notion of Modernity. For Descartes the distinction between Subject and Object becomes logically prior to all others, and it was in terms of the presumed categorical difference between them that the social logic of Modernity was founded. As a general characterization of reality, the Object/Subject relation is specific to Modernity; it is its self-definition and its modality of existence. This distinction is replicated over and over again in the specific practices that mark Modernity as a distinctive way of life: mind and body; use and exchange; appearance and reality, all more or less directly encode the distinction between Subject and Object. Indeed, we might well be tempted to define Modernity as a worldview and a related set of social practices for which the distinction between object and subject is fundamental, as compared to the premodern or the nonmodern, which might be conceived as a worldview and related social practices for which such a distinction has little or no significance. The philosophical issue is crucial just because it involves a recognition that "thought" cannot be detached from experience; that Modernity is a new form of subjectivity as well as a new understanding of the world (Judovitz 1988).

In Descartes's view (the viewpoint of Modernity) everything that exists does so as *res extensa* (space-filling substance) or as *res cogitans* (nonextended substance), usually and somewhat loosely equated with "mind." Both, it should be noted, are defined as substance, and both are characterized in terms of a specific form of motion. Extended substance—what we might loosely call objects, or things, that exist independently of our perceiving them—is a continuous flux of matter in motion, while thinking things are characterized by continuous changes of quality through which a primordial self-presence is disclosed. Subjectivity is distinct from, but inextricably linked to, a specific body and is, therefore, spatially located. Change of position of things in the world can be understood as conforming to a simple underlying law of motion which, whatever the fine detail of Descartes's formulation of the matter, can be treated *in nuce* as a principle of inertia. Similarly, what at first appears to be a chaos of changing subjectivity also corresponds to a simple principle, namely, doubt. Subjectivity—emotions, feelings, intentions, and so on, as well as perceptions and ideas—undergoes a continuous process of erosion and transformation. Its every content perishes at the mere possibility of being other than it is at present, a possibility, it should be added, which is given as an inherent aspect of the content itself. Doubt, we might say, is the inertia of the soul, a subjective principle of motion.

Most commentators, including Descartes's contemporary critics and supporters, have tended to dwell on the difficulties deriving from the presumed difference between *res extensa* and *res cogitans*. Certainly such issues are not to be overlooked. In what sense, for example, can both be thought of as substance, or is the difference Descartes indicates so radical as to rule out any significant commonality? But if that were so, how could the presumed interaction between the two sorts of substance take place? Indeed, the entire development of modern psychology, in the widest sense, has been preoccupied with such matters. But what is important at this point is to emphasize the common "logic" that Descartes applies to both. Not only are both Object and Subject designated as substance, both are characterized in terms of an immanent tendency to change and, furthermore, to change "in a straight line." Inertia and doubt are "rectilinear" in form; Object and Subject persist in ceaseless movement according to the simplest of rules.

Nor is substance of either sort ordered hierarchically according to qualitative distinctions and attributes. Once again we are compelled to understand Descartes's views, and thus the origin of Modernity, in their proper historical context. The notion of substance and the significance of change here gain their full meaning in relation to premodern conceptions of reality as a changeless hylomorphic order. Within such a cosmos substance is not divided between Object and Subject, body and mind; a completely different set of differences orders its structure and distribution in space. Body is not defined simply by extension because space is not a uniform and empty dimensionality; rather, bodies have distinctive characteristics and properties according to their location, so that body and place are inextricably bound together as a qualitatively distinct essence. In fact, body "as such" is a meaningless category for the premodern cosmology. And, consequently, the distinction between body and mind has no fundamental place in its structure (Lovejoy 1960; Gurevich 1985; Haren 1985). Subjectivity is not conceivable as doubt, or even as certainty; it cannot be viewed in terms of the problem of knowledge at all but, rather, takes on the same locational properties as does body. Essences are linked not by an underlying and universal rule of inertia or by general laws of interaction but in terms of a structure of dependency. Each essence owes its existence to a greater being in which it has, in some sense, condescended. Nothing exists "for itself," and the whole is bound together as a "chain of being." There is no fundamental distinction here between space-filling body—which is only that part of reality registered by the human senses—and the, to our view, diffuse fieldlike properties of place with which it is continuous.

Descartes's distinction of bodily and thinking substance, or body and mind, thus becomes possible and, indeed, encodes the emergence of Modernity out of premodern cosmological orders. To view body as independently existing and governed by immanent laws and, equally, to regard subjectivity as driven by doubt that is arrested only when it confronts itself in an act of self-consciousness—all this is unmistakably modern. The distinction between object and subject becomes important just because space is now regarded as everywhere the same, as pure extension, so that the quality of "filling up" space becomes a sufficient definition of the universal properties of body. Extension is the universal and autonomous reality of body, its existence independent of our noticing any specific aspect of an object or thing. Body offers a mute and dumb resistance to our senses; it is impenetrable and indifferent to our look or touch. Body seems to stand over against us as something which cannot be "thought away," and it is in this sense that the "objectivity" of body has been most widely understood.

Descartes's rigorous and philosophically interesting understanding of *res extensa* was rapidly obscured, however, by a variety of empirically significant distinctions embedded in the early development of modern science. The distinction between primary and secondary qualities introduced by Galileo and elaborated by Newton and Locke complicated the picture a good deal. Hardness, impenetrability, and indivisibility, as well as space-filling extension, became viewed as essential characteristics of body (Thackray 1970).

However, from the perspective of the present, what appears to be significant in the notion of the autonomy of body in terms of its "primary qualities" becomes fully meaningful only in the context of the developing autonomy and freedom of the human subject. This is clearly the case in the early emergence, or perhaps we should say anticipation, of Modernity in the Renaissance. Here the idea of the dignity of man required that the human realm be accorded a certain level of independence. The autonomy always recognized in the Christian tradition as the freedom to sin (which meant a negative freedom to bind oneself to nature) was transformed into freedom to move oneself. For the Copernican Revolution—the long-term consequences of the overthrow of the geocentric cosmos in the unification of space and time as empty dimensions (Koyré 1957; Blumenberg 1987)— movement was the natural mode of being. The old distinction between forced (rectilinear) and natural (cosmological) motion was transformed into a notion of the built-in persistence of motion as inertia. Motion was immanent in body in much the same way that purpose or intention "belonged" to an individuated subjectivity. From the point of view of body, Modernity might be viewed as the transformation of human self-understanding (and thus the understanding of nature) from a conception of physical being whose ponderous weight inclined it to rest to one of being whose dignified mass imparted to it an indwelling force of inertia.

This can be understood "objectively," of course, in terms of the transformation of Western society out of communal and organic (feudal) forms of social relationships toward individualized and rational (capitalist) modes of life. The autonomy of nature only became conceivable as a representation of human autonomy, so that the fundamental insight of Modernity can be stated simply in the notion of human self-determination. The human realm is a self-defining domain in the sense that it is not limited by or subordinated to a presumed preexisting and fixed cosmological order. Whatever order is revealed in the human world is the result of human activity itself that, in the event, might have been otherwise.

Although the categorical separation of subject and object is prior to all other modern conceptualizations, two other modes of differentiation have became significant in related but distinctive traditions of Modernity. And, equally, the discourses of Self/Other and Ego/World described particular characteristics of Modernity in terms of concepts that were themselves thoroughly modern.

Self/Other

The Cartesian subject, in addition to being conceived as a generic non-object, was commonly understood as a Self distinguished from the Other (Judovitz 1988). The distinction of object and subject (though not strictly given in this way in the Cartesian or other early modern formulation) came to imply a nonaccidental and individuated interrelation of body and mind. Descartes, indeed, was concerned to avoid the deduction from any conception of bodily individuation that a vacuum was a real possibility and preferred instead to identify the extension of space with the "subtle fluid" of an ether whose presence was identical with the extension of space itself (only body could be extended, so space was coterminous with the extension of the ether). It is worth noting again that premodern notions had favored more or less diffuse and distributed conceptions of reality where neither body nor mind was, so to speak, a crystallized individuality but both were intermingled, rather, as the essential qualities of place. Modernity was characterized, however, by the progressive disentanglement and drawing apart of Object and Subject until they came to confront one another in mutually incompatible Otherness. In the emergence of Modernity, there quickly developed a precise model of the universe in which the correspondence between individuated bodies and equally individuated subjects or minds became compelling. And, at the same time that objectivity became identified with the "outside," subjectivity became one with the "inside," of the human body.

The symmetry of Subject and Object and, more significantly, the growing realization that this distinction was itself wholly internal to the human subject—a division within subjectivity rather than a boundary between an immediately felt self-presence and an alien and impenetrable reality—encouraged a notion of the self as impenetrably "deep." Just as, for Modernity, space was infinite and uniform extension, so the self became an infinite and inexhaustible interiority. As a result, the self—which could not define itself in relation to the nonsubjective (which must remain forever unknown)—could not either define itself through a process of inward inspection which would be indefinite and unending. The real psychological difficulties of any modern conception of the self as interior freedom (in contrast to the exterior necessity of nature) were already clearly stated by Montaigne in his *Essays*. His writings, indeed, remain an enormously rich source of insight into the specific experience of Modernity as a committed and continuing process of self-creation.

If the inner world of the self could never fully disclose its own interiority, it might, nonetheless, establish a stable identity in relation to other discarded forms of subjectivity. In contrast to the dynamic, elusive, and ultimately sovereign Self, the Other was characterized as spatially or temporally outside the community of modern experience. The Other was "old" and exhausted; the Self was "new." The Other was "outside" and beyond civilization (Oriental, primitive, archaic, barbarian . . .); the Self was European (Fabian 1983; Said 1985). But where the dialectic of Subject and Object (founded on self-certainty) promised to replace ignorance with knowledge, the relation of Self and Other (redolent of self-doubt) was a continually shifting boundary between familiarity and strangeness (Kristeva 1991; Ricoeur 1992).

What began as an "encounter" between the Old World (which was in fact full of self-generated novelties) and the New World, in which the Self confirmed itself as modern and rational in comparison to the precivilized, primitive Other, gradually became an internal dialectic in which the Self undermined any possibility of authentication. The Voyage of Discovery became a powerful metaphor for self-investigation of both a physical and a psychological kind (Pagden 1993; Camporesi 1994; Sawday 1995). But the process of self-discovery, rather than revealing the solid foundations of self-certainty, trapped the subject in deepening layers of despair.

And if the self was taken in a more superficial way to be nothing other than an appearance, matters were hardly more satisfactory. The self was familiar rather than definitively known. As novelty, it could never fully anticipate itself and, thus, might appear strange or uncanny even to itself. Ultimately, as in Freud's psychology, the Self becomes estranged and the Other appears familiar. Increasingly, realizing Montaigne's premonition of Modernity, we find reason in the primitive and are more intimate with madness than sanity.

Ego/World

The hierarchical structure of premodern, and particularly feudal, societies was hypostatized as a cosmological plan in which everything was ideally located "in its proper place." Motion, other than the regular circular motion that characterized perfect heavenly bodies, was conceptualized as "unnatural" or "forced." In terms of local displacements of matter, it seemed obvious that all such motion was the outcome of some external and continually acting force. Put simply, it seemed evident that nothing moves unless it is pushed (Koyré 1978). In this scheme of things, nature and society intertwined in a singular chain of being in which the existence of reality at one level was dependent upon a more perfect reality located at a higher and more inclusive level, a hierarchy terminating in necessary Being that was the uncaused cause of all movement and the source of all authority (Gilson 1936; Lovejoy 1936). Socially, as well as naturally, the mass of the people were bound to particular communities and moved from them (for example, in the conduct of war) only as a consequence of the external action of a superior individual.

For Modernity, therefore, Object and Subject were fundamentally united in both expressing the universality and naturalness of rectilinear motion. Not only Descartes but in their own rather different ways writers as diverse as Cervantes and Montaigne are also unambiguously modern in the centrality of motion to their vision of the world. Don Quixote's eccentric journey is a deranged straight line, the madness of uncaused deviations from the propensity for motion to persist. And Montaigne's voluntary retreat from the distractions of society is not a state of rest but a temporary refuge within which was gathered and released in a fresh and more vigorous form the ceaseless inward movement of thought and reflection (Starobinski 1985). The only changeless element in Modernity is the propensity to movement, which becomes, so to speak, its permanent emblem (Spragens 1973).

Modernity, in the sense of the culture and typical forms of human self-understanding that emerged from the collapse of feudalism and developed along with the establishment of market relations, the general production of commodities, the centralization of the state, and the growth of bureaucratic social organizations, may be said to begin with the assertion that the human being ought to possess the freedom and capacity for self-movement. This is a central motif of the Italian Renaissance revival of Platonism, which in many ways anticipated the later development of Modernity in its full sense (Burckhardt 1921). Pico della Mirandolo's oration *On the Dignity of Man* viewed motion as immanent in the human condition, directly reflecting a moral and religious status which, while fallen from a state of grace, was not without hope or the means of self-improvement (Cassirer 1963; Copenhaver and Schmitt 1992). It was inconceivable that the human creature, made in "the image and likeness" of God, should be so deprived of perfection as to inhabit a motionless world in which all change was confined to the superficial transience of generation and decay (Trinkaus 1970).

The Copernican Revolution was inspired by, and extended, Italian humanism into a more general theory of "natural" motion which found its expression not only in new dynamical theories of nature but, equally, in dynamical conceptions of the human individual.

Copernicanism found its logical outcome in the concept of inertia (Koyré 1978; Blumenberg 1987). This development represented a dramatic shift in the perspective and assumptions of premodern traditions. The new view held that "absolute rest," if it is conceivable at all, is nothing but a theoretical limit to the natural condition of rectilinear motion. Again, to put it simply, things move and continue to move until they are acted upon by an external force. It is not movement that is problematical but, rather, interruptions and changes of motion that require explanation. In its turn the concept of inertial motion provided a foundation for two distinctively modern tendencies within psychology. First, as part of the minimal assumptions of a reductionist science for which all reality was conceivable as "matter in motion," it was directly transferred to psychology as the underlying dynamism of the psychic apparatus. And, second, by metaphorical extension inertia played an even larger role as the intention of the human agent.

A more general way of conceptualizing the dynamic aspects of Modernity is found, thus, in terms of a dialectic of Ego and World. Since the Renaissance the World has been construed primarily as a visual image, the "view" recorded by the Ego, which, in some sense, stands apart from it (Edgerton 1991; Panofsky 1991). The activity of the Ego—its self-movement and voluntary changes in orientation—discloses the World from a whole series of such "points of view." Movement, in principle the unrestricted response to some originating subjective inclination, simultaneously differentiates and interrelates the World and the Ego. This reciprocal focus established the individuated subject as a detached and omniscient observer—an Ego. Subjectivity here undergoes a further concretization and specification; no longer merely thinking substance, or civilized humanity, modern subjectivity realizes itself as an active and self-willed individual.

The development of these conceptions of an immanent and autonomous dynamics and the dialectic of Ego and World distinguishes and links together the most important social, cultural, and psychological aspects of Modernity. At the same time, and directly linked to both the discovery of the New World and the rise of the rational sciences, a discourse of novelty arose. Autonomy and dynamism implied continuous self-creation and not just a shifting perspective on a fixed reality. Thus, while dynamics arose as a positive science through which knowledge of nature apparently could be secured, ceaseless inner movement rendered the human subject enigmatic. Endless novelty made the ego a stranger to itself and put self-knowledge beyond the bounds of rational knowledge. Michel de Montaigne already grasped this, the solipsistic character of Modernity, and saw in it the most general source of melancholy, which was the most characteristic of modern feelings (Starobinski 1985).

A notion of self-development, which as "self-fashioning" was equally as central to Renaissance humanism as was Galilean dynamics (Greenblatt 1980), also developed within Modernity as a description of rather different aspects of its inner movement. If human beings were empowered to move themselves, then, for a world not yet wholly liberated from a logic of place, it followed that every movement was simultaneously the expression of a corresponding inner movement of the soul. This movement, continuous and unavoidable, was self-willed rather than inertial and was immanent to the human in a unique way. It was this form of self-movement which was later given a characteristic ethical direction in the notion of *Bildung* as the realization in harmonious action of an implicit and unique selfhood. At the same time notions of growth and development, of a general process of unfolding of natural forms and their realization in mature physiognomic structures, played an important part in the emergence of the Romantic movement in both its literary and scientific aspects (Gusdorf 1985). The dynamics of development and self-development played an important part in modern psychology, again directly in the understanding of the growth of psychic forms and indirectly through the metaphor of desire.

DIVISIONS AND BOUNDARIES

Directly linked to the major issue—how best can Modernity be characterized—and on the assumption that this is in some way bound up with the dualisms outlined above, a related analytic issue arises: what is the nature of this difference, as a difference?

Alterity

The great difficulty is that if Modernity is conceived in terms of the radical estrangement of Object from Subject, then the apparent clarity of the distinction is very quickly obscured by the absoluteness of the boundary that separates them. The world of objects withdrew and became enigmatic; we could no longer participate in their reality; we could do no more than trust in ourselves and assume or hope that the representations of these objects, which seemed continuously and effortlessly to well up from within us as aspects of our own subjectivity, were in some sense authentic representations of the reality from which we had become detached. All experience was not merely subjective in character—experienced, that is, by a subject—but was, so to speak, the experience of subjectivity. Of course it took a long time for these implications to become clear; to a large extent they still present us with difficulties. But in principle we can say that the distinction of Object and Subject means that we know nothing directly of objects, that our world is thoroughly and completely subjective. This, ultimately, is the justification for the "subjective" approach adopted here. The distinction between Object and Subject is unlike the difference, for example, between the left side and right side of a sheet of paper on which we care to draw a straight line. That, true, is a clear categorical distinction; but between Object and Subject is the categorical separation of two realities, not the (ultimately arbitrary) differentiation of a single reality into two mutually exclusive and exhaustive parts. The distinction, thus, is a distinction within and for subjectivity, an alterity of the subject itself. The "not-subjective," that is to say, is itself a subjective representation of an Otherness which cannot be imagined, and can only be the representation of some other aspect of subjectivity itself.

Dreaming

Descartes intuitively grasped the nontransitive character of his fundamental distinction between Object and Subject and presents a very interesting discussion of the abysmal character of subjectivity through an analysis of dreaming. For Descartes the enigma of dreaming (he rightly avoids the casual objectification in referring to a "phenomenon"—the dream) poses fundamental problems for our understanding of the world and of ourselves.

The illusory character of dreams, which is so much more impressive and general than the accidents of waking perceptual error, is seized by Descartes as a stimulus to that metaphysical doubt which is the real starting point of his reflection. For the problem of knowledge, dreams are first of all important as exemplary instances of deception and, retrospectively, arouse the skepticism Descartes wishes to extend to other kinds of perceptions. He declares, thus, to have "resolved to pretend that all the things that had ever entered my mind were no more true than the illusions of my dreams" (Descartes 1985, 127).

Descartes assumes everyone is willing to admit that however unreliable the testimony of our senses, they provide us with some information about the outside world in a way which our dreams never can. But he would like to argue that, contrary to a philosophically naive view, our senses are much more deceptive than is generally assumed: "Every sensory experience I have ever thought I was having while awake I can also think of myself as sometimes having while asleep; and since I do not believe that what I seem to perceive in sleep comes from things located outside me, I did not see why I should be more inclined to believe this of what I think I perceive while awake" (Descartes 1984, 53).

More interestingly, he also argues that by standards that might be applied to sense impressions, our dreams often appear equally as truthful, rather than equally as false. This raises for him the more difficult question of whether or not we can reliably tell whether we are asleep or awake. The deceptiveness of dreams, in other words, goes deeper than at first suspected: "As I think about this more carefully, I see plainly that there are never any sure signs by means of which being awake can be distinguished from being asleep. The result is that I begin to feel dazed, and this very feeling only reinforces the notion that I may be asleep" (Descartes 1984, 13).

Disconcertingly, he suggests just such a criterion—"to feel dazed"—at the very moment of denying its possibility. But this apparent contradiction can be resolved on the assumption that "to feel dazed," while it may be some sort of vague indication of being asleep, can never amount to the "sure sign" that he is seeking. The kind of certainty for which Descartes is searching, and in which he hopes to anchor philosophy, is found exclusively, he contends, in "clear and distinct ideas." This, in fact, presents a new difficulty, because it is in our dreams that we frequently conceive just such clear and distinct ideas, which, by virtue of their clarity and distinctness, ought to be true. Thus, in spite of "feeling dazed," Descartes insists that ideas coming to us in dreams are often "no less lively and distinct" than those we have when awake. It must be remembered, however, that the criteria of "clear and distinct ideas" refers to the Truth, and not the verisimilitude of ideas. It might be said that in dreaming we often experience clear and distinct images but not lucid ideas that, abstracted from sensory images, convince by the clarity of a purely intellectual content.

It now seems that Descartes can unambiguously characterize dreams as internal images devoid of genuinely rational interconnection. At the close of the Sixth Meditation, he reports that as for dreaming and waking, "I now notice that there is a vast difference between the two, in that dreams are never linked by memory with all the other actions of life as waking experiences are" (Descartes 1984, 61).

This seems compelling but does not in the end lay to rest the doubts engendered by his scattered remarks. His various comments have been made from the perspective of someone who believes himself to be awake.

But it is just a characteristic of waking experience that we feel, when awake, that "we cannot doubt whether we are awake or dreaming." The difficulty lies in a fatal asymmetry between the two states. The notion of experience through which these distinct states are joined is by no means the same viewed from the perspective of each. Wakefulness carries with it, as it were, its own warrant of actuality. Thus, while in a wakeful state we may clearly distinguish between, on the one hand, the rational interconnectedness of our own thoughts and their appropriateness to the world around us and, on the other, the disconnected and uncoordinated images of a recollected dream, when we are asleep, nothing strikes us as odd, and the most absurd images may appear perfectly natural and rational. Descartes quotes the example of a man who dreams of a clock striking "one, one, one, one" and sees nothing odd in his reacting with the thought that the mechanism had "gone mad" because it had struck "one" four times, rather than striking "four."

The search for unambiguous criteria of dreaming leads, then, to a more profound metaphysical skepticism; and what began as the most common exemplar of a distinction which might profitably be applied to all thinking ends in a paralysis of doubt: "What if dreaming is a single operation which enables you sometimes to dream that you are dreaming, and at other times to dream that you are thinking while awake?" (Descartes 1984, 335).

The dream, so to speak, contains its own world, its own inner sense of Subject and Object, reality and appearance, being and becoming. To dream is to enter this other world, rather than to experience a specific segment of what, when awake, we imagine to be a singular reality. It is just this radical difference, the separateness and self-sufficiency of the dreamworld, that is productive of so much ambiguity. It is as if in sleep we paradoxically awake to the peculiarities of a reality which has an equal claim on our credulity. The problem of the dream, thus, "is no longer the question of a single consciousness powerless to distinguish between illusion and reality, but of two beings from two different realms" (Caillois 1966, 50).

As all distinctions reemerge within it, the dream itself has no defining opposite. The dream is an inclusive term and exhaustive of its own reality. It is both a world apart and a world to itself, so that "to dream is not another way of experiencing another world, it is for the dreaming subject the radical way of experiencing its own world" (Foucault and Binswanger 1993, 59).

BODY/SOUL/SPIRIT

The difference between Object and Subject, Self and Other, Ego and World, then, is more like the asymmetrical relation between waking and dreaming than it is like the difference between right and left. The fact that we have come conventionally to represent Object and Subject as, respectively, "outside" and "inside" the human body should alert us to the peculiarity of the difference we are drawing. There is no obvious connection between outsides and insides; a closed box might contain anything, whereas the line on an unmarked sheet of paper is an arbitrary division within a uniform medium; things are just the same on one side as the other, the same whiteness, receptivity to ink or pencil, the same flatness, which is, in fact, a continuous surface in relation to which it is only the perspective of the observer that changes.

These conceptual difficulties and ambiguities might readily be multiplied (van Peursen 1966). There is no "place" left outside of the experience of Modernity from which we might analyze its peculiarities and no perspective that reveals to us the "real" boundary of existence and what might lie beyond it. The whole discourse of Modernity, with its insistence on sharp distinctions and clear classification, thus, even before it has properly got going, seems to lose itself in a labyrinth of self-reference.

Such issues cannot easily be clarified; indeed, they cannot easily be stated. But at least part of the difficulty is compounded by a too ready adoption of the language and conceptual apparatus of Modernity as itself the object of study. Thus, rather than embark on a more detailed examination of contemporary human self-understanding in terms of either general notions of Modernity or its encoding in distinction of Object and Subject, its central features might more fully be revealed through the application of an older set of categories that do not depend for their meaning wholly on the constitution of the object of study itself. This, in the end, may not avoid the abyss of solipsism, but it offers at least the prospect of a novel means of falling into it. The specific features of modern subjectivity, of the subjectivity that is Modernity, will be approached, then, by a consideration of Body, Soul, and Spirit. Unlike the dualism, real or imagined, of Object and Subject, Body, Soul, and Spirit are rooted in the prehistory rather than in the history of Modernity. And the character of Modernity thus becomes visible in terms of the transformations wrought in each.

Contemporary debates—still mesmerized by Descartes and, in fact, still coming to terms with the long-range implication of the Copernican Revolution in science and philosophy—are all too often polarized in terms of Object and Subject. As a consequence discussions of the "body" and "mind" and "culture" (late replacements for the categories of soul and spirit that are being invoked here) are forced into an unreal either/or. The approach here is, rather, to draw out and complicate these contemporary oppositions (which are everywhere admitted to be simplistic, outdated, or at the very least equivocal), so that body, for example, is viewed as both subject and object and as neither subject nor object. Similarly, reflecting on the character of soul and spirit dissolves the dualistic structure of Modernity and forces us to conceptualize its essential features in new ways. Only thus, in redrawing the map of contemporary experience and in redescribing its typical forms, can the Procrustean bed be avoided. And in doing so the most characteristic of modern experiences both emerge in terms of their historical peculiarity and uniqueness and yet reveal their continuity with a rich past which the self-founding of Modernity has concealed but not destroyed.

The conceptualization of Modernity as the transformations of Body, Soul, and Spirit carries with it a residue of older meanings which allows for, and indeed requires, a more general historical framework and, thus, reopens issues foreclosed by being understood as the most general form of Subjectivity.

· ONE ·

Body

ALL HISTORY is the history of the body. This seductive paraphrase offers a truism much in need of elaboration. It is true, but its truth, like the body it predicates, is not self-revealing. Whose body? The body of an adult or a child; a man or woman; a European, African, or Oriental; healthy or diseased; loved or unloved . . . ? The list of possible qualifications is endlessly differentiating. And which body? The body as understood by the biologist, the physician, the engineer, the novelist, the advertising executive . . . ? To grasp the historical character of the human body, and the bodily character of history, is an especially urgent and difficult task if a fuller understanding of Modernity is to be gained. Modernity, first of all, required a human body that could be autonomous, self-moving, and conscious of itself. Whether as Subject, Self, or Ego, Modernity was not only a new idea, it was a concept that required embodiment to become fully meaningful; it was, in short, a new way of experiencing the world and human agency.

An obvious starting point, therefore, for a more complete understanding of Modernity should be found in a historical sociology of the human body. A number of the classical works of sociology hint at such a perspective. Karl Marx, for example, viewed the development of Modernity in the context of the transformation of human labor, and Max Weber regarded asceticism as central to its origins. But the corporeal dimension of their writings has hardly been developed in the flood of literature stimulated by their insights. This neglect is due less to the insignificance than to the intransigence of the problems at which they hinted. Indeed, quite apart from the empirical complexity of such a project, the very possibility of a historical sociology of the body is confronted by a double obstacle.

First, the human body appears to us as the most "natural" of objects and, thus, to fall altogether outside of the range of sociological analysis and understanding. We all feel our own bodies as a unique presence in which Nature is effortlessly realized. The body, it seems, constitutes a reality of its own, a reality which appears to us to stand outside of the conventionality of collective life. Overwhelmingly we are aware of our corporeal nature as a given reality, that which we offer or withhold in every action, the vehicle of our volition and pleasure that, even when we admit such actions and feelings partake of a host of variable and perhaps ultimately arbitrary standards of valuation, remains the unaltered natural ground, rather than a fully acculturated aspect or element, of social life.

Second, at the same time and in a quite puzzling and paradoxical fashion, the body, in another sense, becomes for us something transparently malleable and open to new forces of conventionalization. In an era of sex change operations, cosmetic surgery, and the widespread practice of body piercing, the body enters fully into the stream of social life and is defined and transformed not according to the seemingly natural rhythm of growth and maturation but in conformity with the continuously shifting demands of style. The body becomes an addendum to a freely chosen, and freely changing, personal identity—and promptly disappears. The human body loses its specifically given reality and is understood eccentrically in terms of fashion, health, sport, leisure, sexuality, art; anything, that is to say, apart from the corporeal or somatic "as such."

That is to say, either the human body is conceived wholly in terms of Nature and, in its universal givenness, to be of no interest to sociology or history; or the human body is understood exclusively in terms of Culture and, assimilated to a general semiotics, loses its distinctiveness. Oddly, a sociology of the body has emerged at the very moment in which the human reality of the body seems to have diminished in significance or even dissolved into a confusing flux of partial experiences. In fact, we might suppose that the body has become available as a sociological topic only to the extent that it is conceptualized as something other than a living human presence. Thus, in spite of recent influential developments (which in fact owe more to the highly original and important works of Norbert Elias and Michel Foucault than they do to the originating works of modern sociological traditions), a historical understanding of modern forms of embodiment remains to be fully developed and is, perhaps, best approached indirectly through philosophical and scientific movements that are themselves grounded in such images.

ABSENCE AND PRESENCE

Even if Modernity could be construed as a continuous process of differentiation, interrelation, and reconciliation of Object and Subject, it would be altogether too simple to regard Body (and in particular the human body) as Object in contrast to Soul as Subject. Indeed the purpose of reintroducing the tripartite distinction of Body, Soul, and Spirit is primarily to free the work of characterizing Modernity from the temptation of such dualistic thinking. For Modernity the body has become both Object and Subject and, at the same time, neither Object nor Subject; both Self and Other and neither Self nor Other; both Ego and World and neither Ego nor World. The body, it seems, is a living paradox in relation to the entire structure of modern antinomies.

It might fairly be claimed, in fact, that the human body has become celebrated as both the primary site of Modernity and, so to speak, a living key to its interpretation. We need only consider the most obvious facts of bodily experience—and all experience, after all, is bodily experience—to become aware of the true character of modern life and thus escape the illusions of philosophical speculation that ensnared earlier generations of thinkers puzzled by its enigmatic and paradoxical character. Such a view, certainly, seems to be the programmatic attitude of a large number of diverse and important twentieth-century writers, among whom Gabriel Marcel, Maurice Merleau-Ponty, Jean-Paul Sartre, and Paul Ricoeur first spring to mind as innovative thinkers all influenced to a greater or lesser extent by contact with Edmund Husserl's phenomenology, a philosophy which situates itself in relation to the body in a new and intimate fashion.

For such authors the body is "given" in a quite distinctive way; it is the "zero point" and center of our world; it is both an organ of sense through which we apprehend this world and the organ of will through which we act in the world; and it is intimately, unavoidably, and somewhat mysteriously connected with the ego (Husserl 1980, 151–69). And, while for the phenomenological movement the human body has become a particular matter for investigation, there is a more general sense in which, particularly through growing awareness of the writings of Nietzsche, Bergson, and Freud, every contemporary effort of human self-understanding takes the body as its explicit or implicit point of reference.

Thus, in a characteristic statement Gabriel Marcel declares that in the effortless self-presence of the human body, "the opposition of subject and object is found to be transcended from the start" (Marcel 1949, 12). In the body, after all, do not all the contradictions and discontinuities of Object and Subject—the very differences that inescapably accompany every effort to conceptualize the defining character of modern experience as radically new—meet and resolve themselves in the effortless flow of voluntary actions, in the thoughtless awareness of spatial and temporal contents, in immediate sensitivity to the outside world? Should not abstract categories, therefore, and the polemics and rhetoric to which they give rise, give way to the immediate being of the body, to its elemental potency as a world-creating and world-sustaining structure? Careless of metaphysical problems, the lived body continually reconstitutes itself from, and returns to, the elementary structure of experience.

That this philosophical program has borne rich results need hardly be emphasized. Yet within the human sciences that claim kinship with such philosophical developments (sociology, anthropology, literary theory, and cultural history), the body, rather than filling the abstractions of the Enlightenment with a fresh content, has been entered into the framework of a semiotic conception of society. The body here becomes a carrier of social signs, literally and metaphorically stigmatized. It is nothing in itself; in fact we might say that it has simply changed places with the early modern conception of the mind as a tabula rasa upon which can be inscribed and encoded the particularities of every social experience. The body is fashioned and constructed as a representative of a group and as an enabling mechanism for the formation of social relations. It is the bearer of social identity.

Thus, for all its popularity as a focus of reflection and research, the human body that appears to be at the very center of contemporary cultural studies more often than not turns out to be wholly disembodied, itself a formal concept lacking just those self-evident qualities of immediacy and self-presence in which lies its claim to be the arbiter of all "merely" theoretical disputes. Indeed, it seems that the body has become a central preoccupation for sociologists and others just because, rather as Marx complained of Feuerbach's humanism, it has become nothing more than the concept of a body. The body in its immediacy and self-presence disappears in this process of differentiation and identification; it becomes little more than a quasi-natural symbol, a convenient, transportable, and ever-present billboard upon which the self can project its image to the world.

Yet it would obviously be foolish to abandon the insight that the body should be understood socially, as a bundle of conventional practices and meanings that are only fully articulated and understood through a dense system of metaphorical relationships linking, directly and indirectly, somatic structures and sensory qualities with social relationships. This is obviously valuable and cannot be lost in favor of a return to any naturalistic conception of the body as the illusory "thing-in-itself." The body with which we are all familiar, the body that makes itself felt antecedent to any theoretical speculation, and the body that, at the same time, eludes all efforts to grasp and describe its distinctive character—the "given" body of lived experience—is also a wholly socialized and, therefore, historical body.

The question, therefore, remains: what is the body?

The Image

Another paraphrase is tempting: the body is a simple thing, and like other apparently given unities—World, God, Commodity—it "abounds in metaphysical subtleties and theological niceties" (Marx 1976, 163). It is both itself and more than itself. The body is an eccentric being, continually running ahead and doubling back on itself (Pannenberg 1985; Gehlen 1988). Movement beyond itself, quite literally, characterizes the human body. The extended arm and probing hand characterize a general human bodily attitude, an unavoidable and inherently risk-laden process of movement into the world.

This is not just a matter of gesture. The body goes beyond itself, and returns to itself, in a quite specific way. The body, as the most familiar and intimately known object, only comes to itself as a living being in the form of a composite image, itself constructed from many varied and often divergent sources that are, so to speak, fused to the functioning organic substance that serves as their bearer. The body, that is to say, is neither a sign nor a symbol, but an image; an image of itself. It is not a sign, in the sense of some arbitrarily designated sensible quality to which a specific meaning adheres only by virtue of a social convention; nor is it a symbol by virtue of participating in the same essence as the bearer of its living qualities. Of course it may, and does, in different circumstances enter into the system of signs or carry within it a hidden, symbolized reality. But, more fundamentally, the body constitutes itself as an image, most simply as a plastic likeness, a living statue (Rad 1967, 1:145).

An image is a resemblance or likeness which preserves at least some of the sensible qualities of the original. This is an addition by duplication, rather than by the imposition of any "significance" or "meaning" derived from something outside itself. The image, unlike the symbol, is "attached" to its original and depends upon it. The statue is an image of its model, though it may also be a symbol of some virtue and, additionally and without losing its relation to its original, part of a system of signs (Ricoeur 1994; Vernant 1991, 164–85).

The human body in Western societies, and since ancient times, has primarily been known as an "image." The formation of the ancient body image—the reduplication of the body in its own self-image—is, in fact, the relation in which a theory of images takes root. The image (eidolon) is mimetic in character; it is first of all a copy. On the one hand, the image is less than the body, because it is devoid of those animating forces through which the body lives; but, on the other hand, the image is more than the body because it has something of the quality of a supernaturally produced copy.

The oldest of recorded Western body images was not itself regarded as a vital principle, animating the organism, but was, rather, the mere accompaniment of the physical actuality of the body. The image leaves the body at death, and indeed, it is only in the moment of death that the body realizes the completed, but revitalized, form toward which, while it was alive, it unsuccessfully struggled. In Rohde's classic account the Homeric body image is the origin of images as such; it is the natural locus of the process of imaging that the rest of nature, as well as the artist, imitates. *Psyche* is "unnoticed during the lifetime of the body, and only becomes observable when it is 'separated' from the body" (Rohde 1925, 4; Armstrong 1986, 361). And more generally, "according to the Homeric view, human beings exist twice over: once as an outward and visible shape, and again as an invisible 'image' which only gains its freedom at death." This image is associated with breath and "escapes out of the mouth—or out of the gaping wound of the dying—and now freed from its prison becomes as the name well expresses it, an 'image' (*eidolon*)" (Rohde 1925, 5).

The body image is "nothing but" the body it mirrors, but in this duplication the image makes the body more than itself; more, that is, than a physicopsychical unity. The body and its image are uniquely related. The body image is essential to the body, which cannot even become a body without this reduplication of itself. Thus, for example, we create for ourselves a picture of how we look; a postural model (Head 1920; Schilder 1964a). But there is more to the body image than a mental construct of our appearance. As cases of hysteria make plain, the body image is primarily an experiential rather than a pictorial or a conceptual structure. Hysterical analgesias, for example, are distributed according to the map of the "lived" and "felt" body and not according to the (unknown to the patient) real connections of muscle and nerve tissue (Janet 1965, 138).

The discovery of this image—both in philosophy (Husserl 1980; Marcel 1949; Merleau-Ponty 1962) and in psychology (Lhermitte 1960; Schilder 1964a; Straus 1966; Werner 1957)—is announced as the unveiling of a primordial reality. However, it is now possible to see that the givenness of the body, in both its difference from, and indifference to, itself as a reduplicated image, is entirely a historical reality.

It is, that is to say, as an image that we first come to know ourselves; but the history of this body image is not a straightforward narrative of events or of transformations in which one reality replaces another. We are aware of ourselves, rather, as a collection of such images, each one of which has a specific origin in the past and, as such, allows the sediment of a previous epoch to settle within us. Indeed, there has accumulated in our bodies—in the variety of quite different images through which it is animated and ordered—a synoptic history of Western society. Each novel form continues to coexist with older, but never discarded, pictures of ourselves, and thus through our own self-experience we gain "access to the labyrinth of unfinished cultures" (Nietzsche 1973, 134). As a result we cannot grasp ourselves as a totality but only glimpse partial, overlapping, and incompatible possibilities of completeness now foregone.

The Shadow

Within sociology and the contemporary field of cultural studies, the body is viewed as a representation. This view stems from a conception of Modernity as the progressive self-creation of an inherently free humanity. This is, in effect, a modern version of a much older myth; human beings have rejected Nature and, as a result, only know and act in the world through the mediation of systems of representation that, however compelling and operationally effective, are essentially arbitrary and remain detached and distinct from the wholly unknown reality of Being itself. And as the body is part of the world, it also is known only through its representations. The field of representations is an endlessly self-referential system of signs into which the body is drawn as into a hall of mirrors. We experience the world, including ourselves, only as and through the medium of signs. In this perspective the body is reduced to being a purely material carrier of a (variable) sign, and thus, in a paradoxical and initially misunderstood process, it loses its "substance."

But the self-image of Modernity that is rooted in bodily experience cannot wholly be grasped in this current preoccupation with the emblematic character of the body as a kind of social advertisement. In fact, the quality of embodiment is almost entirely lacking from this perspective. We might argue that this is rightly so; that Modernity is all about the gradual erosion of qualitative distinctions in favor of universal quantities. Yet we all remain aware of ourselves as bodies in a quite peculiar way, irrespective of the specific qualifications that are, so to speak, added to it by virtue of our particular social identities. We are aware of a certain weight and a kind of elastic resistance to gravity, a specific orientation in space, a characteristic directionality, and above all we are conscious of ourselves as a uniquely embodied self-presence; we remain inseparably enfolded in our bodies. But these too are socially constructed and conventional modes of experience, and this provides us with an entry point into a more general historical understanding of the emergence and development of Modernity in terms of bodily categories. The manner in which the body becomes the central experience of our world, that is to say, is neither fixed nor "natural" but is, rather, continuously subject to, and a source of, social and cultural change.

The "lived" body cannot fully be represented and cannot fully be understood as itself a representation. This is just the problem that, in a number of fascinating works, Victor Stoichita has recently taken up (Stoichita 1995, 1997). How have Western artists responded to the challenge of representing what is essentially unrepresentable? In the process he outlines an alternative history of Western representation, arguing in particular that the shadow in Western art reveals a presence (albeit indirectly and as an absence) rather than reflects a constructed image. Thus, rather than view reality in terms of a process of "mirroring" or visualization, as has commonly been the case in Western society since the Renaissance, it may also be apprehended as a shadow cast by an unrepresented and unrepresentable presence. The body, then, may be grasped (indeed cannot help but be grasped) as an elemental entity, as a reality beyond representation; a shadow cast by real presence. This view, indeed, recaptures something of the originally undifferentiated notion of *eidolon* that included dream visions and shadows as well as reflections. And in this view the truth in Plato's myth of the cave is that the shadows cast by real figures at least can be grasped in their elemental and ill-defined givenness, while the images in which they seem to be impoverished and dimensionless projections are insubstantial and distracting representations.

The contemporary body (and it must be emphasized that we do not live exclusively through the specifically contemporary form of the body but have at our disposal, so to speak, the entire accumulated history of such forms) is no longer tensed between Object and Subject, reality and appearance, outside and inside; it oscillates, rather, between image and shadow. The substance of the body, its inner mass and dignity, has dissolved, on the one hand, into the dreamlike unreality of a multiplicity of luminous images and, on the other, has softened into an obscure and melancholic shadow. The body realizes itself as nonpresence or as absent presence; it is nothing.

HISTORICAL FORMATION OF
THE MODERN BODY IMAGE

Modernity required a new body image, one in which human autonomy, individuation, and the power of self-movement could be realized. Here Modernity as a specific form of embodiment can be specified in terms of a long-term process of differentiation and interrelation of varied images of corporeality (both as an architectonic principle or "structure" of the body and through its modalities of sensing, feeling, willing, and so on), to which modern forms are both logically and historically related. This entire process may be characterized as the emergence of an experience of the body as a closed and self-sufficient entity. However, before such a form of embodiment could be actualized, the premodern experience of the body as a microcosmic structure first had to be understood as a metaphor for, rather than as a symbol of, the macrocosm.

Microcosm/Macrocosm

In the medieval West the human body was generally conceived and experienced as a fallen and corrupted being. It occupied the very center of the universe, caught within the sublunary world, subject to decay and death, its collective future dependent on the unpleasant necessity of organic regeneration. The human body was joined to the awful recurrence of a purely natural cycle of life and death, appetite and satisfaction, putrefaction and decay. The body, joined to the world, was joined to death and participated in the terrible drama of abandonment and despair.

The sinful body was set at the farthest point possible from God, who presided over his creation, encompassing its totality from an otherworldly location beyond the outer rim of a series of graded, concentric spheres of being that made up the universe. Each sphere, descending from the sublime perfection of necessary Being, held within it created forms appropriate to its own level. The angels, positioned next to God, then the lesser angels, seraphim, and below them the visible heavenly bodies, perpetually rotating in their regular circular orbits. Within the sphere of the Moon, Earth was conceived as an unmoving and all but abandoned rock upon which man was forced to live (Lovejoy 1960; Haren 1985; Gurevich 1986). Eschatological hopes of the resurrection of the body—of raising it to a higher form of earthly existence—had been transformed into extrabodily doctrines of Heaven and Hell (Goff 1984; Bynum 1995).

Gnostic traditions of dualism, as well as orthodoxy, susceptible to both naturalistic Aristotelian and metaphysical and mystical Neoplatonic influences, readily developed into a microcosmic human body image. For the medieval world the image of the body as modeled on the universe as a whole was given a fresh intellectual and social significance and was developed in much greater detail than it had been by classical authors.

The body image here is a symbol rather than a natural unity. It is both part of the fixed structure of being and an image of its totality. And for all its being fallen and corrupted, the body nonetheless revealed in its inner and essential order the mystery of creation. The hierarchical order of the body is a replica of the cosmological design. The "higher" region, the head and its associated functions, is formed in the "image and likeness" of the Creator and exercises a controlling influence over the "lower" internal bodily regions that are the site of generation and decay. The upper, higher, and symbolic region is contrasted to the lower, interior, and material. The medieval microcosmic body is, therefore, distinguished from older traditions of Platonism for which the valued soul is an interior part of the body. The soul exists here as an intellectual function, as a "picturing" or "imaging" device which allows the body image to be conformed to a greater reality. Through contemplation of the Great Chain of Being as a *scala paradisi,* the body image could receive divine assistance in raising itself to eternity. The body as microcosm contained in itself the possibility of redemption and realized in itself the divine plan of the macrocosm; it was both a representation and a differentiated part of the totality of Being.

The ladder of being—the link between body stuff and soul stuff—forced together in the human person but ideally separated in the marvel of contemplative faith, was master metaphor for the age of feudalism (Gurevich 1985). The social hierarchy, similarly, was a ladder of dependent being. Each individual was dependent, not simply in terms of status or legal personality but physically, upon a superior (Bloch 1965). The chain of superiority ended in the absolute person of the monarch, so that society was a replica of the cosmological hierarchy. Each "order" of society was assigned its appropriate "place" (Duby 1980). The entire symbolic edifice, indeed, was essentially a logic of place. The essence of each being was defined by its position within the totality, and ideally, it should not be removed from that place. The social hierarchy, thus, became highly differentiated, and visibly so through the observation of a host of sumptuary regulations that made immediately identifiable any person "out of place" (Goff 1980).

The body image, furthermore, underwent a process of social differentiation through which specific social orders were symbolized. The aristocratic military elite not only looked distinctive because of their weaponry, armor, and horses; they were essentially different, endowed with a natural valor and love of justice which they spread to the wilderness of non-Christian lands (Lull, 1970). The knight was tall, well formed, and clear-eyed, untouched by disease, strong, skillful, and eternally youthful (Auerbach 1968). The religious functionary, on the other hand, was essentially old, withered, and withdrawn, his body composed of skin and bone rather than flesh, a fragile container of a mighty spirit. A fat priest was always corrupt, as was a "sleek" knight, and for both those types women were virginally erotic, even when married. The common people were rough, ill formed, lumpy, fitted for work. Such specific body images, though doubtless exaggerated in later literary stereotypes, nonetheless serve to indicate ideal differences. The body image of the monk, for example, unlike that of the knight or the ecclesiastical functionary, was focused on the inner affections and feeling, on the ancient movements of the heart rather than on the disjunction of body from soul or flesh from spirit. In opposition to its developing scholasticism, the monk viewed the body as a receptacle of feelings and appetites rather than an instrument of thought and action. But even those who attempted to cut themselves off from the main institutions of feudal societies (and by no means all monastic movements did so) confirmed the symbolic logic they shared with all other medieval microcosmic body images; feelings had to be controlled and appetites restrained through an unconditional surrender of the will to a superior individual (Leclerq 1978).

In addition to a significant process of social differentiation of body images, the medieval period also witnessed the development of a much more general countercultural body image. Communities from time to time became involved in festive transformations, Carnival, in which an entirely new body image temporarily usurped the place of all authoritative models. The grotesque body image, which Bakhtin has revealed for us in his startling book, is not just an inversion of the sacred order of feudal society; it is, through an invocation of the primordial organic body image of Western society, a radical denial of the idea of any differentiated social order whatever (Bakhtin 1968).

As the highest values within feudal society are those which transcend temporal existence and are indicated in the symbolic power of thought, faith, reverential affection, and the nonmaterial otherworldly abstraction of Being, Carnival draws its participants into disordered, wholly concrete forms of bodily experience. The immediate world is celebrated in an excess of physicality. Continuous eating and drinking, the bodily powers of generation and decay—despised in the official worldview—are made the central occasion for festivity and laughter. The "inner" parts of the body, rather than the "inner" part of the human being (soul), organize the activity. But the activity is hardly organized at all. The Carnival is a kind of play, in which the participant becomes lost; a form of transcendence symmetrical with the longed for, and forever unreached, promise of the spiritual life. The body "sinks" into pure sensuality and, therefore, loses its individual soulful identity.

Reinvigorating the ancient body image for its own purposes, the Carnival becomes present to itself as the singular body of society, achieving, over against the minutely regulated hierarchy of the official cosmological body, a kind of spontaneous rediscovery of the primordial disorder of natural processes. Where the feudal cosmological body is differentiated, hierarchical, symbolic, and dependent upon the Being of God, the Carnival is unitary, egalitarian, and autonomous. Here "nature," rather than revealing God's design, is nothing other than itself, a pure organic substance, a kind of perpetual digestive-procreative process that absorbs the human body image into itself. The fertile female, continually open and nutritive, which is among the earliest of Western body images, is here powerfully reinvoked. This is why particularly devout women had to starve themselves, not as an ascetic discipline but as an escape from the putrefying and wholly material body that was without spiritual value and that, it was held, played a more prominent role in the everyday life of females than it did for the essentially more contemplative and spiritual men, for whom the intellectual "image" played a decisive part (Bynum 1987; 1992).

Carnival, however, was always a transient state. In temporarily overthrowing authority it served ultimately to reinforce the structural distinctions and valuations of the official worldview and to stabilize the relation of microcosm to macrocosm. For all its subversive antiquity, the medieval grotesque body image remained part of the premodern universe of symbols.

From Symbol to Metaphor

The development of Modernity was marked not only by the emergence of new body images but also by new modes of interpretation through which they were formed and grasped. The relationship between the microcosmic structure of the human body and the macrocosmic structure of Creation, which since Plato had been understood as a symbolic correspondence in which the body played the part of both an element and a structural homology, was viewed afresh as a metaphor. The body, that is to say, still formed according to a divine structural principle, gained a certain autonomy; it became its own substance.

The decline of feudalism, which was the precondition for the emergence of a new and distinctively modern body image, resulted first in the release of older forms that appeared suddenly as adumbrations of, and preadaptations to, new intellectual and social circumstances. All investigations of the structure of reality began to take the body as their point of departure and most significant reference point. The resurgence of Platonism associated with the Italian Renaissance manifested itself in two somewhat different body images: on the one hand, an intact and liberated star-man harmonically attuned to, and master of, cosmological forces and, on the other, an anatomized and helpless creature, forced to yield up its historic secrets to intensified forms of self-examination. These images are linked as foci of a new observational relation to the world. The body became both the key instrument and the prime specimen of a new, practically oriented curiosity. The body, freed from the constraints of earthbound actualities, was projected into space as an observer of the great cosmological body, and opened and eviscerated, it looked in upon itself to observe the host of inferior bodies that it contained (Camporesi 1994; Hallyn 1995).

Harmonic Correspondence

The revival of classical models of culture in the Renaissance involved a profound shift, not only from medieval conceptions of a hierarchically fixed cosmological body toward a humanism founded on the principle of self-movement, dignity, and individuation; it also expressed this ideal in terms of a modern version of the classical Greek body image (Burckhardt 1990; Hale 1994). It was, however, the completed and integrated Greek god-body and not the fragmented and plural organism or insubstantial *soma* (Vernant 1991) that was invoked for the first time as a realistically human ideal. The autonomy of the human form as such, as a self-adhering mass, became for the first time the focus of artistic representation, scientific research, and philosophical reflection (Hersey 1976).

The Renaissance body image manifested itself in a clearly defined outline, a sculptural form in which the proportions of the various parts to each other and to the whole defined harmonic relations that were replicas of the most general structural features of the cosmos. An architectonic model of the bodily microcosm gained a new meaning, and it was in the proportions of the human body that the cosmological structure, as the inner harmony of nature, was revealed. Vitruvian figures—the human form inscribed within a cosmological circle—became commonplace illustrations of the direct, formal, and substantial link between the individuated human body and the totality of the universe (Heninger 1974, 1977). Harmonics, a mathematical and musical term which rested ultimately on bodily proportion and the inner receptivity of the senses to its replication in the world, was held to be a natural and not a symbolic form. And for this reason there was believed to be a direct bodily link between man and cosmos. Human beings, thus, contained within themselves universal cosmological powers that might be unlocked and used to subdue nature and subordinate its entire system of forces to human interests (Yates 1964; Garin 1983; Couliano 1987). And, as distinct from the ancient body image, rather than being penetrated and fragmented by superior powers, the Renaissance body was brought into focus by universal forces immanent in nature. The sculptural form, unified, individuated, and well proportioned, was an animated image of a natural totality.

The Platonic image of the microcosm, thus, was given a new dynamic interpretation. Invoking not only older Pythagorean teachings but Orphic and Hermetic mysteries, the Platonic revival in Italy championed practical harmonics in art and architecture in addition to new astrological and alchemical technologies. Astrological and magical theories were revived and developed on its foundation and on a rereading of Plato in the light of a new bodily illumination. Marsilio Ficino and his followers saw in the human body the key to unlock the universe. This was a far cry from the ignoble and depraved creature of the medieval Christian vision. Human beings could not reach God by contemplation, but they could extend themselves into the cosmos by a growing awareness of the harmonic secrets of their own nature. The direct influence of the stars upon human behavior, the possibility, explored in the Hermetic tradition, of calling down superior astral powers and extending human control of nature, and enhancing natural human powers many times over, all sprang innocently from an understanding of human proportion and its harmonic interrelations with the cosmos (Cassirer 195; Hersey 1976; Heninger 1977; Garin 1983).

For the key figures in the emergence of Renaissance science, Copernicus and more particularly Kepler, harmonics played a fundamental role in the conceptualization of the cosmos (Hallyn 1990). Here, however, the intricate correspondences between bodily proportions and the structure of the world were understood on a purely formal basis. Kepler, for example, though still old-fashioned enough to endow the sun with the "attractive power" of a living being, criticized Robert Fludd's "magical" use of mathematics. He argued that the manipulations of humanly contrived sign systems, while they ideally replicated "real" structural universals, could not in themselves carry any causal implications for the human or natural world. In this regard it is worth noting that early modern science was primarily a practical art (Rossi 1970) and was, thus, linked ideologically with the revival of magic and Hermeticism (Yates 1964). In its more theoretical aspects, however, it drew heavily on the investigation of musical forms and their mathematical elucidation (Crombie 1995, vol. 2). Indeed, rather than viewing the Renaissance in terms of its innovative visual culture, and particularly its elaboration of perspectival space, it is important to grasp its meaning as part of the development also of an aural culture (White 1987; Edgerton Jr. 1991; Leppert 1993, 1996). The visual beauty and physical vigor of the harmonic body could be understood, thus, in terms of its resonance with the "music of the spheres." The human body was an instrument, but one which required tuning before it could "sound" its fundamental tone. These body images, it should be noted, are still present and have recently been revived in the New Age movement, for which being "in tune with nature" is the foundational condition of bodily health.

Self-Examination

Changing historiographical fashions have done little to revise Burckhardt's classic portrayal of the Renaissance as the inauguration of a continuing modern fascination with the self. The individuated subject (a unique individual), ideally liberated from the constraint of tradition and personal dependence, ceded to itself all the capacities of humanity. The self, thus, burdened itself with the obligation of creativity, self-generation, and autonomous action (Greenblatt 1980; Weinstein 1981).

It is in this context that the distinction between the inside and outside of the body becomes significant in a new way. The inside of the body, the metaphorical and actual home of individuated selfhood, is neither formless nor disordered, but it is qualitatively distinct from the outside. The inside of the body represents the hidden truth of the self. At the same time, echoing the bodily grotesque of an earlier era, it represents everything dangerous, unpleasant, ugly, and fascinating. The mystery of interiority could be revealed by the controlled destruction of the external body form itself. Dissection, a literal destruction of the body in the interest of looking inside it, was established as a scientific technique during the Renaissance; and it should be emphasized that just as Copernicanism in imparting motion to Earth began a long-term shift in perspective that emphasized the centrality of purely human characteristics in the formation of the modern world, this was a consequence of, and reinforced, a new evaluation of the human being as an independently worthy object of study. Many of the resulting anatomical texts were illustrated with pictures of self-revealing bodies, bodies that literally anatomized themselves, pulling away the outer surface of the body to reveal the internal structure and interrelations of organs, skeleton, and connecting tissues (Sawday 1995). The interior space of the body was explored as a "new world" as vast and hitherto unknown as the Americas (Camporesi 1994). The idea of self-dissection as self-revelation and self-knowledge, and of the potentially self-destructive character of human curiosity, was, so to speak, built into the new image of the body as an autonomous being.

The human body, which was circumscribed in the universe, enclosed within itself another entire world, so that the individual became viewed as a structure which kept these disparate realms apart. The body could turn outwards and, as in Giordano Bruno's "frenzy" or the more controlled flights of fancy of Cyrano de Bergerac, Burton, or Kepler, imaginatively take up any position in the cosmos and redirect its gaze upon Earth; or it could turn inwards and reflect upon the different kind of experience that seemed to be contained within the body as an inner stream of life. The body, thus, required physical integrity, individuation, and closure. The implications of this changing cosmology for the new body image, just as the implications of the new humanism for emerging modern views of nature and society, developed over a lengthy period; but the fundamental assumptions upon which this development was based were made during the Renaissance.

The new humanism was ideally constructed, thus, through two linked body images, announced simultaneously in 1543 with the publication of the pioneering works of Nicolaus Copernicus and Andreas Vesalius. One led toward the notion of body as dead matter dignified by motion; the other celebrated the self-revelatory power of the human. The medieval microcosm-macrocosm relation was revalued in favor of the intimate human world, a process of intellectual development in which the relation between the two was interpreted metaphorically rather than symbolically and ultimately overthrew the assumptions upon which the distinction and comparison were based. Magical and metaphorical interpretations of the microcosm-macrocosm relation gradually gave way to a new conception of the body image as the bifurcation between two qualitatively distinct realms of Object and Subject. Indeed, to the extent to which conceptions of Modernity have remained within the dialectic of Subject-Object, they have continued to draw their ultimate meaning from the earliest period of the actual historical development of modern society.

CORPOREAL FORMS
OF MODERNITY

Modernity—in the most general sense the culture of modern society—required and called forth new forms of bodily self-experience and self-expression as well as distinctive modes of personal being that have proved to be as characteristic of that society and culture as has commodity production, the money economy, the organic division of labor, or bureaucratic social organization. The distinctive feature of modern embodiment lies in the process of individuation, in the identification of the body with the person as a unique individual and, therefore, as the bearer of values and legally enforceable rights. This was associated not only with a specific ideological complex but with the rise of a rational scientific worldview which was both justified by, and was itself rooted in, just such forms of self-experience.

It is worth emphasizing the extent to which during the early modern period (variously distinguished as Renaissance, Baroque, mercantilism, absolutism) the emergence of the Subject-Object dialectic had already given rise to paradoxical inconsistencies for any related conception of embodiment. The human body claimed the privilege of a paramount reality. The body was identified not merely as a metaphor or harmonic structural plan but as an autonomous being. Weight, substance, dignity, from being diffuse characteristics of extended reality, flowed into and congealed in the body. In the body, thus, the most fundamental characteristics of reality were crystallized and came to life.

The early modern period represents a decisive break with the past in bringing a dispersed and diffuse reality into focus as the "given" structure and appearance of the body. At the same time, however, the premodern sense of reality as mysterious and reticent Being was preserved and even enhanced. Bodily reality, still present in an immediate and nonobjective sense as felt self-presence, was increasingly "subjectivized" as consciousness, feeling, imagination, and will, an interior shadow which became incommunicable, personalized, and individuated as the "soul."

The Atom of Civil Society

It was, in fact, a somewhat inconsistent amalgamation of Cartesian and Newtonian conceptions of body—the empirically given "body-in-space" and the mathematical point-mass—which served as the natural form for the dominant body image of the modern bourgeois era. Body implies both the separation of matter from space and, simultaneously, the differentiation of matter from mind. These distinctions, however remote and abstract the philosophical and scientific domains in which they appeared, nonetheless encode the practical experience of the living body in modern society. For the bourgeois era (as for premodern societies) the world is experienced through the body and is reflected upon only because the body image offers itself as a plausible model of that world. For Modernity the human body—the elementary unit of nature as well as of society—is, in Newton's famous designation, a "solid, massy, hard, impenetrable, movable particle," which, endowed with inertial properties, remains identical with itself irrespective of time and place (Newton 1931, 400). This universal body interacts with other such bodies according to simple underlying laws, so that large-scale stable structures result. And it is understood in this way just because the human body (as the localized embodiment of universal subjectivity) is experienced as a closed, separate, autonomous, and individuated Subject-Object.

Whereas the Renaissance and Baroque body images continually verged on the lawless and disorderly, which had to be held in check by the imposition of powerful external constraints (Foucault 1977; Maravall 1986), the bourgeois body, into which an entire battery of new self-controlling beliefs and values had been inculcated, was liberated into the free space of modern society. For modern society, indeed, the body no longer required to be controlled; it had become self-regulating. This is the burden of Elias's conception of the "civilizing process"; new thresholds of bodily consciousness, a new awareness of and sensitivity to the proximity of others, the integrity of its boundaries and surfaces, the maintenance of proper "manners," and so on, were a bodily expression of the self-controlling mechanism essential to the creation and development of Modernity in general. As it emerged, however, this process was viewed as the mechanical outcome of the universal character of humanity as Reason. The principle of Reason was conceived as inherent in each individual, so that, when allowed freedom to express itself, the body was unfailingly directed to satisfy needs that could only be satisfied through collective life. The autonomous individual, thus, is led to choose to conduct itself in a proper manner and would inevitably choose to act in ways conducive to the maintenance and good order of the modern world of capitalist production.

Automatons

The modern body image is present, then, at the birth of rational science. Newton's *Principia* begins with the injunction to "imagine a body-in-space," a methodological precept which implies, in fact, an extraordinary act of isolation and detachment. You cannot help but imagine yourself, your own body, as the observing subject, isolated in infinite and empty space, alone in the cosmos but for the companionship of a singular lump of matter. This lump of matter can only be conceived in terms of the body image that has been thus fantastically transported into deepest space. The fundamental characteristics of lifeless matter, thus revealed, hardly surprisingly turned out to be just those which, for modern society, seemed inalienably human. The "body-in-space" is our twin, an alienated human body.

Renaissance writers, including Kepler (Lear 1965), had imaginatively transported themselves into space to throw into a fresh and startling perspective their description of Earth's place in the universe. But the science of Newton and Galileo required a flight into the emptiness of space as a methodological necessity. Scientific knowledge began with an act of drastic simplification, the reduction of Nature to the simple givenness of the human body. Observer and observed remain identical; what is new is the socially conceived character of the observer as a closed and self-sufficient individual. The human body image is the starting point for the new science as, in different ways, it was for primitive thought and for mythological reflection. Indeed, in terms of its fundamental intuition of nature, rational science was as anthropomorphic as any premodern cosmology. But, rather than being joined to and directly participating in Nature or part of a hierarchical and fixed order of Being, the body (generative of every image of reality) is now an independent and irreducible quantity of matter. The body is, first of all, a mass, a quantity of self-adhering substance. It also fills a specific amount of space; it has a specific density and shape.

The inherent unity and integrity of the body are not put at risk by joining it to another; it exists autonomously, it is something in its own right. But in relation to another body there is a mutual interaction, a visible attraction or repulsion; a body exhibits gravity as well as mass and inertia. It is extended but is not fixed or limited to a specific place. It is mobile, self-moving in a new way; infinitely self-moving. As both Hobbes and Montaigne had recognized, the human body is "naturally" in motion (Spragens 1973; Starobinski 1985). Equally, therefore, natural bodies are in continuous motion, and an external force is no longer required to move it or keep it fixed in place (Koyré 1965). Liberated into infinite and empty space, every body moves in relation to every other. The character of this perpetual and effortless motion is deducible from the characteristics of the body itself; it is a principle as immanent, obvious, and mysterious as the "intentions" and "motives" that roused and directed individual human action.

Newton's characterization of the "body-in-space" is the prelude to an attempt to reconstruct a "system-of-the-world" from a multitude of such bodies in a process of continuous interaction. In terms both of its originating conceptualization and its systematic elaboration, Newtonian dynamics became the inspiration and explicit model for the development of sensationalist psychology and utilitarian political philosophy, which, in fact, stood in an equally close relation to its hidden understanding of the human body.

For David Hartley, thus, the body is primarily a sensory mechanism capable of receiving impressions that, through the fine structure of its conductive channels, is translated into consciousness as a "picture" of the outside world. The "images" possessed by the body are the mechanically produced imprint of an external world upon sensitive receptors. Human actions necessarily flow from these images: "By the mechanism of human actions I mean, that each action results from the previous circumstance of body and mind, in the same manner, and with the same certainty, as other effects do from their mechanical causes" (Hartley 1810, 515).

The body also becomes conscious of "needs" and "appetites" that spring from within its own mechanism and impart a directional tendency to the ceaseless flow of sensory images. These internally produced images, pictures of things not immediately present but that would satisfy the needs felt by the body, move and guide the body toward what are felt as its goals. "Pleasure" is felt in the temporary satisfaction of a need, which, naturally recurring, sets the whole process in motion again. Both the memory and anticipation of such pleasure might, additionally, propel the body where no "real" need underlies the activity.

The body in all this becomes a self-moving and self-adjusting mechanism, an automaton. Once the body-mind distinction had been decisively drawn by Descartes, it was not long before the mind could be dispensed with and the body image reduced to the body itself, or to a kind of mechanical replica of itself. Indeed, throughout the eighteenth century the technical expertise of watchmakers in fabricating automatons seemed to offer a more or less precise, if simplified, simulacrum of the human body (Vartanian 1953). The technical virtuosity displayed in such dolls for the first time offered a believable material analogy to the human body. La Mettrie, the best known of the materialist philosophers of the body, understood, of course, the difficulties of such a reduction. The adjustment of the body to its environment was not just uncannily precise, it was accompanied by an unconquerable illusion of self-conscious control, directedness, and intentionality. The body, above all, was a machine that "winds its own spring" and is perfectly self-controlled (La Mettrie 1912, 93). In the image of the self-regulating body, the Renaissance program of humanist educational reforms received its ultimate endorsement and realization. The "body-in-space," as self-contained and well regulated as a self-winding watch, is wholly self-contained and needs nothing outside of itself to propel it toward appropriate ends in a controlled manner.

Libertines

Emerging at the same time, and in apparent contrast to the notion of the automaton, a distinctively modern sensuous body image also came to prominence. In the writings of the marquis de Sade as, in a variant form, in the novels of Samuel Richardson, the human body image is also represented as a completely autonomous individual being. But, rather than being prompted to rational action to satisfy internally generated needs, it is driven by wholly irrational and insatiable passions to subdue and join with other bodies in a socially destructive fashion. The body is nothing but a voracious appetite; there is no recurrent cycle of pleasure and satisfaction but a vast and unquenchable longing which ultimately nothing can assuage.

The radically subversive character of such a body image belongs wholly to the modern world. The passions are here brought into the closest possible relation to the bourgeois ego, and it is essentially a bourgeois body image which is sensualized and eroticized. Thus, for example, Madame Delbène gives an account of her libertine philosophy in terms of an underlying sensuous mechanism which appears not unlike Hartley's sensationalism: "I'm not aware of having any soul; I'm acquainted with and feel nothing but my body; it is the body which feels, which thinks, which judges, which suffers, which enjoys; and all its faculties are necessary effects of its mechanism, organization, and structure" (de Sade 1991, 44).

There is no hint in de Sade's characters of a body image animated by a spirit of Carnival excess. The premodern tradition of periodically licensed sensuousness has been abandoned, and its collective body image has undergone an irreversible process of individuation and personalization. And, significantly, de Sade justifies the endless eroticism of his *tableaux vivants* in the same way that his utilitarian and rationalist opponents justify their defense of enlightened self-interest: that it is "natural." De Sade's vision of nature, however, founded in a body image centered upon the helpless dependence on others as the counterpart to the autonomy of self-generated needs, emphasizes the tyranny of its perpetual dynamism rather than the unity and integration that his more optimistic opponents held to be the necessary outcome of the self-regulating interaction of its constituent "atoms." Sensuousness is Nature, Nature individuated and subjectivized as personal experience, and it imposes upon every individual its absolute demand. In a phrasing reminiscent of St. Anselm, de Sade expounds a new ontology of the body image as unbounded natural sensuousness: "There is a certain perversity than which no other nourishment is tastier; drawn thither by Nature . . . if for a moment Reason's glacial hand waves us back, Lust's fingers bear the dish toward us again, and thereafter we can no longer do without that fare" (de Sade 1991, 11).

OBJECT/SUBJECT RELATIONS

These two forms of individuation—the autonomy of self-regulation and the absolute ego of the libertine—are only the most extreme tendencies within an age in which the commodity reached maturity. The thinglike objectivity and independence of the body do not replicate natural being but, rather, constitute corporeal images of the commodity. The living body image experiences itself through the commodity form. The modern "body-in-space" is not simply the human body but the commodity image of the human body. The social character of the body is concealed, so that the body appears to be a singular object, related to other similar objects, according to simple laws connecting their inherent characteristics to each other. The bourgeois body image—a closed, completed, and impenetrable entity—is by no means an asocial conception, nor is it founded upon an implicit withdrawal from social life; it is, rather, the specific social form in which experience is given to the modern subject.

Yet commodities have insides as well as outsides. As exchange values they are pure quantity, devoid of any sensuous character of their own, but as use values they surrender their hidden qualities in the act of consumption. The body, likewise, still has an inside and an outside. While the outside defines the space of the body, a portion of an infinite space into which it has been liberated, the inside at first seems to be full of "qualities," to be a wholly interior Subject. As Object, that is to say, the body image is part of the world of formally identical objects interacting in the infinity of space and time; but as Subject, the same body image is immeasurably enriched with the inner content of lived experience.

The human subject—the "interior" of the body image—was conceived to be a region of pure potentiality, a kind of reservoir of potential experiences, any one of which might be realized, depending upon the circumstances of the moment. There was no inner limit to the human character, just as there was no outer limit to the growth of the commodity world and the infinite space into which it expanded.

Pascal perhaps more clearly than anyone else articulated the experience of the human body image in the modern world as a formal dividing line of this sort, a boundary or limit, which is the consequence of the Cartesian rupture between body and soul. Pascal is aware of a kind of incomprehensible arbitrariness in the body image. Indeed, as a boundary which marks a definite and insurmountable division between an inner world of individual feeling, passion, and sensation and an outer world of cold, infinite space and the endless continuity of identical substance, the modern body image seems to be an inescapable but incomprehensible fact of experience: "Our soul is cast into the body where it finds number, time, dimensions; it reasons about these things and calls them natural, or necessary, and can believe nothing else" (Pascal 1966, 149). But we cannot really understand the limitations that nature imposes upon us: "Why is my stature what it is and the span of my life one hundred and not one thousand years" (Goldmann 1964, 27). Far less can we understand the inner qualities of our own experience: "The feeling of fire, the warmth which affects us in quite a different way from touch, the reception of sound and light, all seem mysterious to us" (Pascal 1966, 244). The body is nothing other than the boundary between these two qualitatively distinct regions of being, a meeting point between two mutually incomprehensible and impenetrable infinities. As the plane of separation between Object and Subject, the modern body image is a boundary which both contains an infinity and moves through infinity.

The body image can direct itself inwards or outwards and becomes in turn bewildered over the succession of possible selves and unhinged by the emptiness of the world. Feeling is "locked away" in the body, not because it is dangerous to "show emotion" and run the risk of humiliation, rejection, or aggression but, rather, because the expressive lability of the emotions, if they were permitted to "surface" from the continuous flux of subjectivity, would present to the world a continuously changing, amorphous body image, without a center or immanent directionality. The very idea of the commodity and of the commodified body image, however, is of a fixed "center of gravity," a focused and integrated "personality" or "selfhood" which maintains itself unchanged over a period of time and turns an unchanging and resolute face toward the world.

The body establishes and keeps apart the absolute difference between Subject and Object. The bourgeois body image, therefore, is tightly closed, hermetically sealed against the inside and the outside. The body image is a third kind of "place," itself neither inside nor outside, protecting both Subject and Object from each other and allowing the convention of an individuated "identity" to emerge between them. It is to the establishment and maintenance of this boundary that much modern practical culture, education, and social welfare have been directed. Skeptical of the moral efficacy of Reason alone, modern authorities have been keen to inculcate a bourgeois sensibility in which hygiene, respectability, and uprightness reinforced and made visible the integrity of the body image as a closed entity (Gay 1986–93; Donzelot 1980). The classical bourgeois body image is the support of an individuated interior ego and the very foundation of character and personality, a view well expressed by the influential French psychologist Théodule Ribot at a time when such assumptions had become commonplace: "The bodily condition, which is without the sphere of consciousness because of its perpetuity, is the true basis of personality—ever-present, ever-lasting, without repose or respite, it knows neither sleep nor exhaustion, lasting as long as life itself, of which it is only an expression. This it is that serves as support for the conscious *Ego* formed by the memory; it renders association possible, and maintains them after they are formed" (Ribot 1882, 110).

The bourgeois body image corresponds precisely to the physical boundary of the individuated body: it fits "like a glove." This shrinking of the body image to fit the frame of the body, a kind of vacuum packaging which fused the body image to the surface of its material bearer, is a practical result of the metaphysical polarities that define the experience of Modernity. For the modern body image the "thickness" of the body shell was, thus, reduced to a thin, hard surface which served to separate an empty interior from an empty exterior.

This entire development has been illustrated in an original and remarkable way by Norbert Elias, whose work suggests a conception of Modernity as the inculcation of new codes of bodily self-control and self-discipline. In his view northern European humanism, associated in particular with the writings of Erasmus, transposed the call to human self-dignity, which lay at the root of the artistic and scientific ennoblement of humanity in the Italian Renaissance, into a universal pedagogy of the body. The culture of Modernity begins in the general demand for good manners; that is, with self-restraint in bodily matters. A continuous and effortless self-control over bodily comportment, gesture, disposition, state of need, and readiness for public activity should be exercised. In a word, decency was the first requirement of modern society, a requirement which in turn demanded constant vigilance. In a society where the sumptuary regulation of social life had broken down and strangers of unknown rank more frequently interacted, bodily gesture and conduct became matters of practical importance.

These developments shifted the locus of social control and effected "a change in the relation between external social constraints and individual self-constraints." Psychic mechanisms correspondingly became socially more significant. The "threshold of shame" was lowered and made more specific; it became "bad manners" to relieve oneself in public, spit in the street, and so on (though not all at once and not all the time). Conduct was continually regulated by the effort to avoid embarrassment over any untoward negligence over appearance, behavior, or temporary loss of self-control. However, bodily self-control was at the same time a spiritual liberation and the realization of a particular kind of individuality. Control over the body was achieved by the agency of the body's own self-presence; manners provided, above all, a modality for the development and expression of a new form of personal identity.

It is worth emphasizing that the interiorization of social control through the mechanism of shame represents a more pervasive and certain means of coercion than does any external agency. This is nowhere better illustrated than in the conduct of war; in combat the sense of shame at, and fear of, the loss of bodily self-control becomes a paramount concern. Before going into action soldiers frequently feel the fear of embarrassing themselves—at "not coping" in some obvious physical way—more acutely than they do the fear of injury or death (Holmes 1985; Hynes 1998).

Substantively, Elias brings to light the crucial historical significance of the social processes through which an unambiguous boundary between one body and another was established. It was a boundary which was, in fact, a kind of reflexive formation of new social interests and social requirements. The social character of the body and the social relations that were inherent in all bodily experience were manifest first and foremost in its isolation. The apparent independence and self-subsistence of the human body were, in fact, the consequence of new forms of social regulation. Self-control was a principle of social control; close attention to conduct, appearance, and the etiquette of everyday interaction created a new individuated body image and a new society. The history of manners, that is to say, was at the same time the history of state formation.

Elias's discussion of the modern "individual" and the self-perception of the modern subject as *homo clausus*—"a little world in himself who ultimately exists quite independently of the great world outside" defines classical modern body image as a closed structure. Typically, modern society is composed of "people to whom it seems self-evident that their own self (or their ego, or whatever else it may be called) exists, as it were, 'inside' them, isolated from all the other people and things 'outside'" (Elias 1978, 205). That the sense of individuality is itself a social relation was already stated by Durkheim but is usually taken to refer to a nebulous sense of "self" rather than to the more concrete and everyday sense of "body." Yet the history of the twentieth century is so many reminders that the body, no less than the soul, is an interdependent and interrelational reality. The tenacity of self-perception as a *corpus clausus*, rather than being evidence of a presocial foundation from which and out of which social relations are developed, is a kind of ideological reflex of the particular social relations through which the body is constituted.

The social division between the individual and others is replicated internally as an immediately felt relation between an "interior," nonmaterial individuality and its own body. The human being is locked up within a protective corporeal shell. Thus, Elias remarks, "his true self appears likewise as something divided within him by an invisible wall from everything outside." But what is the nature of this wall: "Is the body the vessel which holds the true self locked within it? Is the skin the frontier between 'inside' and 'outside'? What in man is the capsule, and what the encapsulated? The experience of 'inside' and 'outside' seems so self-evident that such questions are scarcely ever posed" (Elias 1972, 84).

Elias argues the sense of inside and outside is itself a product of the civilizing process and the self-restraint or "repression" of emotional and aggressive expressions that are still felt as "inclinations" that are controlled.

GENESIS OF THE POSTMODERN
BODY IMAGE

Toward the end of the nineteenth century, the serene objectivity of classical Modernity was disturbed by a series of diverse scientific, literary, artistic, and philosophical movements that came in time wholly to undermine its assumptions. A new body image was as central to this radical cultural transformation as it had been to the emergence of Modernity itself.

The Body-in-Space and the Force Field

What is evident from the most cursory review of fin-de-siècle culture is that a new language of corporeality was being forged in the culturally most advanced urban centers of Europe: in Berlin, Paris, and above all Vienna. Already, at the dawn of the twentieth century, the "rediscovery of the body" had been announced by the most daring thinkers in diverse and apparently unconnected cultural fields. The human body was the concrete reality above all others that demanded investigation and promised the most in self-understanding. The classically modern "body-in-space" dissolved not into empty abstraction but to be reborn as new and provocative body images.

The Newtonian cosmos had been conceived as the infinite extension of formally empty space and time within which appeared a vast collection of things: bodies, each one of which was fundamentally identical to every other. The "body-in-space" was, simultaneously, the "claustral" body fundamental to the development of modern society and culture. A body was an identifiable "thing" known through its "primary qualities," above all through its possession of mass, or what in social terms might be referred to as dignity. Body was simply a quantity of self-adhering matter whose motion was governed by immanent, universal laws and interacted with other bodies according to simple underlying laws of nature.

By the end of the nineteenth century, however, physical reality was coming to be described in terms of nonlocalized fields of force. Bodies, in this view, were qualitatively indistinguishable from space; they were local deformations or concentrations of space that gave rise to the phenomenal properties hitherto interpreted as inherent qualities of matter. By the end of the century, it was clear that in the full understanding of the pioneering work of James Clerk Maxwell, a completely new foundation for the physical sciences had become imperative. What is significant here is less the specific character of this transition in the physical sciences than the observation that a similar "dematerialization" of nature was also apparent from other perspectives and that the new developments that occurred in almost all fields during the same period reveal complementary aspects of a new body image, and a new form of human embodiment, which was to come into its own during the twentieth century.

The body in the twentieth century opened itself into, and became relationally defined through its participation in, an extended "force field." Particularly as described in the eclectic psychology of Paul Schilder and the encyclopedic psychopathology of Karl Jaspers, the body image—the structural, emotional, and interactive "model" of the body that we constructed and through which we experienced reality, including ourselves—was no longer identical with the material form of the body but, rather, continually dissolved and extended into the space surrounding it or withdrew into an unknown interiority. The classical modern body image might be thought of as shrink-wrapped to the surface of the material body, while the contemporary body image is much more loosely related to its corporeal form. This is now a quite familiar feature of everyday life. We frequently refer to our "personal space," which is both more extended and more variable than the severely localized space of bodily experience established during the classical period of Modernity. The automobile, for example, further extended this space, while the telephone and new electronic media of communication do so with at present incalculable effects (Kern 1983; Castells 1997).

Between the Conscious and
the Unconscious

Friedrich Nietzsche had already anticipated much of this revolutionary change in modern culture. Before the close of the nineteenth century, he had begun to view the body as a living resolution of the philosophical dualism introduced by Descartes into the heart of modern thought and practice. The body, for him, was not reducible to simple matter any more than the mind or soul could free itself from purely material entanglement. Nietzsche's radical dissolution of all materialist and idealist duality, however, had to wait a century to become generally influential, and the reorientation of consciousness toward a new recognition of embodiment and a recognition of new forms of embodiment can more readily be traced in a number of writers who, coming from different traditions, coincidentally produced major works around 1900.

The publication of seminal writings of Bergson, Freud, and Husserl (in another context Simmel and Veblen might also be mentioned) within a few years of the end of the nineteenth century is certainly suggestive. They are all, in fact, part of the dramatic transformation in every aspect of culture, as was, a little later, the daring literature of Kafka, Proust, and Joyce. The human body was not simply given a new centrality and prominence as the foundation of thought and experience in these writings but in the process was conceptualized and experienced in novel ways.

Henri Bergson, for example, broke with the major traditions of empirical psychology by stressing the extent to which "experience" is composed of memory as much as it is of direct sensation. But, rather than describe the novelty of contemporary body images in terms of archaic models (as Nietzsche had attempted in his distinction between Apollonian and Dionysian cultures), Bergson introduced a provocative metaphor. Inasmuch as consciousness had in the past been viewed unambiguously as a "mental" phenomenon, it belonged to the soul, and the modality of the soul was time. Personal identity and the sense of self for the modern period (certainly since Rousseau's *Confessions*) depended upon an art of memory, on the recollection of a continuous train of interior feelings. However, in contemporary society the soul has, so to speak, risen to the surface and merged with the body; it has assumed a spatial rather than a temporal form. The characteristic way of grasping consciousness (and of consciousness grasping the world) has, thus, been transposed from temporal to spatial categories. Bergson launched a major critique of the contemporary "spatialization" of experience, but what is important to note here is that his rejection of this tendency was founded upon a recognition of its current actuality. Bergson, directly influenced by novel technical means of recording human and animal locomotion devised by Etienne-Jules Marey, correctly identifies the special character of contemporary experience and its description as "cinematic"; it is decomposed into a series of "frames" that are then arranged in sequence, like the beads of a necklace (Rabinbach 1990). In this process the soul is materialized and matter is dissolved; the body emerges as a genuinely interactive surface.

Bergson's influence has been diffuse and is only now being reassessed (Deleuze 1993). Freud's work, always well known and hugely influential in many academic disciplines and cultural practices, rather oddly remains known more by reputation than at first hand. His name is now frequently invoked to lend authority to perspectives remote from his own. It would be too easy to regard Freud's work as a psychology of the Unconscious, and the Unconscious as Nature, thus assimilating (or simply ignoring) his subtle interpretations of contemporary embodiment to an "objective" science of evolutionary biology (Sulloway 1979). Freud's writings, however, are overwhelmingly concerned with what might be called a psychology of consciousness. The Unconscious by definition is beyond experience and is consigned to a vague and indeterminate region between nature and humanity. What interested Freud, however, was the characteristic forms of conscious experience that might be represented as "deformations" of the classical modern ego; that is, of an individuated and embodied subject, self-possessed and activated by specific needs and wants, the Subject (housed in shrink-wrapped body armor) of classical utilitarian philosophy and political economy. Contemporary life provided many examples of states of mind and feeling, as well as bodily actions and inactions, that could not be understood from this perspective and that seemed to suggest the persistence of forms of "pre-egoistic" or "non-egological" consciousness. Dreams were the most obvious and the richest source of such material.

Freud's analytic efforts, therefore, were focused on the interpretation of dreams and of neurotic symptoms, jokes, and parapraxes (including inadvertent bodily gestures as well as slips of the tongue or pen, small failures of memory, and so on). And what emerged was not a simple contrast between, on the one hand, an ego-centered form of conscious experience fixed in the individuated "normal" body form (the Newtonian body-in-space) and, on the other, some more primitive, nonlocalized form of consciousness but, rather, a contrast between the former and a series of fairly well defined forms of consciousness each appropriate to a specific body image which remained accessible (in specific circumstances) to the adult. The so-called stages of psychosexual development are a schematic presentation of this archaeology of the body image and chart the surrender of the ego to alternative forms of embodiment.

The oral, anal, and genital "stages" represented particular "mapping" of the body in terms of its sensitivity and excitability. The persistence of earlier stages, which were systematically repressed in the interests of the developing ego (and its fittedness for active social life, work, and world making), provided sources of specifically "perverse" forms of sexual pleasure. Marcuse, indeed, later argued that the realization of human emancipation required a process of "desublimation" in which these sources of pleasure would become freely available. Properly speaking, in fact, these experiences based on pre-egological body images cannot be immediately felt as pleasure in the conventional sense because pleasure is, by definition, a relation of the ego, a form of ego mastery, ego satisfaction, and ego possession. The "perversions" in their original form might perhaps be thought of as more like the ego-surrendering experience of the "sacred." In any event, this century has not been witness to any such general process of liberation. The forces of repression have intensified and become more pervasive and intimate and (as Elias points out) are not negated by the general growth of "informalization." What has occurred is a kind of colonization, and consequential distortion, of the preoedipal world by the ego itself, so that the perversions become erotic fantasies of the ego, rather than non-egological forms of consciousness (Whitebook 1996). The classical ego and its closed body image, that is to say, have remained orthodox and dominant.

Freud demonstrates, nonetheless, the myriad of ways in which the everyday world is continually intersected by other worlds; it vibrates with what are felt as "undercurrents" of feeling. Yet in the romantic sense of being buried beneath the ego in a deeply recessed and profound "soul," which is the wellspring of individuality, there is nothing "underneath" here. These currents, rather, are so many alternative forms of association, linking, and connection, which operate through memory and imagination, dissolving the "solidity" of the everyday world and opening the body to its own past and to the world (Ferguson 1996).

The phenomenological movement, like Freud's psychology, has exerted a continuous influence throughout the century. Phenomenology drew itself together and gained its seriousness as a reflection upon, indeed, upon its reclaiming of, the human body as the primordial subject matter of thought and the elemental given reality of human experience. Experience was always bodily experience, and therefore, the body placed itself between the great unknowns of Nature and the Soul as both the obstacle and the means to knowledge of Being. Experience was both bodily experience of the world and the body experiencing itself, a process in which the Object-Subject distinction that inaugurated Modernity and modern thought was effortlessly dissolved.

Husserl's influence in relation to a clear conceptualization of the body did not fully develop until recent years with the publication and translation of many of his writings, which had remained unknown except in lecture form during his lifetime. His is a philosophy which seems, in principle, to be opposed to Freud's psychology, a determined attempt to grasp the fullness of consciousness rather than a pursuit of the Unconscious. Such a view, however, hardly does justice to either. Both, in fact, were concerned primarily with the character of human experience in contemporary society and to that extent can usefully be compared. Husserl's approach, deriving from the central tradition of modern philosophy, is by way of epistemological issues rather than directly through psychology. Indeed, as the prime critic of "psychologism" in philosophy, he has too readily been assumed to have an antipathy toward psychological works. Whatever the differences in background and aim, however, Husserl too dissolves the "body-in-space" and seeks for new descriptions of experience. Rather than describe consciousness as a mirroring of nature and the outside world that is the source of all our experience, he focuses on the objectivity of our experience, on the extent to which it does not lie in an interior mind but is constituted and continually reconstituted through all the activities of the human Subject. In this process the body plays a vital role; no longer conceived as the indifferent housing for the conscious observing ego, the body image, rather, comes to itself as the foundation of the world of experience itself.

For Husserl the body is a "thing" in the sense of being fully integrated into the nexus of causal relations, and we are aware of our bodies in this purely objective sense. This much he is willing to concede to modern materialist psychologies. However, the body cannot fully be understood on this basis alone. Husserl stresses that the body (our own body) appears, first of all, as the center of orientation. It lies at the center not only of immediacy but of the entire multiplicity of actual and possible orientations of sensing; indeed, it has "the unique distinction of bearing in itself the *zero point* of all these orientations" (Husserl 1989). It is the body (and not the ego) that is always and absolutely present "here" as against everything else which appears "there." The body cannot be distanced from myself. That is, "the Body as *my* Body, is something particularly subjective, inasmuch as it *mediates* my perceptions and actions which extend into the world of things" (Husserl 1989). The body, taken at its simplest, is always a "two-sided reality" and a "turning point," an ill-defined zone of contact with the purely conditional relations between the external world and the human subject. But it is rarely so simple; it is both an organ of sense through which we apprehend the world and the organ of will through which we act in the world. In the effortless accomplishment of voluntary movement, the body reveals itself in quite a new way, as it does, also, in acts of imagination, memory, love, and so on. The body is many-sided and in continuous metamorphosis among its many possible phasic states. Husserl's powerful analysis here replicates (and reveals the experiential foundation for) the contemporary physicist's rejection of Newtonian mechanics and the simpler forms of empiricism; all material bodies, and not only the human body, exist variously in a number of distinct possible states and are never given "once and for all."

Husserl's influence has been enormous, not only in philosophy, for which he defines one of the major developmental streams of the century, in relation to which succeeding generations of innovative thinkers have developed their own positions (Marcel 1949; Sartre 1958; Merleau-Ponty 1962; Ricoeur 1967; Lévinas 1973), but in psychology (Straus 1963, 1966; Strasser 1977), in biology (Buytendijk 1994); and in a somewhat more general way he is connected with radical reformulations of a general anthropology (Pannenberg 1985; Scheler 1987; Gehlen 1988).

Freud and Husserl, in different ways, define the possibilities of embodiment inherent in contemporary society. Freud views the body as an elemental multiplicity, and this multiplicity is the foundation for the impregnation of the world with imagination, fantasy, and dreams. The "derealization" of the world (its characteristic contemporary distance, sense of unreality, and heavy melancholy) stems from the historic layering of the body image and its uncontrollable fluctuations between these levels. For Husserl, however, the body remains one and is constituted out of the continuous interplay of memory, fantasy, dreams, and the "free variation" and "modalization" of raw sensation. The world gains reality, as does the body, to the extent that it can be fantasized; the "unreal" is the substance and not the image of reality; the body, rather than disintegrating into a series of tenuously connected images, comes to itself in a renewed substantiality through these very images.

UNFOLDING THE CONTEMPORARY
BODY IMAGE

The context of the dematerialization of nature is also significant for the development of new psychological studies of the body image. This not only is evident in the emergence of Freud's insights but is equally important to the development of other novel approaches that the subsequent celebrity of Freud's works has tended to obscure.

A common theme of both pre- and post-Freudian psychological studies was the emerging autonomy of the body image as the central focus and mechanism of human experience. The notion of the body image that emerged by the 1920s and 1930s had its roots in the same fin-de-siècle culture as Freud's work and might also be seen as part of a reviving interest in morphological and organismic approaches in biology which can be traced back to Goethe and the emergence of European Romanticism (Uexküll 1926; Goldstein 1939).

In this perspective the body image is viewed as linked directly with, but not mechanically related to, sensation. It is not identical with any particular sensory experience, nor is it a simple sum or more complex accumulation of such raw experiences. Here the body image is grasped as a lived unity prior to, and a precondition of, the meaningful perception of particular objects, movements, and so on (Straus 1963).

The centrality of the body image as the foundation of the perceptual world became more obvious through studies of its pathology. Whatever the origin and "meaning" of, for example, hysterical symptoms (which also played a central role in the development of Freud's psychology), they demonstrated the extent to which a "normal" body image was an essential and continually renewed construct in relation to which the normal world of experience became possible. And it was not only the hysteric who willfully, if unconsciously, created a body image which at points was at odds with the "facts" of the world. Early studies of epilepsy and aphasias by Hughlings Jackson opened up a rich seam of research into the pathologies of orientational body images and in the process made much clearer the process of assimilation and integration that went into the maintenance of a normal postural self-consciousness (Jackson 1931). Although frequently taken to be the point of origin for the development of modern neuropsychological studies with a pronounced reductive tendency, Hughlings Jackson's sensitive descriptions of the reported experiences of his patients proved to be equally influential in encouraging a more phenomenologically orientated psychology of the body image (Sacks 1985). Importantly, Jackson introduced the idea of a series of levels at which bodily experience is integrated, each with its own characteristic patterns of assimilation and typical pathologies. Each level was the locus of specific integrative functions, so that pathological functioning at one level did not necessarily affect a "lower" or "higher" function. All parts of the body are "respectively represented, re-represented, and re-re-represented" (Jackson 1931, 2:99). The resulting body image, therefore, is not a matter of simple spatial "modeling" of particular streams of feeling but is, rather, the result of a series of constructive processes in which first one part or aspect comes into prominence and then another. Breaking with the dominant tradition in empiricist psychology since Locke, he insists this image or representation is not an "idea"—"we have, indeed, no ideas of any parts of our bodies" (Jackson 1931, 2:208)—but a living form through which the self, organic processes, sensations, emotional life, and the world are experienced in their immediacy and continuous transformation.

Henry Head later extended and elaborated on Jackson's pioneering research. Equally, he insisted that the body image (he was the first to use the term in the sense that Schilder and others were to take up) could not be understood as the outcome of a "mechanical" process of association and remained independent of any particular sense or sensory system (Head 1920). The relative stability and meaningful coherence of the world, rather, depend upon the development of schemata that are anchored in, and define, specific forms of bodily consciousness. Most celebrated for his studies of aphasias of speech, Head used an approach that was in principle applicable to postural, affective, and other aspects of body images and partial body images. In the more sophisticated development of his approach, a stronger sense in which such images were both directly experienced and constructed through complex developmental and integrative processes (in which the action, and particularly the voluntary movement, of the person played a central role) became evident.

From Organs-without-a-Body to the Body-without-Organs

The contemporary body image might be regarded not only as a fragmentation and opening out of the classical modern body image but as a logical inversion of the ancient Western body image. The ancient body image was a collection of organs each linked separately to a specific divine source of vitality. The body as a form and structure was little remarked and did not constitute a fundamental point of reference for thought and reflection on experience (Vernant 1991). The unification of these vital forces within an idealized body form was a realization of divinity rather than of human corporeality. The historical transformation of this "organic" body image, through the religious and spiritual revolutions of the ancient world to a unitary structural principle in Plato, together with forms of dualism in later religion and philosophy that were subsequently integrated into Christianity, is fundamental for any understanding of the development of Western culture but cannot further be reviewed here (Ferguson 1997). The contemporary body image, at another extreme, loses its unity through "emptying" itself onto the continuous "surfaces" of modern life. It becomes a "body-without-organs" (Deleuze and Guattari 1977).

The most compelling descriptive account of such a body image is to be found in the rich eclecticism of Paul Schilder's psychology, whose *The Image and Appearance of the Human Body*, first published in 1935, remains a largely unacknowledged classic. If he never fully succeeded in his ambition "to unify in one framework, phenomenology, psychoanalysis, experimental psychology, and brain pathology" (1953, 19), his attempt was fertile in suggestive insights, none more compelling than the central place to which he accorded the body image as the focus of his psychology. Developing what he termed a "constructive psychology," he focused on the elementary processes that in a formal and substantive sense are the preconditions of experience. At the heart of all such processes lies the given objectivity of a body image which is itself the result of a largely unconscious and continuous process of construction and transformation. Thus, in opposition to the dominant behaviorist paradigm of stimulus and response, the activity of the person as an embodied Subject is regarded as the continuous requirement of all experience: "Sensations are not isolated since they are always closely related to the body-image and are not in direct correlation to the stimulus" (Schilder 1942, 3). "A perception," Schilder points out, "always belongs to an individual with a body" (Schilder 1942, 84). No "object" can emerge at all from the instability of the sensory flux except in relation to the body; "stabilization of the object parallels the stabilization of the impressions of the body" (Schilder 1942, 137). And, similarly, "every action is based upon the body-image. Action means a dynamic change in the body-image" (Schilder 1942, 231).

This complex interrelation of the body sensing the world and the body sensing itself through sensing the world gives rise to a dynamic process: "Physiological impulses of tonic, rhythmic, and phasic character, which are in such close relation to the impressions of the senses and the formation of the object, determine space in its properties and the dynamic relation of the body-image to space. The body-image continually creates a new space equilibrium around itself" (Schilder 1942, 234).

The unity of the body image is, thus, contingent and equivocal; it is "in perpetual inner self-construction and self-destruction. It is living in its continued differentiation and integration" (Schilder 1964a, 16). This process outruns our conscious control and manipulation: "It might be that there is in our body-image more than we consciously know about the body" (Schilder 1964a, 13). The image is an "immediate experience of the human body," and as such is not only a "postural model" but an identifiable complex of feelings. As a lived and fragile unity, "we have to expect strong emotions concerning our own body. We love it. We are narcissistic. The topography of the postural model will be the basis of emotional attitudes towards the body. Our knowledge will be dependent on the erotic currents flowing through our body and will also influence them" (Schilder 1964a, 15).

And again: "It is one of the inherent characteristics of our psychic life that we continually change our images; we multiply them and make them appear differently. This general rule is true also for the postural model of the body. We let it shrink playfully and come to the idea of Lilliputians, or we transform it into giants. We have, therefore, an almost unlimited number of body-images . . . but emotional processes are the force and source of energy of these constructive processes, and they direct them" (Schilder 1964a, 67).

This freedom of variation is a central part of Schilder's conception and brings him into a closer relation with Husserl, for whom the "objectivity" of the object is, in large measure, the result of a series of perceptual variations freely carried out by the human subject; indeed the host of imaginary objects, or the object viewed imaginatively from a multitude of divergent (and in a practical sense often impossible) perspectives, add to and provide the spatial and material "thickness" and "substance" to the image.

Among the most important "objects" that thus come into being through the free variations of the body image is the body itself, whose "substance" and "solidity" depend upon the continuous construction and reconstruction of its image from a multiplicity of varying perspectives. Interestingly, therefore, Schilder (like Husserl) views the fragmentation of the classical bourgeois ego—the "point-mass" of the closed and singular body image—as the precondition for the experience of the body as a fully realized unity. The dissolution of the ego does not result in a loss of the body but, rather, in the body regained and reduplicated.

Schilder insists, therefore, that we can, and normally do, view our own body in exactly the same way as any other object. And, in contrast to the popular existential philosophies that largely obscured his work, he does not regard the givenness of the body as essentially different from the givenness of any other object. Schilder, in this regard, points to the curious sense of detachment and distance from our bodies that we occasionally experience, an intimate estrangement which, we might add, is itself conditioned by the specific form of contemporary embodiment in its difference from the classical bourgeois body image. Thus, as our body image changes, so does our perception of the object or thing.

The Newtonian object corresponds to the closed body image of the bourgeois era; similarly, the "dematerialization" of the body in Maxwell's physics is an anticipation of the dispersed character of the contemporary body image. In this context Schilder is led to interesting and novel insight into the contemporary "emptying" of the body image. When people are asked to describe themselves from an imaginary position directly in front of their own bodies, Schilder reports, they frequently detach an imaginary eye and use it as a peculiarly intimate sensing device:

> There is very often a spiritual eye, which is in front of the subject and looks all over the body. This spiritual, inner eye need not be outside. It can be inside. It is like a psychic organ, which wanders round in the body and sees the outside of the body from the inside. It looks through the body, which is in some way empty, yet it does not see the inside of the body, but the surface. This immaterial eye wanders according to the point on the surface that has to be observed. The impression of emptiness in the body which occurs in

these experiments is very queer. We are led here for the first time to the problem of the perception of the inside of our body. (Schilder 1964a, 84–85)

This remarkable passage, anticipating aspects of Deleuze and Guattari's notion of a "body without organs," expresses specifically contemporary phenomena of multiple and shifting perspective, detachment, and the peculiar sense in which embodiment becomes an open surface of the world rather than a closed container against it (Deleuze and Guattari 1977).

In fact the entire boundary of the body, so well maintained theoretically and practically during the classical period of Modernity (which remains central to writers as diverse as Mary Douglas and Norbert Elias), increasingly becomes less well defined. Schilder himself remarks on the "astonishing results" of carefully examining the sensations of the surface of the body: "There are vague feelings of temperature. It is more or less the feeling of warmth. But the outline of the skin is not felt as a smooth and straight surface. This outline is blurred. There are no sharp borderlines between the outside world and the body" (Schilder 1964a, 85).

There is, in fact, a complete "indistinctness of feeling" of the surface of the body. Further, there is no neat match (now) between the optical and tactile image of the surface: "The skin that is felt is distinctly below the surface of the optic perception of the body" (Schilder 1964a, 86). We are "inside our skins" yet know nothing directly of the inside of our bodies (Schilder 1964b, 59). We become curiously dispersed over the surfaces of things, and in fact, "we do not respect our physical boundaries" (Schilder 1964a, 52). Our body image is continually subject to constructive and deconstructive transformations. Schilder's incisive analysis might be regarded as a "normalization" of Karl Jaspers's exhaustive documentation of radical "deformations" of body images that he records in his *General Psychopathology* (Jaspers 1963). Every possible whole and partial transformation is actually experienced to some degree.

This represents a decisive change from the classical self-contained and self-controlled bourgeois individual, the "point-mass" that was the impenetrable atom of modern society. Rather as particles radiated, for example, from an X-ray source remain in a "virtual" state till the moment of contact on a sensitive surface, so the surface of our body remains indistinct until it is touched; then, "at that very moment, the surface becomes smooth, clear, and distinct" (Schilder 1964a, 86). But this identity of optical and tactile sensation does not imply a fusion of body surface and object; rather, "there is a distinct space between," as they remain "psychologically separated."

More remarkably, although we know nothing of the inside of the body—which appears uncannily empty—we do feel the presence of an indeterminate "heavy mass" as the perception of gravity in our own body. The heavy mass is distributed in a characteristic fashion: "When one is standing, one feels that the heavy mass is chiefly in the legs and more especially in the feet. It diminishes from the feet upwards. Another center of gravity is the abdomen . . . and the head." But when one is lying down, the heavy mass immediately gathers toward the back. And "this is all we perceive of the inside of our body. Our body is nothing more than a heavy mass . . . we have a feeling of emptiness in ourselves" (Schilder 1964a, 92–93). Interestingly, this is just the way we perceive any other heavy object; we "imagine" its mass is concentrated in the lower portion.

More generally he remarks that "certainly the body-image in its final outcome is a unit." But this unit is not rigid: "it is changeable . . . every unit has parts and sides which are comparatively independent of each other. . . . Another important feature is the comparative looseness with which the single parts of the body are connected with each other . . . psychological dismembering can take place" (Schilder 1964a, 114).

Schilder has described very well the "postural model" of the contemporary world. The body image is experienced as a sensitive layer, just below the skin, and it is in this narrow surface that pulses of life and energy are felt. But now the body no longer encloses anything, not even an empty and enigmatic space productive of its own mysterious symbols or soul stuff. We are confined to the narrow division between two forms of absolute Otherness; it is the very hostility of these vast and impenetrable regions that holds body and soul together. But the body image is not fused to the body; it continually strays "beyond" its material form: "The space in and around the postural model is not the space of physics. The body-image incorporates objects or spreads itself into space" (Schilder 1964a, 213). However, its reach is, so to speak, along the same plane and belongs to the same dimensionality as the body itself. The body and its image are two linked, but loosely linked, localizations of the same interactive and sensitive surface. The surface of the body is not uniform; its characteristic feelings differ in different regions and are experienced through "libidinous flows of energy" focused on openings and specially sensitized areas. Indeed, "the narcissistic libido has as its object the image of the body" (Schilder 1964a, 122).

The contemporary body image, in contrast to that of classical Modernity, is quite distinct from the material integument that is its bearer. This is nowhere more dramatically demonstrated than in reports, well known after studies carried out during the American Civil War, of "phantom limbs" (Mitchell 1872). It was the persistence of feeling in the absent limb, particularly the localization of pain in the absent limb, which encouraged a good deal of psychological research on the body as a lived image (Lhermitte 1970; Kolb 1954). The "phantom" persists as a playful variation on the body image, the persistence of the lived image beyond its "material" organ. Especially in dreams "the old lability of the body image comes back, and the body contracts and expands according to our emotional needs" (Schilder 1964a, 114).

Summarizing an impressively wide-ranging discussion, Schilder argues that

> the building-up of the postural model of the body takes place on the physiological level by continual contact with the outside world. On the libidinous level it is built up not only by the interest we ourselves have in our body, but also by the interest other persons show in the different parts of our body. They may show their interest by actions or merely by words and attitudes. But what persons around us do with their own bodies is also of enormous importance. Here is the first hint that the body-image is built up by social contacts. (Schilder 1964a, 137)

The intersubjective character of the body image does not depend upon the existence of some organizing "soul" or ego that is in some mysterious way "elsewhere" than the part or image itself. It is also the precondition for the peculiarly sociable nature of the contemporary body image, which continually participates in interaction with others. When Schilder claims that the body image is social, he means that "our own activity is insufficient to build up the image of the body" (Schilder 1964a, 116). Others are an essential aspect of its identity, and that intercommunication is central to its existence; "body-images of human beings communicate with each other in parts or in wholes" (Schilder 1964a, 138). But here the social character of the body image is taken in a more general and stronger sense. There "exists a deep community between one's own body image and the body image of others" (Schilder 1964a, 217), a continuous effort to incorporate others into it.

The social reality of the body image emerges as a continuous process of self-creation and realizes itself in and through the psychic constitution of the interactive subject. Imitation, identification, and projection are the fundamental social mechanisms through which the body image is constructed.

THE SHADOW OF THE BODY

The body is no longer distinguished from the nonbody as Object from Subject or matter from space; for the specifically contemporary form of embodiment, the difference that remains significant is that between the body-as-image and the body-as-shadow. The body-as-shadow is a negative presence, the return of a lost substantiality in illness, suffering, and death. Here the body is universalized and corporealized; purified of difference, it is reduced to being nothing but the body "itself." The body-as-image is particular; it is always some specific body defined in terms of its distinguishing marks. But the body-as-shadow is simply body "as such": depersonalized, immediate sensuousness.

The unnameable presence—primitively felt as the "weight" of the body—has dissolved into nothing, or almost so. The image is in the ascendant, and its luminous variety distracts us from that which cannot be represented. The entire development of Modernity can be, and often is, understood as nothing other than the gradual, but ultimately complete, realization of human autonomy as self-generated systems of representation. Now there seems to be nothing left over, nothing to obscure the spread of Enlightenment or to offend, by its mute and unresponsive presence, the therapeutic largesse of an all conquering Reason. Every effort to grasp the fugitive bodily character of reality refines and elaborates the catalog of historic images from which it is composed and, thus, diverts it from one of its fundamental tasks. However "antimetaphysical" in intention, contemporary attempts to "return to the body" lose themselves in the playful freedom of insubstantial ideas and, rather than outwit the modern urge toward abstraction, end by further extending its empire.

It is all too easy, indeed, simply to deny the reality of bodily self-presence as anything other than an interesting, if somewhat obscure, idea. Yet, at the limit of embodiment, we confront obvious and unavoidable realities that resist our imagination and exist for us as brute facts, as dark and impenetrable body shadows. Thus, rather than rediscover the mystery of self-presence in the everyday experience of the body and the body's everyday experience of its world, we put off confronting this enigmatic being to the mundane but singular moment of death or glimpse it fleetingly in the penumbra of sickness and pain.

Whereas for the premodern West reality continually spread "beyond" empirical actuality, Modernity increasingly identified the real with the actual and, thus, could fully represent and imagine existence. For the premodern world, therefore, bodily presence could be understood as the "dark matter" essential to every form of reality; it was not "less real" by virtue of its reticence. Modernity, however, does not surrender any substantial reality to such a purpose. All reality must be bodily reality and, at the same time, capable of reflection as an image. Because bodily self-presence remains mysterious, it is effectively excluded from life and manifests itself, if at all, at the boundary of existence. Now, therefore, we can only seize upon the universal transition to nothingness as the empirical "foundation" for our persistent and otherwise groundless residual feeling of somehow "containing" more than we can imagine and of being something other than ourselves. Now, rather than view death as the release of *psyche*, we see it as the moment when the body, after all, is most fully itself. And as death sustains a real presence, it becomes tainted with metaphysical abstraction and doubt; it becomes as "unreal" as any premodern "superstition."

It is, therefore, in the larger framework of the development of Modernity, and not in any contemporary squeamishness (which in other respects is far from evident!), that we can understand the strange ambivalence in contemporary attitudes toward death. The struggle between the body-as-image and the body-as-shadow—which is also the struggle of Modernity to establish its independence from the past—reveals itself more clearly in this ambivalence.

The Shadow of Death

In an extraordinary fashion we have come to deny the reality of death. It is not simply that during this century many infectious diseases which had previously killed millions have been subdued and even eliminated (though in many areas of the world, including the most advanced societies, some, such as tuberculosis, are making an alarming comeback). Nor is it that life expectancy has increased dramatically throughout the development of Modernity or that infant mortality has been reduced to a level at which its incidence becomes a scandal or a tragedy. Changes such as these might encourage a growing sense of physical security but cannot explain a reorientation to life which seems to exclude as a possibility the most certain of eventualities.

Death is not only delayed, it is denied. In being wholly secularized, death loses all significance and, thus, no longer finds any place amid the meaningful images of life. The pure nothingness of nonexistence cannot appear as an image, and because we live in the medium of images, death consequently is banished.

We are unable, therefore, to enter into the death of those close to us. As Philippe Ariès has pointed out, death has become a private act, an ultimate withdrawal from society rather than, as in premodern societies, a final rite de passage. We rarely see a dead body. Most people die in a hospital attended, if at all, by medical staff. Grief and loss, correspondingly, are individuated and interiorized. The fact of death goes unrecognized and unremarked. Where a ritual once marked the death of an individual and allowed a collective adjustment to the loss, now social life is quite independent of any of its individual members. There is no ritual of readjustment because no readjustment is necessary; the routines of social life continue in an uninterrupted fashion. We live in and through such routines and to that extent participate in a process which is immune to death. Thus, inasmuch as the body is experienced as an image or a series of images and is assimilated to the circulatory logic of social exchange, it triumphs over death. We lack, therefore, any positive conceptualization of death. And to that extent we experience life as something insubstantial but eternal.

Death becomes the reality of the body that we cannot experience; its substantiality and presence, banished from a Modernity for which every reality becomes accessible only as self-created images, are fully realized in the moment of absolute negation. It is, therefore, with something akin to an ancient sense of wonder that Hans Castorp (in Thomas Mann's fundamental reflection on Modernity and death, *The Magic Mountain*) is fascinated by viewing his own X-ray: "The flesh in which he walked disintegrated, annihilated, dissolved in vacant mist, and there within it was the finely turned skeleton of his own hand . . . he gazed at this familiar part of his own body, and for the first time in his life he understood that he would die" (Mann 1960). But such uncanny experiences are rare; more commonly death is reduced to a paradoxical phenomenon. An ultimate self-certainty, death, which cannot be experienced, like an insignificant dream fades into nothing.

This is true on a historical scale as well as at a personal level. The twentieth century is witness to human destructiveness of unprecedented scale and inventiveness. The toll of avoidable death is staggering. Intellectually we may acknowledge this. Even intellectually, however, we normally fail to confront the extent and ubiquity of mass killing. Of course the "senseless destruction" of the First World War is vivid in the collective memory. The Somme, Verdun, Ypres, Passchendaele remain, like superstars of contemporary sport, instantly recognizable singular proper names. Yet we underestimate; the encounter with mass death was unprecedented. It requires a historian to remind us that "more than twice as many men died in action or of their wounds in the First World War as were killed in all major wars between 1790 and 1914" (Mosse, 1990). More than 300,000 died in the first two weeks of the Battle of the Somme. But already these numbers belong to history rather than to memory. Death on this scale defeats the imagination. We memorialize, in order to forget rather than to recall, the human abattoir. The First World War was transformed, even as the fighting continued, into a literary classic, a kind of gothic masterpiece, which supplies us with arresting images (that is, with specifically disembodied and undying representations) of slaughter. These *tableaux de mort* have become part of a new myth of war, not of death made meaningful through struggle and liberation but of friendship, courage, and stupidity rendered "timeless" as human virtues and follies altogether detached from the reality of annihilation.

War is continuous with the development of Modernity (it is absurd to pretend otherwise) and in its most advanced forms illustrates the tendency of the body to lose its well-defined boundaries and to enter into a general process of merging. The distinction between the soldier and the civilian is abolished, first through a general mobilization in the First World War; indeed, the concept of world war is incompatible with that of professional armies engaged in limited combat. The mobilization draws the civilian into the midst of war and, later, releases the soldier back into a civilian world which has been transformed. Furthermore the civilian population, as workers and enemy citizens, becomes a target and is drawn inexorably into the maelstrom of destruction. Second, there is no period without war; its intermittent character is an illusion. In these respects, just as the limited national warfare of the seventeenth century was an important instrument of modern state formation, so the total war of the twentieth century is the perpetual act of violence that in its more benign aspect is called globalization; it is a continual breaking down of previous solidarities, a dissolving of the territorial and cultural boundaries that restrict the flow of commodities. By the time of Vietnam, the Americans were able to take advanced consumer society with them; every unit was serviced with Coke, beer, hamburgers, American films, music, and drugs. The global expansion of production and consumption uses war to obliterate distinctions and establish freedom of movement, uses it to destroy the older nationalism in the empty name of which many of its conflicts in practice were fought.

The Western Front remains the inadequate archetype of a century of incomprehensible destruction. The archetype is embellished—the Nazi death camp, Hiroshima, the Gulag—but does not fundamentally alter the dreamy emblem of a century of total war. There is no question here of confusing image with reality. Reality was destroyed. We live through images just because they are substantially unreal. The image of war, like any other image, knows nothing of death. Indeed, the place of death, like any other place, suffused with the cold indifference of modern empty space, is distinguished only through a kind of retroactive labeling process. The "real" Somme, the "real" Auschwitz, the "real" Hiroshima: names once redolent of death become so many tourist destinations to be ticked off the itinerary of world travel and compared, unfavorably in terms of their banal artificiality, to the film versions.

We live in the era of total war but contrive to insulate ourselves from its potent actuality. The twentieth century is a continuous present; its war is global, but war for us is always "in the past" or "somewhere else." Death is multiplied, mechanized, industrialized, computerized until, thankfully, it is virtualized. The century that rediscovered genocide and ethnic cleansing—Armenia, the Jews, Gypsies, Nanking, Cambodia, Burundi, Slovenia; the list could be extended—also experienced on an unprecedented scale famine, disease, and "natural disasters" attributable in whole or in part to a variety of governments' calculated actions and inactions. It is difficult to calculate the number of avoidable deaths; the most determined and comprehensive research reports that "in total, during the first eighty-eight years of this century, almost 170 million men, women, and children have been shot, beaten, tortured, knifed, burned, starved, frozen, crushed, or worked to death; buried alive, drowned, hung, bombed, or killed in any other of the myriad ways governments have inflicted death on unarmed, helpless citizens and foreigners. The dead could conceivably be nearly 360 million people. It is as though our species has been devastated by a modern Black Plague. And indeed it has, but a plague of Power, not germs" (Rummel 1994, 9).

These same governments have also revived and refined the old arts of torture, not as a public display of absolute power but covertly and from weakness as a routine means of dealing with opposition. Thus, to the hundreds of millions killed must be added the countless number of "survivors" broken by grief, hardship, and suffering.

Yet the extraordinary festival of death does not touch us. It is as if the entire population of North America were to be wiped out, but so long as it is not us or our children, we need not notice. We cast death into the void and rid ourselves of all encumbering presence. The sublime transcendence of death remains infinitely remote, at once a confirmation and a negation of the body's share in Absolute Being.

The Shadow of Illness

Death is the body's most turbid shadow and one, so to speak, too dark to be visible. Yet it remains our most intimate companion. And now, rather than visit as an exterior and alien being, death awakens within us as from a dreamless sleep. Now, our encounter with death is played out in relation to its minor figure, in the penumbra of illness and pain.

It is in the form of illness that we can become acquainted with death and, unavoidably, with bodily presence. And Modernity has discovered new forms for this introduction. In advanced societies cancer, heart disease, and injuries from accidents have largely replaced infectious diseases as the leading causes of death. And, more generally, stress, food additives, and sedentary lifestyles, it is frequently claimed, constitute the "unhealthy" aspects of contemporary society that facilitate, if they do not themselves cause, a wide range of viral illness and give rise to diffuse chronic pain. Analgesics are among the most widely consumed and profitable of contemporary commodities. New diseases and new concepts of disease have developed as new body images have become established. The closed "body-in-space" suffered from "internal" organic complaints, from secret and hidden disease processes, particularly those associated with eating, digestion, and elimination, and from "unhygienic" aftereffects of social contacts: syphilis, gonorrhea, and infectious diseases. The contemporary open and extended body image, in contrast, is prey to a host of "superficial" psychosomatic conditions and suffers particularly from diseases of movement and hyperactivity: anxiety, stress, and tension.

We most commonly think of death as the natural outcome of a "terminal" illness. Death is the extremity of illness, and illness is a kind of anticipation of death. Some illnesses, in respect of this proximity, are accorded a certain ambivalent privilege, a superiority indicated by more than the granting of a license not to work. Tuberculosis, for example, retained an association with Renaissance melancholy and became the archetypal Romantic disease, afflicting especially those sensitive souls capable of the most refined culture and feeling. For the wealthy, in particular, tuberculosis indicated a level of distinction and civilization which made ordinary life more or less unbearable (Sontag 1980). The sanitarium so perfectly described in Thomas Mann's magisterial novel, therefore, is a superior reality where the arts of civilization and manners have been preserved and developed in contrast to the gathering forces of barbarism below.

Illness is dense with the shadowy presence, rather than the lively image, of the body. The closer it draws to death, in fact, the more ghostly does the body become. Severe and prolonged illness reduces the body to pure materiality and, paradoxically (like the pure sensuousness of intense pain), annihilates corporeality at the very moment of bringing it fully to itself (Scarry 1990; Morris 1991; Rey 1995). It is the process of corporealization, in fact, that, by liberating the previously enclosed soul, can give rise to the impression of brilliance and sensitivity in the dying. The refinement and cultivation on the Magic Mountain are deceptive; they are simply the illusion wrought by the forcible separation of soul from body. In illness the soul becomes more visible because the body falls back into a purely organic state. Thomas Mann once again provides the essential insight: "A human being who is first of all an invalid is *all* body; therein lies his inhumanity and his debasement. In most cases he is little better than a carcass." On the other hand, such a being, equally, becomes all soul, and "a soul without a body is as inhuman and horrible as a body without a soul." The living body is as remote from the pure materiality of organic processes as is the abstraction of the soul.

Illness and pain can themselves enter into the processes of life as images, but their secret complicity with death restores to them the sense of a primitive substantiality which cannot wholly be eradicated. Illness reasserts itself against the claims of medicine and science (Gadamer 1996). In illness it is the shadow of death, not the image of life, that has come to bear the stamp of reality.

The Living Shadow

For all the apparent ascendancy of life and its images, the strange denial of death, and its residual conceptualization as illness, the body-as-shadow has not wholly been excised from modern experience.

Perhaps, for the advanced societies, the most general recognition of this presence is manifest in the determined pursuit of physical comfort that has become the real aim, certainly, of domestic life, if not the guiding purpose of social policy. Contemporary life seems preoccupied with the elimination of discomfort. Modern domestic machinery and the modern products of industrial machinery have the common aim of promoting human bodily comfort. Comfort is the manifest goal of contemporary social life and consists simply in becoming unaware of our corporeal nature (Giedion 1948). It is as if our bodies had become intolerable to us, not the fluid self-transforming body images in constant superficial interaction but the body shadow that in its lethargic heaviness offers a certain resistance to the freedom and mobility of such images.

Comfort means, first of all, weightlessness. There were no chairs in medieval society; people sat on the floor or on benches, even in formal settings. The Baroque development of the chair offered continuous support to the body while the classical modern chair allowed greater relaxation and flexibility. During the twentieth century tubular steel frames and the cantilevered chair support an apparently weightless body. The reclining seat, a medical innovation, becomes domesticated so that the body is fully supported along its length and held suspended in space. Other aspects of modern domestic technology and materials led to "streamlining"; to the home and workplace being organized in terms of extended "surfaces" rather than in terms of isolated, independent, and closed "pieces" of furniture with a multiplicity of secret internal compartments. Built-in furniture, streamlined surfaces, cantilevered chairs, and advanced systems of communication became the home environment of the contemporary "dematerialized" body. The pursuit of comfort, that is to say, is a constant oscillation between the body-as-shadow and the body-as-image, an acceptance and, at the same time, an overcoming of the substance of the body.

It seems that we can neither escape nor resolve this paradox. The rational goal of physical health falls into compulsive unhealthiness. The compulsive character of Modernity comes to light in the meaningless repetition of actions that are, in themselves, functionless. Informed neither by conscious goal nor by access of pleasure, the human body is driven ultimately by an inertial principle of repetition. Thus the liberty of play and the determined pursuit of a "healthy" lifestyle is worn away by the dark shadow of bodily presence; it becomes a weekly, twice weekly, then daily submission to discomfort. Exercise, not sport, appears essential to well-being. Precisely measured units of pain (a specific number of repetitions, periods of time, gradations of weights) are endured in a strange ritual reenactment of the debilitating work discipline from which sport seemed originally to offer an escape. The soaring spiritual freedom of the athlete becomes tainted with the glamour of death. We long for death because we cannot help but want to have the fullness and weight of the body restored to us. We seek our own presence, but having denied presence to everything except death, we seek death.

Freud's understanding of the contemporary body, and of its essential link with modern society and its culture, was nowhere more clearly revealed than in his controversial insistence on the reality of the Death Instinct. Perfectly attuned to the least obvious but most significant aspects of the new century, Freud, in addition to deciphering hysteria and normalizing it as dreams, detected "the urge to repeat" as the most pervasive contemporary manifestation of Thanatos.

HISTORY OF THE BODY AND
THE BODY AS HISTORY

The contemporary open and sensitive body image not only registers everything which is novel in contemporary social life, but also, as specific qualitatively defined "regions," it remodels its own past and preserves as possibilities of experience all previously developed body images. The contemporary body image has become a temporal, as well as a spatial, representation of itself; it offers itself as a kind of accumulated history of itself. It is in this context that the divergent and even contradictory views of, and interests in, the contemporary body can be understood in terms of the quite different historical locations of the body images that each invokes. Schilder, thus, describes not one but a host of body images "in perpetual self-construction and self-destruction" (Schilder 1964a, 16).

The characteristic historicism of the contemporary body image, however, has tended to be obscured and misrepresented as a philosophical or sociological dispute over which of its many forms best describes contemporary reality, or which most completely characterizes its "real" nature. New and old body images are described as if they were "natural" phenomena outside of the stream of history. Marcel, for example, brilliantly uncovers by his phenomenological method a primordial body image that is perhaps anterior to and simpler than the most ancient of recorded images. His mistake, we might say, is in regarding this as a given reality which is not itself the product of a historical process, the very same process, it might be added, that came in time to obscure this particular givenness with a new order of reality that appeared, for that epoch, an equally natural and incontrovertible mode of being. For most academic psychologists the "natural" body image is rooted in the classical period of Modernity; it is just the closed instrumentality of the body, its responsiveness to reason and command, that is its primary datum. In everyday life, on the other hand, medieval and Renaissance body images, redolent of older religious and magical worldviews, reappear, particularly in relation to experiences of human weakness such as illness and death. The contemporary world, indeed, provides us with access to an almost complete inventory of Western body images.

The body image is the empirical foundation of our historical imagination, as of our natural knowledge. Each form retains its historical integrity; each, in fact, plunges us into a world complete in itself and provides us with the hermeneutic keys to an understanding of distant epochs. These forms cannot be added up, synthesized, or combined. They bear a certain relatedness one to another as aspects of the continuous development of Western society, but the living body retains this multifaceted and many-sided aspect; it is, or rather would be, a mass of contradictions, were it not that each form, ignorant of a logic rooted in one of their number, remains indifferent to and coexists alongside all the others. Schilder, thus, remarks that "one may be enshrouded by various body images. They cannot form a unit, but they may form a sum" (Schilder 1964a, 237). The distinction among body images, that is to say, is somewhat like the distinction between waking and dreaming. When awake we can distinguish the peculiar class of recollections we call dreams and recognize them as being quite distinct from the recollection of waking experiences; but when we are dreaming, the entire world of waking perception ceases to exist.

It is, in fact, only from the rather peculiar perspective of the present, for which multiple perspectives and the conventional character of social behavior have become more evident, that the existence of other bodily forms and images appears at all.

In contemporary society body images drawn from different epochs become available in two quite distinctive ways. First, as spontaneously experienced, specific body images appear preadapted to particular social circumstances and relations. Our everyday experience is a continuous switching among such body images, each of which has its origin and draws its meaning and significance from particular and widely divergent historical periods. We respond in a quite thoughtless way to all these forms; the ancient body image, for example, becomes available as a language of the "heart." We have "gut feelings," "heart-stopping moments," and describe dramas as "breathtaking." At other times medieval body images become uppermost. We are "touched" by some monumental work of art or "impressed" by some natural scene to the extent of becoming small and insignificant; helpless and impotent in the face of some great disaster, suddenly transfixed, unmoving, "rooted to the spot" for a moment, we contemplate the world in a new way and, more than that, feel its presence in us as a strange and disconcerting intruder. We become light-headed and directionless, disoriented—and suddenly we respond with our bodies and to our bodies as symbols rather than as signs. But the moment passes, an interior life opens up once again establishing the spontaneous flow of its own images as if from an independent and inexhaustible reservoir of experience. We recover ourselves as self-moving intentional objects, as bodies in space going about their daily business with weight, dignity, directionality; bodies into which all the inertial forces of Modernity are gathered and upon which they are focused. Then we go shopping or fall asleep and dream, and the body image unfurls itself onto a new world. The antinomies of object and subject collapse onto the surface of the body, which becomes the fundamental reality for modern culture and gives rise to a body image adapted to an age of consumption: fashionable, excitable, irritable, a moment within a dematerialized flux of experience.

Second, historical body images are invoked to characterize particular, frequently subordinate and devalued, social groups. Children, for example, until very recently were given the toys, pastimes, and clothes that once characterized the (equally dependent) premodern rural adult; their body image was defined through quite elaborate sumptuary conventions that made visible and emphasized their subordinate status and lack of legal personality. Similarly, the symptoms of the insane now consist primarily in their being overwhelmed by, and "stuck" in, the ancient body image (Storch 1924), which simultaneously establishes their remoteness from modern "reason" and a romantic overvaluation of their experience as "original." The characterization of the "Other," that is to say, is always founded upon an aspect of the "Self," upon an actually experienced body image now (usually mistakenly) regarded as marginal to the character and integrity of that self.

Body, which is central to the emergence of Modernity as a spatial category—as simple extension—is, thus, also and just as significantly a temporal category. We grasp contemporary reality through a kind of historicist architectonics of the body plan, each moment of which brings into prominence a different structural feature of the body and defines its form in a particular way. The contemporary body image reveals itself as a series of topological possibilities running from the ancient "organs without a body" to the postmodern "body-without-organs". This series may be schematized as follows:

Ancient /organic, unbounded

Christian / flesh, closed, filled

Gnostic–Neoplatonic / flesh, closed, empty

Medieval / skeletal, microcosmic, collective-symbolic

Grotesque / visceral, open, material

Renaissance / anatomical, microcosmic, individuated-metaphoric

Modern / epidermic, closed, individuated, male

Postmodern / epidermic, open, deindividuated, female

It need hardly be added that in relation to each period and accumulating along with these main forms, a host of variations, inversions, and transformations arise and also persist as continuous possibilities of and for human experience. This complexity cannot adequately be reflected in a dialectic of Subject and Object or any of its cognate forms, all of which, in fact, are rooted in, and give formal expression to, just one of these images. As a characteristic form of embodiment, Modernity, rather, should be viewed more broadly as the accumulation, differentiation, and interrelation of these forms.

That the body can only be understood historically is hardly a novel idea. But this is too often taken as a weak demand for the restoration of a properly contextual presentation of facts of bodily experience, as if such facts and their relation to what is defined as an appropriate context were not in themselves problematic. But, in fact, the body should be understood in a more radically historical way, as a historical object in the fullest sense. Experience is ordered and becomes available to us "ready-packaged," so to speak, in a specific bodily form. Each form can be understood in terms of its origins at different epochs in the development of Western society, so that normal experience continually invokes worlds that we had imagined no longer existed, not as nostalgia but as living history. The development of Western society can be viewed, thus, as the emergence and development of new body images, each linked with a specific form of social organization and a particular cosmology; each literally "embodies" a specific understanding and experience of life, a specific world.

Standing apart from this sequence and offering an inarticulate but persistent challenge to its Aristotelian orderliness (as well as, of course, to its reductive simplification), there lurks another and more vital difference, the distinction between absence and presence, between the body-as-image and the body-as-shadow. Every modern effort to banish presence stumbles over the peculiar givenness of the human body, and at the same time every attempt to articulate that givenness ends in unmodern metaphysical abstraction. The most elementary of bodily experiences, thus, are appealed to as incontrovertible "evidence" in support of radically incompatible understandings of experience. Like an Escher engraving, spontaneously alternating foreground and background to reveal incompatible realities, the body oscillates between image and shadow, absence and presence.

A proper appreciation of the peculiar characteristics of modern body images, however (and a fortiori of Modernity more generally), requires not only a reconstruction of the original context of their various sources and an acknowledgment of their incompleteness; it also stands in need of a related historical understanding of the "soul." Indeed, the contemporary body image remains fundamentally obscure until it is recognized as nothing other than the soul, an insight expressed with exceptional clarity by Nietzsche: "Granting that the 'soul' was only an attractive and mysterious thought, from which philosophers rightly, but reluctantly, separated themselves—that which they have since learnt to put in its place is perhaps even more attractive and even more mysterious. The human body, in which the whole of the most distant and most recent past of all organic life once more becomes living and corporeal, seems to flow through this past and right over it like a huge and inaudible torrent: the body is a more wonderful thought than the old 'soul'" (Nietzsche 1973, 132–33).

TWO

Soul

$\mathcal{M}$ODERNITY can be understood in terms of specific transformations of the body image, as a particular mode, or modes, of
embodiment with everything that implies for self-experience and the experience of the world. In a related way Modernity may also be conceptualized
as a history of the human soul, as specific transformations of human feeling. And as "in many societies, the soul has been thought of as an image of
the body" (Durkheim 1995, 48), these transformations are, not surprisingly, closely related. Indeed, because reflection on the body held center
stage in the most prestigious of modern intellectual movements—the
rational sciences—for many the most compelling and the only fully justifiable way of gaining human self-understanding in terms of the soul was
(and has remained) to conceive its qualities as aspects of the emerging
understanding of body as a physiomechanical system. For some this
amounted, ultimately, to denying the categorical distinctness of the soul
and reducing it to a monistic view of reality. But this need not imply a radical "materialism" (the body image and not matter itself is the model of reality), nor, more significantly, was this program generally pushed to its extreme. More generally the modern soul was conceptualized in relation to,
but as distinct from, the body. And new knowledge of the body provided
fresh clues to, but not a complete explanation of, the mystery of the soul.

For Modernity the soul was not simply linked in some way to the body,
it was related specifically to the "body-in-space," that is, to the individuated
and closed body form of the bourgeois era. The soul, on this model, was

defined as an intentional and feeling body, a body peculiarly conscious of its own movement and able to affect it in terms of its "inner" wants, purposes, or intentions. The soul became a kind of vector associated with a specific body and was characterized, above all, by the possession of the universal attribute of reason. Human action could then be understood in terms of the more or less logical realization of intentions that were, so to speak, representations in the mind of the soul's inclinations.

The body is a complex image inextricably bound to the field of cultural history, so that body and soul seem to define each other; the soul is understood on the model of the body, but the body, as a nonmaterial and intuitively given image/shadow, is in its turn understood in terms of the soul. This circularity can be broken, or at least avoided, by a contextual understanding. The perspective of the body as the "body-in-space" is founded upon the same social reality that makes it meaningful as a model for the soul. It is not that the "materialism" of the body perspective provides a concrete and successful intellectual model which can be extended to the less understood world of the soul; it is rather that both body and soul become viewed in terms of new social relations in which individuation, the market, money transactions, and the circulation of commodities play a central role.

Thus, as distinct from, and at times in opposition to, the dominant tradition of scientific rationality that explicitly took its point of departure in a reductionist materialism, the modern soul seeks to grasp itself and the world through the immediacy of inner feeling and emotion. It seeks to do so in terms of time rather than space, and with respect to the characteristic dynamics of organic growth and development rather than through the sheer persistence of rectilinear motion. Thus, rather than reflecting critically on the Subject-Object distinction, a focus on historical transformations of the soul is best understood in relation to the modern dialect of Self and Other.

What is involved here is two contrasting visions of human subjectivity in modern society. One is "scientific," rational, and materialistic, for which the soul (when it is admitted to exist at all) becomes transparent, communicable, and lucid, nothing other than the self-presence of the cogito. The other is "romantic," irrational, and ideal, for which the soul remains hidden, inward, and personal, the mysterious inner depth of being.

It is important to recognize that both of these conceptions are thoroughly modern in character. Indeed, the complex of cultural movements associated with, but not identical to, what is generally referred to as European Romanticism can only be understood in relation to the same historical context that gave rise to the modern transformation of the body image outlined in the previous chapter. And, just as the body perspective included within it a specifically rational vision of the soul, so the perspective of the soul encompassed its own irrational conceptualization of nature. Thus, although the perspective of the modern soul sought its ultimate ground in the distinctive interiority of human feelings, it would be quite misleading to regard this perspective as exclusively about human feelings. Not only does it involve a decisive transformation in people's views of their society and its history, it also involves a new conceptualization of nature, a view which, culminating in the writings of Goethe, Schelling, and the *Naturwissenschaften,* short-lived though it was, has exerted many long-term influences in the development of modern scientific as well as humanistic and literary culture (Gusdorf 1985). This influence can still be detected, in fact, in those disciplines in which morphological as distinct from analytical accounts of nature and human experience have been preferred (Lenoir 1982; Nyhart 1995).

In all this the perspective of the soul is not (or not necessarily) a subjectivism of the individual concrete ego but, ideally, a metaphysics of a transindividual subject conceived as the universal "depth" of human interiority, above all as shared imagination (Gusdorf 1948; Lockridge 1989). But however much its most ardent and sophisticated champions insisted upon the nonconcrete universality and conditioning absoluteness of the soul, it became identified with a purely secular striving for *Bildung* and the realization in concrete terms of a determinate self.

In discussing the modern soul, therefore, particular attention must be paid to these variations and inconsistencies. More obviously than in the case of the body, every attempt to characterize the specifically modern character of the soul is a contested defense or critique of Modernity itself.

THE PREHISTORY
OF THE SOUL

It would not be helpful or indeed possible even in a schematic form to rehearse here the long history of the Western soul. For the most part the prehistory (that is, the premodern history) of the soul will simply be taken for granted. It is, however, worth emphasizing the extent to which in some important respects what has previously been termed the "body image" is (or was), and does not simply imply, the soul.

For the ancient world body and soul were, so to speak, jointly dispersed in the organic fragmentation of life. The rationalization of the body image and its gradual unification under both religious and secular philosophical assumptions (both of which were linked to the centralization of authority and the spread of the money economy) resulted in a splitting apart of material and nonmaterial aspects of life.

What might be termed the Greek tradition, not simply in terms of the original context of Western ideas but as a long-term and continually renewed development of Platonism, provided the fertile soil for the development of a systematic interpretation of the body image, or *psyche*, as a nonmaterial conception of the soul. In this tradition the soul was established both as the animating presence within the body and, more significantly, as the seat of a unified and individuated consciousness, the carrier of self-identity. It is also worth recalling that the notion of *psyche* developed as a plastic form in which the body image and the world were conformed to each other.

These rationalizing processes did not at once result in a wholly nonmaterial and abstract conception of an interior soul. The rationalized body image linked the immediate apprehension of reality to the world of eternal forms. In this linking capacity the soul is reflected back into the body and is felt as *eros*, as a longing for union with those ideal forms of which the soul is itself a partial replica. The human soul, that is to say, lifts itself beyond the body in which it is first mirrored and turns itself toward the image of the world that it makes permanent as a rational (bodily) order, or *logos*. While *eros* represents the "feeling" image of the body and has direct links with older organic body images, *logos* represents a new confidence in the realized principle of bodily integration and unity. The *logos*, it should be noted, is first of all a principle of bodily integration and order rather than the operative mechanism of an abstract "mind."

Reality, in other words, presents itself to us through the intermediary of the body image, which is the only link between the imperfect corporeal form of human being and the perfect, essential form of ideas. But reality cannot be grasped in its totality and simplicity. Reality can become present to us only by way of *eros* and *logos,* both of which are extensions of a more primitive *eidos,* or direct apprehension of the plastic form originally linked to bodily states. Indeed, the essential being of things can only ever be grasped in this primitive form, and ultimately, therefore, Plato does not seek to replace a more inclusive mythological mode of expression with any technical or dialectical use of language (Plato 1973, 136–42). The soul, which is linked to the perishable form of the body, is thereby limited: "Above the world of being towers that which is beyond everything and, therefore, cannot be grasped even by the *Logoi*" (Friedländer 1958, 63; Plato 1993, 56). Reality is felt, in consequence, as something demonic, as the articulation of a force within us which has its ultimate source in a realm of necessity with which we have at best a secondhand acquaintance.

The soul, here, is still nothing other than the "body's exact non-material replica" (Robinson 1970, 30), which is to say the body image has become "thought" as the soul. Plato insists that the soul is "permeated by the corporeal"; the body is "ingrained in its very nature through constant association and long practice." And, moreover, "the sensual element is not merely a mask or veil. It is a stepping stone to a higher level, but a necessary stepping stone whose absence would make that higher level inaccessible" (Friedländer 1958, 49). The body is necessary but only as an ancillary form through which the soul can be reached. There association and interpenetration of body and soul may, ultimately, be nothing more than a bad habit which the philosopher might succeed in overcoming. And if such an overcoming were possible, none would doubt its value; the soul is inherently superior to the body: "The soul is most like that which is divine, immortal, intelligible, uniform, indissoluble, and ever self-consistent and invariable, whereas body is most like that which is human, mortal, multiform, unintelligible, dissoluble, and never self-consistent" (Friedländer 1958, 3:49).

Interestingly, modern developments did not (or not until recently) challenge the underlying assumption of superiority of the "self-consistent and variable" over the "multiform" and "unintelligible"; they merely inverted the attribution of these qualities. For Modernity nature (body) is characterized as a realm of invariant necessity and self-consistency, while subjectivity (soul) is an incoherent realm of freedom; the soul became bodylike, and the body acquired soul-like characteristics.

Plato is led by the urge toward perfection that he feels in his own body image to the realm of pure forms. This is not a theory of "ideas" in the modern sense but of forms that "catch the eye," those "visible forms" that can be seen with the eye of the soul and that remain suggestive of the bodily schema that gave them birth. The soul is an embodied idea, or the idea of a body. The implication of this, however, is to grant a greater reality to the soul as an idea (in the original sense of plastic image), thus rendering the body a mere "phantom" of its ideal form. This view, additionally, encourages a certain asceticism, as immediate bodily pleasure can be dismissed (some of the time at least) as insubstantial "so-called pleasures."

More significantly, once the soul has entered the realm of ideas and there become a kind of human image, an observational outpost of the body, it can construct a humanly comprehensible "picture" of what it finds. For Plato the soul is not only an idealized body, it is both a mirror and a structural model of the cosmos. In the *Timaeus*, thus, knowledge of the world is one with self-knowledge of the most intimate sort, and both are modeled on the body image as a cosmological soul (Plato 1965).

In a different way Aristotle also stressed the intimate mutual implication of body and soul. The psyche is that which arises from a particular organization of the body and "belongs" to it in the same way that sight belongs to the eye. The psyche, or soul, is not in Aristotle's view an immortal and immaterial addition to the body. It is not located somewhere "in" the body but arises from the normal functioning of the body itself. And inasmuch as Aristotle's philosophy is an attempt to clarify just those distinctions which exist "in nature," he seeks to make the psyche the mirror of the world. It is the functional interdependence of nature and body, body and soul, that gives to the soul its capacity to "understand" the world. The soul conforms itself to the natural world through the sensory openness of the body. Seeing affects the organ of sight; it takes on the attributes of the thing it sees. It is the plasticity of the human soul, its almost infinite adaptability, that is the special feature of the human body image through which we adapt to, and ultimately master, the world (Aristotle 1986).

Both Aristotle and Plato connect the psyche directly with the capacity of living beings for self-movement. In the *Phaedrus,* for example, Plato claims that only "a body which moves itself from within is endowed with soul, since self-motion is of the very nature of soul" (Plato 1973, 49). And while Plato sees in the soul an intermediary between the body and the world of ideal forms, Aristotle insists that the soul arises from itself and is the intermediary between the body and the equally changeable forms of nature. Neither, however, proposes a dualism, which as a categorical disjunction between "body" and "soul" or between "matter" and "form" characterized, for many centuries, the standard interpretations of their works. The subsequent misinterpretation of their thoughts seems most obviously connected with the rise of Christianity and a series of attempts to rationalize its religious message through Greek philosophical categories, most notably in Plotinus.

Psyche in this development is no longer a bodily fluid but a "life force" free of specifically organic qualities but inextricably bound with the powers of thought (*phren*), will (*thumos*), consciousness (*nous*), and so on. Whereas *soma* (originally the unity of body attained in death; a corpse) becomes the "frame" of the body, the overall structure uniting its parts, it was the *psyche* that became the bearer of "personality" and the carrier of a unique character.

For Socratic philosophy, the "care of the soul" takes precedence, or ought to take precedence, over the "care of the body." The body image, in this decisive movement, gains a new reality. It comes to occupy a higher place than the body itself, which, now divided from its own image, is reduced to brute organic matter. The soul alone is then responsible for actualizing intellectual and moral value; it alone is "capable of attaining wisdom," and equally, it alone "is capable of attaining goodness and righteousness" (Burnet 1916, 140).

FORMATION OF THE
BOURGEOIS EGO

In the emergence of a modern society, the "soul," resting on and transforming this complex prehistory, came to refer to the localization of all psychic functions within a "body-in-space." Rather than being entangled with the body, the soul is then characterized as the specifically subjective aspects of the world, as nonextended interiority. The soul is inside the body but is distinct from the body, and at the same time the soul registers and responds to the outside world, including its own body. While the body occupies a location in space and is thus subject to necessity, which is comprehended by the soul as universal and rational laws, the soul itself, as interior depth, realizes in its own restless inner movements an incomprehensible and precious freedom.

Self-Fashioning

Renaissance humanism may be viewed as an anticipatory form of Modernity, not only in the sense of constituting the cultural framework of the Copernican Revolution, with its implications for the development of new body images, but equally in its revival of Platonism and, paradoxically, in its fostering of magical arts including alchemy, astrology, and numerology, all of which might be considered as aspects of the liberation of the soul from the controlling authority of feudal institutions and its empowerment as the force and agency of "self-fashioning." The dignity of man required the freedom of self-movement, and self-movement implied the soul; the soul was the modality and the instrument of human autonomy.

In its initial expression, in fact, Modernity reached back to the earliest pre-Christian roots of the Western tradition in defense of a sensuously vital conception of the soul. For Ficino, Bruno, and other Renaissance virtuosi, steeped in Hermeticism as well as Neoplatonism, the soul regained its material qualities. As an inner fluid the soul was responsive to, and physically linked with, cosmological currents. Celestial forces were transmitted through universally dispersed "soul stuff," providing a physical link between microcosm and macrocosm as well as a kind of viscous medium that joined individual souls together in a natural collectivity. The soul, that is to say, was not yet wholly individuated and unambiguously located within the singular body.

The long-term tendencies of the Renaissance and its extension into northern humanism, however, were toward individuation, which decisively shaped the modern soul into the form of the ego as its concrete realization, a form in which all the conceptual and practical ambiguities of Modernity were to crystallize. Already in Montaigne the premodern collective religious quest for salvation had turned inward and become secularized as an onerous search for personal identity, a precarious dialectic of Self and Other.

Infinite Inwardness

For Modernity the world of objects is distributed in an infinite space. Extension, the modality of body, is unlimited and undifferentiated. In Newton's terms it is "absolute." It is the absoluteness of space, indeed, that guarantees that the laws through which we grasp the reality immediately presented to us are not merely local regularities but genuine laws of nature. At the same time the interior world of the soul became infinitized. But even if the soul's self-presence is necessary to, and in some sense underlies, the qualities of individuated consciousness, the infinitization of this self-presence and of the potential field of consciousness has the result of rendering the soul unknowable.

The problem of human freedom and self-understanding is, therefore, not solved by confining the soul to the body and protecting it there from the contamination of other bodies. Preserving its absolute freedom within a spaceless abyss presents the individual person with the difficulty of realizing his or her freedom in relation to this new absolute. The self-presence of the soul, linked to the apparently endless succession of images through which this presence could momentarily be realized, transferred the freedom and autonomy of the human from the realm of the body to an inner realm which, in effect, became as infinitely removed from the subject as did the cosmos of objects. The human was somewhere between body and soul, and the actualization of autonomy meant combining in some way the distinctive orientations toward these two unknowable domains.

Pascal, more clearly and more poignantly than anyone else, expressed the human situation in terms of a boundary between these two infinities. The human is indeterminate because "nothing can fix the finite between the two infinities which enclose and evade it" (Pascal 1966, 199). The soul gains "depth" as the cosmos gains extension, and in infinite depths the soul loses itself in obscurity. Modernity involves the paradox that human autonomy, which expresses itself most clearly in the development of reason and rational science, is self-limiting. For Modernity, "knowledge" is (apparently) the only certain link with reality beyond our immediate consciousness; but for human interiority as well as for the exterior world of nature, this imperfect link has been fashioned only because we cannot reach reality itself. Enlightenment, that is to say, depends upon ignorance of the primordial character of reality.

These issues (ignoring Pascal's subtle understanding of the matter) were generally conceptualized in the development of Modernity in terms of what might be called an "ego psychology." Here human autonomy was, so to speak, focused on the issue of personal self-development, of forming a personal identity distinct, on the one hand, from the ineluctable forces of nature that formed bodies and, on the other, from the absolute freedom of an equally unknowable subjectivity. Two major traditions of self-fashioning developed within bourgeois society to cope with these demands. These might loosely be termed "Puritanism" and "Romanticism." Each in its distinctive way and with different results sought out and surrendered to the infinity of inwardness.

Puritanism

The Reformation, which threatened established authorities by proclaiming the sovereignty of the individual in matters of faith (as a practical reality rather than as an ideal), in fact became the foundation for new and far more efficient forms of social control through self-imposed disciplines. Puritanism in its most general sense shifted the entire locus of authority from the management of public order to the self-imposition of regulation and particularly of bodily self-regulation. Puritanism was first of all self-control in the sense of bodily self-control, and it was through such measures that the individual could "come to themselves" in faith. Not the least paradoxical aspect of Puritanism is that the realization of human autonomy here expresses itself as a complete subordination to the will of God. But as this will (which was the purest form of the notion of the infinite depth of the soul) was unknown and unknowable, the individual had no option but to exercise his or her freedom in defining themselves in relation to it. This relation crystallized the self in a completely new way. Faith was the only grounds of self-certainty; in fact, it was a groundless inner conviction that one was chosen.

Of course, being chosen meant choosing oneself; choosing the self as chosen from a potentially limitless range of possibilities the very identity and selfhood of which was preordained as authentic. This is the most powerful and absolute expression of what became a very general, pervasive, and important tendency within Modernity. Stripped of its religious preconceptions, Puritanism became a duty of self-development and self-realization, what is perhaps most familiar in the notion of *Bildung* but which is, in fact, a common psychic motif in modern culture. The common theme of all such discourses is to "draw out" the one form of selfhood that, so to speak, belongs to that particular individual. The task is to create the self in such a way as to realize just those potentialities for selfhood already present to the individual; to become just the person one could become and, indeed, ought to become. Thus, just as the modern discourse of the body concealed (as a shadow) but did not eliminate real self-presence, so the transformation of the discourse of the soul, for all its insistence on the immanent process of self-fashioning and self-creation, raised the issue of the self's transcending reality in terms of its own characteristic language of authenticity.

The difficulty of self-fashioning, in other words, is not the restrictiveness of the body and its laws but the infinite freedom of the soul. The Puritan took the strongest possible view of this situation: once inner freedom was attributed entirely to God, freedom was converted into an absolute demand for obedience. By emphasizing the estrangement and transcendence of God (as an object), the Puritan redefined faith in terms of inward experience. Faith was an essentially private and inscrutable matter, a secret between the individual and God. Max Weber famously argued that asceticism developed in the fertile soil of the deep anxiety into which the believer was thrown by the doctrine of predestination. Asceticism was, in effect, a continuous self-discipline which came in time to be an adequate substitute for (rather than an irrational sign of) the inner certainty of faith.

It is also worth noting that it is through this process that a specific kind of self-identity was fashioned. What should be stressed, however, is that making faith inward and personal, in a very real sense taking God into the individual soul rather than leaving him suspended as an extracosmic figure, did not imply intimacy with the divine Being. Rather, in being infinitized the soul was effectively shattered.

Few could tolerate the anxiety provoked by absolute freedom of the secular soul any more than they could the anxiety of uncertainty over salvation. The subversive tradition of self-fashioning that was inaugurated by the Renaissance was progressively transformed by the beginning of the nineteenth century into bourgeois philistinism and conventionality with its halfhearted, insincere, and wholly respectable talk of "freedom" and "self-fulfillment."

Romantic Selfhood

Romanticism might, in this context, be viewed in the most general sense as an attempt to rediscover the infinity and freedom of the soul within a bourgeois culture which required of individual subjects nothing "deeper" than easy conformity to the, by then, well-established norms of market rationality and a respectable family life. Of course, in a broader perspective, as Gusdorf's impressive studies document, Romanticism is a permanent feature of Western culture, a "transhistorical category" which comes to prominence in every periodic revival of Platonism (Gusdorf 1982, 1983, 1984, 1985). But at the end of the eighteenth and beginning of the nineteenth century it takes on a specifically modern form, even where (perhaps especially where) it is fiercest in its criticism of modern life and modern conditions (Abrams 1971; Schmitt 1986; Löwy and Sayre 1992).

For Romanticism the inner infinity and absolute freedom of the soul were not empty metaphors or formal images of an empty interior symmetrical with the infinity of extended space beyond the body. There was no vast emptiness over which the self was, so to speak, suspended and into which it threatened to fall. These depths, rather, were filled with images of their own, with a continuous and continuously productive psychic process of which the conscious self—the ego created by the practice of bourgeois discipline—registered only a fraction. Yet in a curious way, just as the selection of sensory data to which one attended was in some way controlled by the self, so the stream of inner images, which appeared to renew itself continually with effortless spontaneity, was also self-generated, at least to the extent of selecting and editing its content.

Dreams, myths, and spontaneous imagery were revalued as the fundamental contents of the Romantic notion of consciousness and selfhood, contents which, though self-produced, could not wholly be brought under the control of a rational ego and thus remained enigmatic. The problem was to become aware of this process of self-formation and to wrest it from extraneous, superficial influences and restore to it a proper autonomy. These themes emerge clearly in the work of Rousseau, the writer to whom all the Romantics turned for inspiration.

What is clear, from Rousseau's first influential work—his prizewinning essay on the Arts and Sciences—is that bourgeois respectability is the negation rather than the realization of the inner freedom and autonomy of the soul. The difficulty with modern society, Rousseau argues, is that everyone is forced to play a part; dissimulation is universal, not because people wish to conceal their true selves but, more fundamentally, because the conditions of life do not allow the free expression of their inner thoughts and feelings. There is no facet of public life that does not require us to wear a mask. Rousseau at once drew the obvious conclusion: that the realization of authentic selfhood depended on the formation of a free society of equals. He portrayed such a possibility in his immensely popular and influential novel *La nouvelle Helöise*. In fact his imagined community was, by today's standards, neither free nor egalitarian, nor was it intended as more than a thought experiment. This, however, was important enough; after all, the scientific revolution in which the modern body image had first borne fruit as a new model of nature had been established by Galileo through just such a procedure. What better method could there be for establishing the true nature of the modern soul as the inner freedom of the imagination?

But inner freedom by its very nature demanded actualization in some form or other. And the actualization of this freedom presented enormous difficulties. Few could aspire to a protected life beyond the corrupting reach of society at large. More systematically and completely, therefore, Rousseau took up another method of self-understanding and self-actualization: memory. The self is formed, in this project, through tracing out its own history. The "secret train of its emotions" (emotions are the inner register of the soul as compared to perceptions of the outside world) provides, beneath and within the narrative of life events, a history of the unfolding selfhood which in a thousand normally undetected ways shapes this narrative of conventionalized falsehood, preserving within it, nonetheless, a truth of its own. The authenticity of the self defined in relation to the truth of the soul takes precedence over the dissimulation of social roles, in which the self plays a part in relation to the outside world.

Truth is thus preserved in two ways. First, by the evident distinction between reality and appearance, between the inner life of feeling and the external signs in which it is normally denied. Second, and more importantly, its truth is preserved and crystallized in a self-conscious history of these feelings together with their dissimulation. The recollection of falsehood transforms all those required and empty conventionalizations into a higher truth, into a coherent self-presence which brings to consciousness in an entirely new way the being that chose and ordered these falsehoods. The shadowy being of the self is given depth and substance through recollection of the entire history of just those lies and deceptions which might have destroyed it.

Rousseau's *Confessions*, therefore, is a key work for the understanding of the modern soul. He begins by discovering the moment in which the total transparency and unity of consciousness of childhood—a consciousness which is not yet divorced from external reality, and for which the distinctions of reality and appearance mean nothing—the moment in which that unity is broken (Starobinski 1988). He finds it in injustice, in the impossibility of convincing adults that an accusation of wrongdoing was false. Inner conviction is no guarantee that the truth will appear to another; the more he protests his innocence, the more his guilt becomes evident to others. At the same time he discovers a powerful erotic element in his punishment at the hand of Mme Lambercier. Falsehood and the deceptions of society, thus, become invested with a positive value of their own, and subsequently the relation between inner truth and outer false-hood is never straightforward. However much Jean-Jacques would like to live in a spontaneous manner, his every action expressive of the state of his soul, he cannot do this, not just because he cannot overcome the conventional forms of expression in which this inner truth is swallowed up and transformed into something else, but more importantly because he is continually misled by pride, by the investment of the self in values that have their origin elsewhere than his own soul. Rousseau thus distinguishes between *amour propre* and *amour du soi même,* between a proper regard for authentic selfhood and the vanity of wishing to please others. The self is trapped between the demands of the soul and the demands of those social conventions in which it is essentially implicated.

Thus, just as the modern body image turns out to be a history of itself in a general cultural sense, so the soul is realized as the self that is a living biography of itself. Biographical time, it would seem, is the nutritive medium of the soul. In a more general sense, in fact, the soul that is not extended in space unfolds itself in time. Time is, so to speak, the soul's specific form of extension, and Rousseau made far more sophisticated our understanding of biographical time. Unlike the rationalist psychologist, there is no straight line of development here. The self does not realize itself in a continuous process directed by an intentional Subject; it is not the outcome of a plan or purpose (plans and purposes can only be formulated as a consequence of the soul's preexisting history). The history of the self, rather, is a secretive and complicated narrative, a series of misapprehensions and mistakes through which a coherent self-image gradually and mysteriously emerges.

The followers of Rousseau frequently were less subtle than their reckless master. The concrete self or ego became identified with the entire being of the soul, and its practical demands were transformed into the ultimate values upon which every human action should be based.

Romantic selfhood, thereafter, was construed as a struggle for the gradual (or not so gradual) release of the soul's authentic tendencies from those stultifying conventions beneath which it was presumed to lie, hidden but fully formed. The soul was literally buried underneath the self. The disjunction between the world of the self—the ego that emerged in the process of normal development within bourgeois society—and an authentic inner individuality in which was expressed the soul's original freedom provided a critical path for the development of popular Romantic writing.

In this development temporal issues gave way, once again, to a new kind of spatial metaphor. For Rousseau, as for Augustine, time is the essential modality of personal existence, the medium of the soul. But for the Romantics time is reduced to a "moment," the temporal equivalent to the "point-mass" of body in the new cosmology. "Real" existence and authentic selfhood can be realized only in the moment, in the instantaneous self-apprehension of freedom. Hence their rejection of systematic philosophy, as well as conventional morality, as a threat to the "unqualified immediacy of feeling" and its replacement by a practical "philosophical struggle for the reality that is inaccessible to abstract rationalism" (Schmitt 1986, 53, 54).

In the complex of discourses contained in German idealism, Romantic literary theory, and Romantic literature from the 1770s to the 1820s, this transformation takes place in a quite remarkable way. Romanticism, in its varied forms, is often now seen as rejection of Modernity and as involving, at least, a thoroughly conservative critique of Modernity (Schmitt 1986; Löwy and Sayre 1992). Indeed, the leading voices of both Continental philosophical idealism (particularly Schiller and Fichte) and of English literary Romanticism (Coleridge) can easily be understood in terms of a nostalgia for a premodern world of community and fellow feeling and the invocation of a kind of participatory consciousness—an immediate sensing of reality—which is not so far removed from the ideal of mystical union that animated at least one element within the premodern religious tradition. At the same time, however, these writers stressed the autonomy of the human subject in an unprecedented way and valued striving, self-realization, and the creativity of human individuality. Fichte's response to Kant electrified the younger generation of European intellectuals, who may well have misunderstood his notion of the ego as a transindividual, metaphysical principle and concluded that the entire world of human possibilities lay within their own concrete and determinate individuality. The popularity of the *Bildungsroman* and its youthful hero (Moretti 1987) indicates a decisively modern sense in which Romanticism—in rejecting the standard version of Enlightenment rationality and bourgeois respectability—sought both a vision of nature and a conception of morality and society which were unprecedented, owing nothing to the fanciful reconstruction and misrepresentation of premodern societies. It fueled the demand for "total revolution" that survived well beyond the period of high Romanticism (Yack 1986).

A Science of Desire

The dialectic of Self and Other that emerged in these discourses provides a quite different picture of subjectivity and its relation to the social world than had emerged in the rationalist and utilitarian positions. The primacy of the inner world of the soul was expressed in and through desire, which was both its fundamental reality and its immanent dynamic principle. Desire was an inherent tendency toward self-completion on the part of the soul that came to consciousness as an inner lack or want. The self was necessarily linked to and dependent upon another self (Girard 1965). And the social relation founded on interdependent desire, rather than on mutual self-interest, was the ideal human image developed within the Romantic tradition, a view which was also taken up and expressed with particular force and clarity by Hegel, its first important philosophical critic.

This dialectical conception, indeed, created a powerful tension between a conception of the soul as an essentially social identity and one in which the indwelling singularity of the person posited itself as a unique, self-willed process. In terms of its spontaneous imagery, the soul revealed a common ancestry, and a common humanity, which did not depend upon the (superficial) conventionality of society. The Romantics often preferred to describe the soul in terms of its "deepest" and most secretive contents, through dreams, folktales, myths, and poetic imagery. Many of their stories were set underground and described heroic rescues from the deepest dungeons and the discovery of strange, forgotten creatures. Dreams belonged to this remote reality more fecund of profound human images than were the rational constructions of the waking mind. The dreams of collectivities, the myths and symbols of past ages and of the contemporary world could, then, be interpreted as the spontaneous outpouring of a superabundant and ultimately irrepressible soul (Bousquet 1964). At the very moment that science seemed to be on the point of defining and describing an order of autonomous objects, withdrawn into a cold, distant, and empty space, Romanticism sank itself into modern subjectivity and sought to liberate the spirit from the obscurity of its self-enclosed depths. The Romantic dream was not, as it was for Renaissance writers like Giordano Bruno or Marsilio Ficino, a literal flight from the world into what the astronomer Kepler called the "dull immensity of space"; it was, rather, an escape by collapsing inward, upon the self, revealing in its interminable fall the inexhaustible immensity of the subjective world.

The inner world of human subjectivity knows the world of objects only through itself. It can become aware only of its own inner movements. The world of objects, withdrawing into itself, exists only as the dubious postulate of the senses that, entirely reliable in their own terms, are powerless to convey the quality of created being. The human predicament is not so much to be confronted with a world of enigmatic but interpretable symbols as to be wholly contained within a world of arbitrary signs, from which real presence is rigorously excluded. In this context the dream is not distinguished from waking reality directly as Subject is to Object, for waking reality too is wholly subjective. As the most notable student of Romantic dreams rightly points out, for them "the dream was not a phenomenon of sleep" but was, rather, a privileged form of representation (Bousquet 1964, 35).

But it was not only in stimulating a new academic interest in myth and folktales, as exemplified, for example, in the writings of Carus and Schubert, that Romanticism had a lasting impact on the sciences. It is important to realize the extent to which, in spite of the continuing rise of "inertial" models of Modernity, many of the fundamental ideas of the Romantics affected the development of the natural sciences, particularly medicine, throughout the nineteenth century (Gusdorf 1985). Romanticism was marked above all by a determined search for the unity and coherence that, it was felt, must somehow still lie behind the analytical fragmentation of reality at the hands of the natural sciences. In this sense Romanticism was only the latest manifestation of a recurrent longing for organic unity which had its immediate predecessor among its German adherents in Pietism and the early modern mysticism of Jacob Boehme

(Abrams 1971; Kirschner 1996). It did, however, give a particular and modern turn to the periodic resurgence of Neoplatonism. Schelling's idealist philosophy expressed the dynamism of Modernity in terms of this tradition with particular vividness. The search for unity was not simply an intellectual conceit—not, as in Coleridge, an appeal to the synthesizing power of imagination—but a genuine force of nature, in which every real form emerged through a dialectical process of unifying and transcending the polarities of lower forms. A process not unlike the Plotinian dialectic of the descent of the soul is here given a naturalistic modern and ascending human form.

More specifically, the impact of Romanticism in the biological sciences and in medicine was highly significant and outlived the relatively brief period of the *Naturphilosophie* movement. The foundation of the Vienna Medical School, for example, whose influence was felt throughout Europe, coincided with the upsurge of Romanticism, and Vienna's leading physicians during this significant period, Johann Peter Frank and Franz Josef Gall, looked first to French and Scottish paradigms of medical practice. They championed the view that bodily health was based on an optimum degree of "excitation" (conceived as a combination of the natural irritability of bodily tissues with suitable intensities of appropriate stimulation), rather than of the harmonious mixture of bodily fluids. John Brown, an Edinburgh graduate whose ideas were influential in Vienna, argued that diseases differed fundamentally only in the extent to which stimulation departed from the healthy norm, giving rise to symptoms of "sthenia" (overstimulation) or "asthenia" (understimulation) (Lesky 1976, 8–11). More general and theoretical approaches in biology sought in Kant and Schelling, rather than in the major empiricist traditions of Modernity, for a comprehensive grounding. Intuitive reasoning, a general morphological approach to the understanding of living beings, and the recognition of spiritual and nonmaterial causes in both normal and pathological organic processes were accepted, as was a general perspective within which a parallel was drawn between the development of the individual and the evolution of the species.

There and elsewhere laboratory-based science never wholly ousted the humanistic clinical tradition, especially in terms of therapeutics. And it must be remembered that the teachers of Freud and the generation who were to transform European culture at the end of the nineteenth century shared with their students not only a deep conviction of the scientific validity of the Romantic tradition in biology but confidence in a much broader German education which revered Goethe and classical studies as the inspiration behind both the literary and the scientific traditions of Modernity (Lesky 1976, 280).

DISINTEGRATION OF
THE BOURGEOIS EGO

All these tendencies, varied from an ideological viewpoint, came together in the notion of the soul revealing itself in the actions of an intentional ego. Intentions were understood as ultimately derived from bodily privations—needs, wants, passions—but expressed themselves in actions that were immediately meaningful in terms of inner motives and universal criteria of reason. Whether the self was authenticated in a blissful moment or not, everyday life demanded a functioning ego in which the complex and apparently disconnected lines and sites of activity could be bound together as a unity. The ego had the function of coordinating and controlling the seemingly chaotic flux of experience, transforming it into a meaningful reality which persisted in time.

The task of ego construction was as much an operation of memory and imagination as it was of perception. The process of selection and editing of raw sensation, of ordering the world in relation to personal needs and interests, hinged on the formation of an ego as a self-identity which persisted for specific period of time, which seemed to develop according to an inner dynamics of its own, subduing the element of arbitrariness in the world and bringing into focus the significance of a host of experiences in terms of an unfolding personal narrative. This narrative, in turn, could be projected into the future, ensuring the continuing connectedness of events. It was an essential aspect of Modernity that the ego be invested with a specific value of reality, that it become the carrier of a primary and taken-for-granted world, the "here-and-now." Whereas in premodern societies reality had been, so to speak, more widely dispersed and had occupied a whole range of extended locations, for bourgeois society the ego was the world and was located inside the body as a sensitive soul.

Of course a strain of skepticism in modern thought challenged the self-certainty and self-evidence of the ego. Most notably David Hume argued that the ego was nothing more than an arbitrary perspective on a world that was inherently disconnected. But such arguments carried little weight for the vast majority of people, for whom the value of the ego was daily authenticated, if not in a momentary inspiration, in transactions (particularly market transactions) that seemed to presuppose its existence. From the mid-nineteenth century, however, this self-certainty began to drain away, and by the end of the century the coherence of the ego, far from being the unexamined enabling assumption of an entire world of thought and action, threatened to dissolve into nothing.

Perspectivism in Nature

Where bourgeois self-centeredness had found its fullest justification in the intellectual triumph of modern science, which seemed both to presuppose and to vindicate a natural individualism, the advances of the physical sciences after the mid-nineteenth century provided the greatest challenge to the perspective of the ego.

The development of the natural sciences, from the intellectual revolution of the seventeenth century up to the mid-nineteenth century, can be conceived as a dynamic theory of the closed body. The singular "body-in-space" was not only the object upon which the inquiring scientist's gaze was fixed, it was, like the vanishing point of a perspective painting, a mirror image of the inquiring observer. But throughout the second part of the nineteenth century, as the bourgeois ego became aware of itself as an unfounded and ultimately arbitrary bundle of sensations, and the singular and privileged point of view from which the classical sciences had reconstructed reality fractured into a multiplicity of perspectives, the natural bodies that had been the object of such precise observation themselves began to fragment and dissolve.

The new perspectivism in the natural sciences was linked to the "dematerialization" of nature. The point-mass gave up its residual "material" qualities and was, so to speak, reextended as a "field" of nonmaterial or quasi-material forces. Matter or body could then be redefined as the local effects of forces widely distributed in space. This much at least could be conceded to the Romantic tradition. The fragmentation of the body image that these tendencies indicated was, simultaneously, a transformation of the soul, a transformation which the modern scientific worldview was forced to take into account. The arbitrary position of the isolated observer itself became a subject for scientific reflection and precipitated thorough-going relativization of all empirical data. The result was a growing awareness of (and bewilderment over) the role of the subject in the scientific understanding of nature. Worse, not only was nature irremediably tainted by ultimately arbitrary and limited human points of view, these perspectives multiplied and came into conflict with each other in an alarming fashion.

The unity of nature, which was the unquestioned assumption underlying the development of classical mechanics and the physical sciences, was seriously challenged for the first time. By the end of the century the search for a "system-of-the-world" as a coherent and consistent statement of simple "laws of nature" was all but abandoned. And in the emergence of new concepts that were to lead to the development of quantum physics, radical discontinuities in natural processes were recognized, and ultimately, multiple, coexisting, and contradictory theoretical models of the simplest observational data were acknowledged. Not only was the soul an integral part of nature (as the Romantics had claimed), the soul was no longer singular or self-consistent, and therefore nature could no longer adequately be conceptualized as a simple and coherent mechanism.

Hysteria and Hypnotism

The disintegration of the classical bourgeois ego became evident less as a consequence of philosophical skepticism or psychological analysis than it did so directly as new and puzzling illnesses that became the focus of discussion well beyond the medical field in which they were first described. Symptoms of "mental dissociation," peculiar losses of memory, disturbances of voluntary movement, localized loss of sensation, hypersensitivity, and, most dramatic of all, apparently well-attested cases of multiple personality were at the center of, particularly French, efforts to understand the character of Modernity in terms of new conceptions of the soul.

But hysteria, which was the general term under which these varied phenomena were grouped, was and remained a fact of life before it was an anomaly or a series of anomalies that were to prove critical for classical understandings of the ego. Indeed, interest in the somewhat diffuse range of symptoms generally referred to under this head first developed within traditions of psychology that were firmly rooted in all the classical certainties of the bourgeois age, in its unexamined prejudices as well as in its explicit commitment to the perspective of an intentional ego. Early studies of hysteria, thus, drew attention to the inadequacy and constitutional weakness of young women and to the difficulties they had in coping with the conditions of modern life. Hysterical symptoms were quickly hypostatized as the hysterical person, and that person was typically a young, unmarried, middle-class woman, economically dependent on her parents, with no fixed occupation or responsibilities outside the home, who devoted her time to the cultivation of minor talents, good works of a respectable and undemanding sort, and, not infrequently, providing companionship and nursing for an aged relative. Hysteria, that is to say, was most likely to affect those least involved in the rational institutions of bourgeois society, those who, as a consequence, were weak and "overemotional." It was, in fact, just those aspects of bourgeois family life (economic and emotional dependence, the development of privacy) which had been institutionalized as emblems of respectability and as a support to personal identity that came, in time, to undermine the security and coherence of the ego, the psychological complex that, in its turn, had been the foundation and support of post-Reformation secular culture (King 1983).

Throughout the nineteenth century two leading conceptions of the origin of hysteria were developed, both of which sought to account for the variety of its symptoms and its apparently disproportionate concentration among young women in terms of a singular underlying cause. One traced the onset of symptoms to a "trauma," most frequently a physical shock of some kind, while the other claimed symptoms could be explained in terms of the "suggestibility" of the patient. Linking both views was an underlying assumption of constitutional weakness as the general predisposing cause.

The traumatic theory of hysteria owed its popularity to the authority of Jean-Martin Charcot, the greatest of nineteenth-century clinical psychopathologists. He had spent his internship at the Salpêtrière Hospital in Paris from 1848–52, returning ten years later as attending physician and professor. This huge hospital, which his assistant Gilles de La Tourette called a "pandemonium of human infirmities," was for Charcot "a sort of museum of living pathology" that contained some five thousand patients upon which he could exercise his diagnostic and taxonomic skills (Charcot 1987, xxiv). In general, he regarded hysteria as "an affection remarkable for its permanence and obstinacy." Many of its local symptoms were typically "mobile and fleeting," and "the capricious course of the disease," he claimed, "is frequently interrupted by the most unexpected events" (Charcot 1889, 3:223).

In what were themselves somewhat theatrical performances, Charcot would remove hysterical symptoms from hypnotized patients (usually prepared before the lecture by an assistant) and, conversely, induce symptoms in apparently normal individuals. The connection between hysteria and hypnosis, Charcot suggested, lay in a constitutional weakness of the nervous system of the individual. Only potential hysterics could be hypnotized, and in this abnormal state their latent disorder would manifest itself (Ellenberger 1970, 89–102).

According to this view hysteria, though an ancient disease, was increasing dramatically due to the intense pace of modern life. Many potential hysterics, who in premodern society might well have gone through life without developing any symptoms whatever, fell ill as a result of the "nervous shock" of modern living, a view quickly taken up in an American context (Beard 1881).

Charcot's conception became the point of departure for an important tradition in French psychology, neurology, and psychiatry. In the present context his significance lies primarily in drawing attention to the "disintegrative" effects of modern life. The primary features of hysteria were a loss of control, sensitivity (alternatively hypersensitivity), and responsiveness of some part of the body. It was as if part of the body had a mind of its own and refused to respond spontaneously and effortlessly to the will of the patient.

If Charcot's elaborate botanizing in the Salpêtrière had its alarming aspect, hinting at a deeply disintegrative tendency in modern life, he at least viewed its effects as confined to a minority of unfortunate constitutional sufferers. Some bodies, sensitized by overly delicate souls, were so formed that they responded in this way to the overburdening stimulation of life. Hippolyte Bernheim, on the other hand, placed no such optimistic limit on the spread of hysteria. Or, rather, there were no constitutional limitations on suggestibility, which, Bernheim argued, was the real foundation of most of Charcot's observations.

Bernheim insisted that "suggestibility" was the fundamental phenomenon of hypnosis, and that "nothing could be further from the truth than the assertion that only hysterics are hypnotizable" (Bernheim 1980, 122). The already classic diagnostic portraits from the Salpêtrière were, in fact, "cultivated hysteria." Charcot's patients may have been unusually suggestible and, unwittingly prompted by Charcot's own discourse and his assistants' diligent preparation of the subject, produced the symptoms as an artificial construct of the situation. "We do not realize how easy it is to make unconscious suggestions," he argues, and "by projecting onto the patient our own conceptions, we fabricate an observation with the preconceived ideas that we have in mind" (Bernheim 1980, 127). It was hardly surprising, therefore, to find that, in the Salpêtrière at least, "it is rare for hypnotic suggestion not to rid the patient of the principal manifestations of hysteria" (Bernheim 1980, 160).

Charcot and Bernheim presented two alternative and distinctively modern accounts of significant alterations in the classical bourgeois ego. For Charcot hysteria became a typically modern disease; it was a bodily protest against the "unnatural" excitement of modern life. For Bernheim hypnotism was a phenomenon of suggestion, and suggestion was, in different ways, also increasingly a feature of public life (Gauld 1992). More and more people were being urged to walk about in a "waking dream." The somnambulist was becoming in many respects an ideal citizen of the modern world.

Toward the end of the century, indeed, there seemed to be a near epidemic of hysteria. And as more investigative studies and reports were published, the more unusual and dramatic the symptoms seemed to become (Kenny 1986; Hacking 1995).

Dissociation

In 1860 Azam, a doctor in Bordeaux, reported the puzzling symptomology of one of his patients, Felida X, who subsequently became one of the most celebrated and widely discussed cases in French psychology. Azam's patient oscillated unpredictably between two quite distinct states, in which, to all appearances, she seemed to be two quite distinct personalities. It was as if she were two individuals, complete in themselves, each with their own store of memories, although "in one she possessed her memory entire; in the other she had only a partial memory of all the impressions in that state" (Ribot 1882, 103). An outsider was forced to treat her as either of two individuals, depending on which persona she presented on any one occasion. In fact Felida X was not the first or clearest case of "double-consciousness"; McNish had reported the similar case of "an American lady" as early as 1830. In that case while one of the "individuals" had complete knowledge of the other, the "secondary" personality believed herself to be in sole possession of the American lady, and from her point of view (amnesia of all intervening periods being complete) was convinced of her own continuous and uncontested presence (McNish 1830). But the significance of such bizarre symptoms could hardly be guessed at while the assumptions of bourgeois egoism held sway. And when, during the latter third of the nineteenth century, these assumptions did begin to disintegrate, evidence of "dissociation," "double-consciousness," and "multiple personality" was promptly found everywhere (Prince 1906; Hacking 1995).

Common hysterical symptoms were reinterpreted as minor forms of dissociation, and multiple personality became seen as full-blown hysteria. Hysterical symptoms were viewed, in other words, as the result of some sort of "breaking apart" of consciousness. In most cases, in fact, they might be seen as disturbances of normal memory. The integration of consciousness as an ego had been seen to depend on the continuous functioning of memory, which, linking together the various states of consciousness in an unbroken sequence, created an irresistible impression of a singular inner observer. It seemed, rather, that the memory worked in a selective fashion, binding together as a continuous narrative only those events and experiences which could be meaningfully integrated with some specific image of the self. Those elements in the past which fell outside of such an image, or seemed even to contradict it, would form the center of a mentally dissociated state with its own bodily consciousness, recollection, and self-image. For most individuals such dissociated elements remained insignificant and unobservable in relation to their "major" ego, but in some individuals they formed the nucleus of hysterical symptoms, which were the beginning, so to speak, of an alternative body image and an alternative personality.

Binet suggested that "a kind of spontaneous breaking up" of the personality was not uncommon. Frequently, he thought, the dissociated part of the personality was pathological in some way, so that the whole process could be seen as a spontaneous exercise in psychic hygiene. The transition from one personality to another, in some cases at least, "is made in an instant, almost unconsciously" (Binet 1977, 44). And in place of the singular identity of a "body-in-space," he proposes a new and striking image, related to Freud's own preferred archaeological metaphor: "The personality of our subjects of observation and experiment seems to me like a complicated and frail building, of which the least accident might overthrow a part; and the stones that have fallen away from the mass—and this is a very curious thing—become the point of departure for a new structure, which rises rapidly by the side of the old" (Binet 1977, 347).

The most sustained and exhaustive studies of all the various disintegrative tendencies of the modern psyche—and thus of the modern body image—were the work of one of Charcot's students and his eventual successor at the Salpêtrière, Pierre Janet. Though loyal to the pioneering insights of his master, he demonstrated a considerable shift in emphasis in his writings. From early attempts to specify the conditions under which more or less independent "automatisms" emerged, controlled by preexisting bodily disposition, he became increasingly interested in reconstructing the "mental structure" of hysteria and, thus, in making sense of the individual symptoms. In this way Janet found many instances of a personality dissociating under the impact of "fixed ideas" that were themselves related to a traumatic event.

The dominance of "fixed ideas" or "intellectual automatisms" gave to the hysteric the character of dreamers. They exhibited a tendency to "ceaseless reverie": "Hystericals are not content to dream constantly at night; they dream all day long. Whether they walk, or work, or sew, their minds are never wholly occupied with what they are doing. They carry in their heads an interminable story which unrolls before them or is inwardly conceived" (Janet 1977, 201).

Hysterics had succeeded in detaching themselves, or part of themselves, from the reality in which, for the most part, they still managed to live. They drew back from the complexity of real life and substituted for it "variable, incoherent images," which become typified and systematized into fixed ideas: "It is always the same monotonous story" (Janet 1977, 202). The hysteric becomes indifferent to the world, endlessly repeating a reverie, every detail of which could be controlled, its outcome assured from the very beginning.

HIEROGLYPHICS OF
THE MODERN SOUL

Freud's psychology represents the most significant synthesis of all those late nineteenth-century movements which undermined the classical integrity of the ego. In his writings the soul takes on a bodily form while the body, in a completely new way, was viewed as saturated with, rather than wrapped around, the soul.

From the mid-nineteenth century hysteria attracted the most progressive and innovative medical minds. It was a condition prodigal of the most varied and bewildering physical symptoms. In ancient society it had been viewed as the prototypical women's disease, the effects of a detached womb which, wandering about the interior of the body, attached itself to various internal organs, giving rise to local external symptoms such as paralysis, hypersensitivity, and respiratory problems (Veith 1965). The protean character of the condition remained its distinguishing and somewhat paradoxical characterization, but just as physicists were forced to abandon mechanical models of nature, so doctors were unable to link these varied symptoms to an underlying "disease process."

Modern Body Language

Freud, influenced to some extent by Brentano, viewed the situation in a new way (McGrath 1986). Freud's psychology is essentially descriptive; for him the contemporary body image has an entirely plastic and free relationship to the world, which remains, in its objective and subjective dimensions, completely unknown. The transition from classical bourgeois to contemporary body images is a movement from closed to open, male to female, desire to wish.

Freud's starting point was in the sophisticated studies of hysteria that had developed during the 1880s in France. By the time Freud visited Paris to study briefly under Charcot, both "shock" and increased "nervousness" could be interpreted in a purely psychological sense; and the secondary symptoms of hysteria were viewed as meaningfully related to the "exciting" occasion, rather than as the mechanical outcome of a physical cause. Moebius, for example, referred to hysteria as a "malady by representation" in which a host of "accidental" mental associations had formed and taken root in the body as physical symptoms (Janet 1977, 486–88).

Freud, impressed by both Charcot and Bernheim—the latter of whose major work he translated into German—combined elements of both the traumatic and the suggestion theories when he turned to the practical study of hysteria. More importantly, however, in developing his own "archaeological" approach to understanding the superficiality of modern life, Freud unearthed the meaning, as well as the cause, of bodily complaints. Symptom formation, which he treated as a hermeneutic problem—that is, as a text which could be understood in its own terms—was a double process of inscription and encoding. The pliant female body, unprotected by a hard reflective shell of intellect, was continually falling into a state of helpless torpor in which it was receptive to a multiplicity of uncontrolled and disordered impressions. If these external forces reached traumatic intensity, a lasting trace would be left on the body in the form of an energetic somatic "conversion" which did not simply register but also signified its "exciting cause": "The symptoms which we have been able to trace back to precipitating factors of this sort include neuralgias and anesthesias of very various kinds, many of which had persisted for years, contractures and paralyses, hysterical attacks and epileptoid convulsions, which every observer regarded as true epilepsy, *petit mal* and disorders in the nature of *tic*, chronic vomiting and anorexia, carried to the pitch of rejection of all nourishment, various forms of disturbance of vision, constantly recurrent visual hallucinations, etc." (Freud 1953, 2:4).

The inexhaustible array of bodily symptoms was chosen primarily for their powers of signification. From his first full-length case study, in fact, Freud assimilated the interpretation of symptoms to the recounting of each patient's "story." Frequently many physical symptoms could be understood as unambiguous "mnemic symbols" of an original, emotionally painful situation which had been subsequently forgotten.

In the case of Frau Emmy von N., for example, her ticlike facial movements and hand clasping were a simple repetition of aspects of a traumatic scene, the death of her husband, which, Freud conjectures, was too painful for her to recall as a plastic image but whose memory had survived in the abbreviated form of physical reactions to the original event. However, her symptoms were also, in part, an attempt at "fending off" these very memories and constituted a kind of "protective formula" through which she could retain her peace of mind. Other characteristic symptoms, including an intrusive "clacking" sound Freud observed in another of his cases at this period, were better understood as "putting an antithetic idea into effect." Thus, the effort of remaining completely silent while watching over her sick child expressed itself through its opposite, as an involuntary disturbing noise. Freud assumes, further, that it was her horror at the noise that made its production traumatic, and that the effort to control it resulted in her equally characteristic stammer, which was, thus, "made into a symbol of the event for her memory" (Freud 1953 2:93). These symptoms "were like a series of pictures with explanatory texts" (Freud 1953 2:177). In their "Preliminary Communication," Breuer and Freud had provided what was to become a famous formulation: "Hysterics suffer mainly from reminiscences." That is to say, it was a disease of the soul rather than of the body or, rather, a disease of the soul as the body.

In understanding hysteria Freud viewed the symptom as a sign, rather than the residual effect or trace, of the original event. Nor is the symptom simply a reminder of some sort, an aide-mémoire such as tying a knot in a handkerchief or scribbling a note on a pad. According to Freud the particular way in which the event is encoded in bodily experience serves a double function; it both carries the event forward in time, as it were preserving the moment as an authenticated experience, and at the same time it conceals the event itself by transforming it into a physical form rather than a plastic image.

More generally Freud viewed the formation of hysterical symptoms at this point (prior, that is, to his systematic study of dreams) in terms of defense, as "the refusal on the part of the patient's whole ego to come to terms with this ideational group" (Freud 1953 2:237). In the early case that most closely resembled the classic French type, that of Fräulein Elisabeth von R., the "splitting of consciousness" was just one consequence of this defensive measure and not itself the cause of the primary symptoms. Thus, "in place of the mental pains which she avoided, physical pains made their appearance. In this way a transformation was effected which had the advantage that the patient escaped from an intolerable mental condition; though, it is true, this was at the cost of a psychical abnormality—the splitting of consciousness that came about—and of a physical illness—her pains" (Freud 1953 2:237).

Hypnotic therapy was not wholly successful in treating hysteria because, quite apart from the unpredictability of the technique, the patient would spontaneously produce new symptoms as soon as existing ones were cleared up.

These early studies of hysteria are remarkable now for their reliance on a realistic approach to the understanding of the emotional and moral conflicts current in the lives of their dramatis personae. Frau Emmy's symptoms were related to the conflict between responsibilities to her sick husband and to her simultaneously sick child. Fräulein Elisabeth von R. was torn between similar demands to nurse her father and the freer and wider role that had become available to young women of her class and to which she felt temperamentally suited. Freud remarks on these characteristic circumstances, fertile, he believes, of hysterical symptoms: "I have described the patient's character, the features which one meets with so frequently in hysterical people and which there is no excuse for regarding as a consequence of degeneracy: her giftedness, her ambition, her moral sensibility, her excessive demand for love which, to begin with, found satisfaction in her family, and the independence of her nature which went beyond the feminine ideal and found expression in a considerable amount of obstinacy, pugnacity and reserve" (Freud 1953 2:161).

It is quite commonly the duty to care for sick relatives that sets up painful conflicts within such gifted and ambitious individuals. Here, in spite of the misleading pronouns, Freud expresses himself in a somewhat more sympathetic manner:

> Anyone whose mind is taken up by the hundred and one tasks of sick-nursing which follow one another in endless succession over a period of weeks and months will, on the one hand, adopt a habit of suppressing every sign of his own emotion, and on the other, will soon divert his attention away from his own impressions, since he has neither the time nor strength to do justice to them. Thus he will accumulate a mass of impressions which are capable of affect, which are hardly sufficiently perceived and which, in any case, have not been weakened by abreaction. . . . If the sick person recovers, all these impressions, of course, lose their significance. But if he dies, and the period of mourning sets in, during which the only things that seem to have value are those that relate to the person who has died, these impressions that have not yet been dealt with come into the picture as well; and after a short interval of exhaustion the hysteria, whose seeds were sown during the time of nursing, breaks out. (Freud 1953 2:161-62)

Yet more is revealed by, and concealed in, hysteria than these conscious conflicts suggest. Prolonged and intensive study convinced Freud that quite other circumstances are typically involved in the genesis of hysterical symptoms. Characteristically the originating trauma, simultaneously concealed and revealed in physical symptoms, could be traced to the arousal of sexual feelings that, for reasons of propriety, could not be adequately expressed.

Increasingly impatient with Breuer, Freud by the mid-1890s had developed his own theory of the sexual etiology of hysteria. Hysteria was the consequence, he argued, of a specifically sexual trauma which had occurred in childhood, the conscious memory of which had been suppressed, but the emotional response to which, unexpressed at the time, provided the "psychical energy" expended in the process of "conversion" into physical symptoms. In hysteria, then, "what is played out in the body takes the place of a discourse that cannot be uttered" (David-Ménard 1990, 3). It is the hysterical body, inscribed with visible signs of its own past, rather than the secretive spatial consciousness of the rational mind, which is the true analogue of the modern world.

Freud's so-called seduction theory of hysteria has been extensively discussed in recent years. In the present context it is worth noting that it represents, in the combination of trauma and the development of meaningful symptoms suggestive of the event, the most fertile point of contact with his two French mentors, Charcot and Bernheim. It is also worth noting that by displacing the genesis of the symptoms onto childhood, Freud views hysterics as victims of the breakdown of idealized bourgeois family relations, rather than as victims directly of the overexcitement of the modern age.

It was not from congenital weakness but, more simply, as a consequence of their greater exposure to the genuinely novel elements of Modernity that middle-class young women were particularly prone to hysteria. It was this new leisure class, able at last to claim a position in public life, albeit that of the transient *flâneuse*, that first entered the world of modern consumerism and spectator culture. More than their husbands and fathers, for whom the shock of the new was absorbed, to a large extent, by a network of professional and public relationships which sustained for them the myth of bourgeois egoism, middle-class young women were abandoned to the new world of magically produced commodities. This was a liberation into an unreal existence of endless, aimless, and ultimately self-defeating pleasure (Ferguson 1996).

For this most advanced of modern social groups, the highly valued (by men) realm of rational self-control and equally rational self-expression was held (also by men) to be of little significance. Such young women, not surprisingly, experienced intense conflict between the demands of domestic life and their new public freedom as consumers of modern culture. Bourgeois egoism played little part in either. At home they were constrained by premodern forms of relations, entirely dependent for their being upon the status, wealth, and personality of their menfolk, while in public they became absorbed into the new play culture of instantaneous wish fulfillment. The conflict between these two worlds, as well as the ambiguities of "pure" Modernity, were literally bodied forth as symptoms.

Most significantly, hysteria indicated a body image or series of images in which the soul (the repository of feelings and emotions) had come to the surface and fused with visible flesh. The body, as well as registering the presence of the external world, received impressions from within itself. And in neither respect could it be considered a mechanical system conformed to an ideal standard of reason.

Freud's theory of hysteria became the starting point for the development of his own theory of the contemporary body image, which focused on developmental issues. He characterized periodic transformation of the body surface according to new levels of libidinal organization that gave the body, at each phase, a specific form and organization, each with its specific focus and characteristic processes; this development selected in turn a body opening as the focus of erotic interest, curiosity, and world-building potentiality.

Contemporary life impinges on the body most completely in what appears to be its favored deviant form: hysteria. But whereas the hysteric fuses past and present, interior soul and external social relation, in a specific symptom which encodes the entire history of the self as stigmata, the normal body image of the postmodern world has become more generally hysterical, that is, susceptible to the molding influence of external and contingent events.

It is the "normality" of contemporary hysteria, its special adaptation to postmodern conditions, that makes Janet's (as well as Freud's) conception of hysteria once again relevant. Janet, admitting that hysteria was the embodiment of specific "representations" rather than the mechanical effect of a specific physical shock or lesion, regarded the precipitating events and the particular form of embodiment to be largely accidental (Janet 1898, 2:214). They represented "fixed ideas" that were "permanent dreams" and thus enigmatic to the patient, giving rise to isolated, detached, and fragmented symptoms (Janet 1977, 201). The most characteristic symptom, indeed, is not the quasi-epileptic seizure or "crisis" that Charcot had claimed but the state of somnambulistic detachment from life (Janet 1965, 36).

Hysteria, the most contemporary of phenomena, is "ephemeral," and all its symptoms are transitory; its causes are accidental, and its main mental symptom is a "fixed idea" which is itself in striking contradiction to the conditions of existence that the disease represents (Janet 1965, 19; 1925). It is a kind of reluctant pliability in the face of the continuous changes of modern life. Analogous to the fixed idea is the local paralysis of a limb, part of the body, or even the whole body that the hysteric effects. Interestingly it is the patient's own conception of the organ or body part, which frequently does not correspond to actual nervous connections and muscular links, that is paralyzed. This, indeed, makes it clear that the paralysis or analgesias are hysterical in character rather than the result of constitutional factors or local lesions. They are distortions of the body image and not deformations of the body mechanism (Janet 1965, 138).

Morton Prince, similarly, supported a mixed theory of more or less accidental "shocks" linked to the "suggestibility" of young women in particular (Prince 1910, 15). But a great many of the physical and mental symptoms were the result of "dissociation," the automatic functioning of parts without relation to the whole organism and, therefore, not brought under conscious control (Prince 1906). The body image, in this view—like the mind and the world of objects and events—was undergoing continuous processes of fragmentation, regrouping, forming nuclei and foci of feeling and activity at lower levels in a more or less autonomous fashion.

Ego and Psyche

Hysteria raised a host of problems that Freud spent the rest of his life working through in a quite systematic manner. What should be stressed here is the novel manner in which Freud developed a conception of the psyche in which modern bourgeois notions of both body and soul were dissolved and reformed in a startling way. The symptom, we might say, in making the event permanent—in transforming a temporal experience of the soul into a spatial representation on the body—allowed the patient to forget the event it recorded. The neurotic symptom is a way of recording events in a language we have forgotten, a language which, as Hebrew (which as a boy he learned and subsequently forgot) was for Freud, we do not realize we ever understood.

What is difficult in this idea is not the tenuous nature of the interpretative links through which Freud reconstructs the original trauma but the contradiction it seems to involve in claiming the symptom to be both a means for remembering and a mechanism of forgetting. This difficulty is linked to two assumptions, common to the classical ego psychology of Modernity: first, that experience is a function of the ego and, second, that the body is an instrument of the soul. This meant that bodily acts were expressive of intentions and motives; that they had, therefore, a communicative purpose. But Freud's analysis of symptoms suggested quite otherwise. Here the communicative or expressive act of the body seems to be deeply ironic, to be self-defeating in a profoundly baffling way. Who is being addressed in this peculiar and unknown language? If the symptom is a memory, it ought to be immediately comprehensible; if it is a way of forgetting, it should be an arbitrary and uninterpretable sign of its predisposing cause.

Freud's original solution to this difficulty was to suppose that the ego was in some way split in two. In much the way that the French psychologists had discovered cases of multiple personality, Freud viewed neurotic symptoms as small-scale and partial hysterias, and hysterias as initial indications of an underlying tendency to neurosis; that is, to the splitting of consciousness. The symptom, thus, might be construed as the record of another ego, an alternative self which could not intrude on the normal world of the primary ego, but whose evanescent existence was recorded in its own peculiar language or, rather, in a bodily translation of that language.

The development of Freud's psychoanalytic theory is, among other things, a rejection of this view in which the underlying logic of ego psychology had been preserved. Gradually Freud developed a view in which the ego (by definition) remained singular but was not regarded as exhaustive of the psyche; there are, that is to say, "non-egological" forms of experience that cannot be subsumed under a rationalistic linguistic framework.

Hysterical symptoms provided one general puzzle and clue to such overlooked aspects of psychic life; a psyche, that is, which should not be conceived as a localized and internalized soul but had in some sense spread out and become identical with the extended surface of the body.

The soul, in other words, was another body image; and it was as a living body image, rather than a mental construct, that body and soul interacted.

In Freud's analytic work bodily symptoms conveyed a meaning which could be perfectly well understood in normal language; the problem, then, was to understand why this meaning should be disguised. Freud's original answer has become well known and to a considerable extent has restricted the reading of his later revisions and elaborations in which somewhat different views were presented. The idea of repression or, rather, suppression was simply that certain unpleasant events were thrust aside from, and by, an active ego which found them intolerable. This idea was easily expandable into a view of repression as the censorship of consciousness by a vigilant superego, which was just another word for the social conventions of everyday life.

However, if the ego is conceptualized as a specific focus of psychic life that develops relatively slowly and is inherently unstable, then the matter is more difficult. Then we must begin with non-ego forms of psychic life and explain the emergence of this peculiar psychic structure, which (prior to its formation) cannot be the agency of repression. The ego, in other words, should not be considered to be both the agency and the product of the process of repression. This became a central theoretical issue for Freud, and one which he never fully resolved to his own satisfaction. Here the significant point about the development of his argument is the increasing significance he accords non-egological perspectives in the description of psychic life.

These developments made clear that at the same time as differentiating his views very clearly from classical bourgeois psychology of the utilitarian school, Freud was at pains to distinguish his approach from its Romantic counterpart. A non-egological perspective—what he perhaps unadvisedly but correctly called the Unconscious—is not underneath consciousness; it is not buried, hidden, or confined inside anything, whether that anything is the soul as ego or the body as an image of itself. The term "repression" is perhaps even more misleading here. The Unconscious is simply psychic life outside the ego: either a psyche in which an ego has not yet formed (as in infancy) or psychic life viewed from a non-ego perspective (as in dreams and hysteria). The point can be illustrated in relation to memory. When

Freud assisted his patients in the recall of the events of their early lives, two different forms of memory were involved. First, and most obviously, a process of conscious remembering took place, prompted by appropriate questions. Here the ego traces back its own life history in a way inspired by the example of Rousseau. Freud also invoked a form of recollection, however, which depended on the spontaneous association of ideas and images that, rather as dream images appear to us in the waking state, seemed disjointed and inconsequential. These fragmentary recollections, Freud claimed, were interpretable in much the same way as bodily symptoms in hysteria. The first form of memory is an imaginary process of time travel; the ego projects itself into the past and takes notice of what is there. But eventually it reaches a barrier; it cannot penetrate the boundary of childhood amnesia created by the very formation of the ego itself. Yet a second form of memory—spontaneous recollection—reveals a permanent record of events in this period, and the manner of their recording provides us with a certain kind of understanding of non-egological psychic life. The unconscious does not necessarily become unconscious because it is full of dangerous ideas and images but, more simply, because the ego, in becoming conscious, claims a monopoly of our attention. The non-egological forms of psychic life continue; and in the contemporary world, as the ego breaks down under the sheer weight of complexity with which it has to deal, these processes become ever more evident. Increasingly, therefore, as the soul rises from the depths to which it had been consigned in the development of Modernity, individuals became opaque to themselves.

Freud's dream theory, in this context, provides a picture of contemporary existence. The dream, which only gradually came to be exclusively associated with the individuated soul in a sleeping state, is presented as a general model of psychic life. Again it is worth emphasizing that this is in sharp contrast to the Romantic theory of dreams, for which the dream image is the inner soul or kernel of consciousness, its most authentic and "deepest" level. But if this were so, then the authentic soul would be irrecoverably lost, and like the Romantics we would be condemned to nostalgia and unfulfilled longing. Freud's theory, however, amounts to charting a contemporary redistribution in the peculiar quality of reality to non-egological forms. The dream is important not because it is a clue to a lost world, but because it is an image of a world still present and becoming ever more available. To see this, Freud insists, we continually have to overcome the temptation of completely translating the unconscious into conscious linguistic forms. Nor does the unconscious belong in the past; it coexists, rather, side by side with the apparently more familiar (because rational and communicable) world of the ego. The "splitting" of consciousness that had been seen as the underlying process of hysteria was really a shifting between the perspectives of the ego and the non-ego, or "psyche." A strange and paradoxical dualism developed within consciousness itself, a spontaneous shifting of perspective not unlike that which affects the contemporary natural sciences.

This development in Freud's thought—charting what might be termed the opening of the contemporary soul—was accompanied by a determined effort to construct a general theory of the psyche. All his initial efforts, to interpret symptoms, dreams, and parapraxes, depended on a large number of seemingly arbitrary elements. This contingency, indeed, had persuaded many psychologists that they need not bother with his work, which remained hopelessly "unsystematic." The meaning of a dream or symptom depended on reconstructing a very exact life history and bringing to light the specific circumstances, which had often taken place many years previously, to which the current material apparently referred. But on the basis of such minute autobiographical details, how could a general understanding of the contemporary soul, of psychic life in general, be constructed?

In one sense, of course, it could not; and Freud, superbly trained in nineteenth-century scientific medicine, did not try to produce a deductive model of the psyche. But what did emerge, he claimed, were certain nonarbitrary constancies through which the nature of non-egological psychic functioning could be illuminated.

Freud talked of hysteria as a kind of survival of an ancient body image, an architecture and an archaeology of primitive body images. Neurotic symptoms, for all their particularity and interpretability in the context of the history of a singular ego, displayed certain common features whose significance was related to forms of bodily experience that preceded the emergence of any ego. These body images were also the source of spontaneous fantasies that formed the meaningful content (rather than did conscious ego thoughts) of dreams. It was this original body image and its successive transformations into the bourgeois form that Freud treated in his theory of sexuality. The process of differentiation by which the ego form of sexuality arises (its isolation ideally in the genital function and justification rationally as reproduction) does not obliterate earlier forms of eroticism and the body images with which they are associated.

These body images are the source of adult sexual perversions but also play an important and largely unnoticed background role in normal experience. Such older body images can dominate and obscure genital sexuality in being, so to speak, harnessed to the ego as an exclusive source of pleasure. The body image then loses its historical dimension, and each of its "epochs" is represented as an equivalent and equally available possibility. Pleasure is associated with each of its phases. Notably it is the surface of the body and the different ways in which it can be topologically defined through eroticism that are most significant. There is no separation here of body and soul, of sexual appetite and love. Once again the notion here of repression can be misleading. Older forms of pleasure are not "repressed"; rather, genital sexuality becomes the specific focus of gratification that we come to know as pleasure. This is accomplished through a process of differentiation from an original primitive form of bodily experience for which "pleasure" as a specific psychic quality hardly exists. The series of transformations through which particular organic functions become well defined, are brought under control, and are ultimately constituted as adult sexuality is the process of creating rather than of repressing pleasure. What is "repressed" are forms of experience we (as egos) would not recognize as pleasure at all (and only become so in the perversions). These other forms —non-egologic forms of bodily awareness—are made safe by the emergence of an ego structure for which, in a sense, they do not exist and are therefore barely noticed (hence, indeed, Freud's great achievement in elucidating their continuing existence in the psyche and in the body).

Pleasure is the result of repression, not its victim. Now, and here Freud reaches an important consideration, the association of pleasure with particular bodily states is ultimately arbitrary. Indeed, the peculiar meaningfulness of certain states of the soul as "pleasure" depends on specific historical and social circumstances. "Pleasure," indeed, is a relatively recent psychic complex, linked specifically to the ego, and is likely to dissolve along with the historic fragmentation of the ego. Freud saw clearly that we have to learn to love pleasure, that the taken-for-grantedness that we like pleasure should not be regarded as given but, like the specific content of experience that at any moment might prove to be pleasurable, is itself a variable phenomenon.

This constitutes a strong attack on the utilitarian underpinning of all bourgeois psychology. The utilitarian defines pleasure in a solipsistic fashion (as a "natural" phenomenon), whereas Freud treats it as a specific, variable, and nonessential quality of experience (like the quality of "reality" or of the emotions). The perversions, thus, are a peculiar form of egoism, in which the ego derives pleasure from non-ego-based body images, in a sense taking pleasure in its own destruction, which is nonetheless construed as its gratification.

Bourgeois psychology, as much as classical physics, had dealt with realities that were given to consciousness in an unambiguous fashion. Subjective feelings pointed with unerring accuracy at the content of the soul, just as much as the senses presented us with a picture of the outside world more or less "as it was." While this realism in relation to objectivity was always undercut by philosophical skepticism that, theoretically compelling, was nonetheless of little practical import, the realism and even "naturalism" of subjectivity were accepted much more readily at face value.

Implicit in Romanticism and idealism was a view of the soul as infinite, and as infinite freedom, which in principle could not be represented in consciousness. But for the most part subjectivity, the entire flow of the inner life as feeling, was regarded as a nonproblematic "reality." Freud's work, however, provided a significant and rich psychology of another sort, one in which the soul was as detached from "deep" subjectivity as it was from the objective world. The flow of feeling in Freud's writings constitutes a reality sui generis in which little is said about the ultimate constituents of the human subject. In some sense subjectivity was "represented" in the psyche, much as the "thing-in-itself" was represented in the perceptual world; but nothing much could be said about the transformations of a primal reality which this process was usually thought to mirror, if not to constitute. Freud's psychology is above all, therefore, a psychology of consciousness (with the proviso that not all consciousness is a function of the ego as a coherent self-image).

Thus Freud points to "objectless" feelings, states of feeling that not only have no evident connection with the circumstances of social life but that, in a more difficult sense, cannot be integrated into a coherent picture of the inner life as a quasi-logical system. These might be regarded as fragments of the soul, rising, so to speak, to the surface of life and finding there a convenient niche, a form of "rationalization" in which they can be accepted in the psyche. But Freud does not suppose these fragments indicate the real underlying causes of psychic life, that in some sense they are more profound than the normal content of experience. Rather, in floating to the surface, "feelings" take on the superficial characteristics of all experience and, to the extent to which they become familiar to us, reveal nothing of their original nature.

THE SUPERFICIALITY OF
CONTEMPORARY LIFE

Freud's psychology, though centrally concerned with the experience of the postbourgeois world, has frequently been viewed as an extension, rather than as a critique, of Romantic inwardness (Kirschner 1996). A postmodern reading of his work becomes all the more plausible, however, when it is placed in the context not only of pre-Freudian studies of hysteria but, more generally, of the many-sided and radical changes in cultural orientation that affected European societies at the end of the nineteenth century and that appeared nowhere more decisively than in Vienna (Schorske 1980; Rider 1993). The transition from a classical bourgeois culture founded on the closed "point-mass" body image and the enclosed, individuated, and "deep" soul to a contemporary culture of an "open" body image coinciding with a "superficial" soul forms the real subject matter of Freud's work, as it does of so many of his imaginative contemporaries and near contemporaries. In different ways, for example, Bergson and Proust also describe the extent to which the body has gained a new sensibility and has, so to speak, taken on many of the functions of the soul and now can be understood only in relation to memory, to its own past, and to its imagined future; it is extended in time as well as space. At the same time the soul, rising from its hidden depths, reveals itself by flowing into and assuming bodily forms.

A more complete understanding of this transition requires fuller detailed examination of the interrelations, in particular, between Freud's psychology and Husserl's philosophy. It is clear that advocates of both Freudian psychology and phenomenology have failed to grasp the significance of each other's perspectives, and with few exceptions (Ricoeur 1970) little effort has yet been made to bring together the twentieth century's two most original and significant approaches to the understanding of human subjectivity. Certainly such an objective cannot be pursued here, but what can briefly be illustrated as an indication of the wider context of psychoanalytic ideas are a number of important connections between the Freudian understanding of the postmodern soul and both its striking anticipation in the writings of Friedrich Nietzsche and its imaginative realization in the fiction of Robert Musil.

Filaments of Life

Nietzsche intuitively grasped the character of the postbourgeois psyche. He saw, first of all, that the dissolution of Nature in the contemporary sciences was itself an indication of psychic fragmentation. The natural world had dissolved into a flux, from which the traditional physicist wrenched a "reality" of massy objects only "by violating nature . . . by isolating more or less artificially a phenomenon from the whole" (Meyerson 1930, 31). Indeed, "we operate only with things that do not exist: lines, planes, bodies, atoms, divisible time spans, divisible spaces . . . in truth we are confronted by a continuum out of which we isolate a couple of pieces. . . . The suddenness with which many effects stand out misleads us; actually, it is sudden only for us. In this moment of suddenness there is an infinite number of processes that elude us" (Nietzsche 1974, 172–73).

More generally the division between appearance and the "thing-in-itself" had become absolute, so that in terms of human experience (which was the only reality given to us), both ceased to exist. If the "thing-in-itself" was banished as a metaphysical illusion, then one could no longer talk of the "appearances" for which that putative reality was held to be responsible; both had to be abandoned in favor of the given phenomena of life as a continuous process of becoming (Nietzsche 1968, 310–16). Just as significantly, by describing contemporary experience in terms of the culture of "decadence," Nietzsche can be viewed as establishing the point of departure for a new psychology. Whereas in the philosophical tradition of Modernity the human psyche was conceived as an imaging device which, as if viewing in a mirror or through a window, was presented with a picture of the world, Nietzsche began to chart the landscape of an alternative sensibility, founded upon a tactile register of shocks and excitations. In some ways recalling more ancient modes of grasping reality, Nietzsche suggested that knowledge of the modern world is not so much encoded within the soul in terms of a specular *logos* as it is inscribed directly on the surface of the body image.

Though Nietzsche found it difficult wholly to abandon specular imagery, he clearly anticipated its demise. The "selfless man" is "a precious, easily damaged and tarnished measuring instrument and reflecting apparatus which ought to be respected and taken care of . . . a delicate, empty, elegant, flexible mold which has first to wait for some content so as to 'form' itself" (Nietzsche 1973, 116).

His is a philosophy, as Freud's is a psychology, awaiting the plastic age. For both, experience leaves its trace not only, or mainly, in terms of an ideal memory but also, and more significantly, in a morphological history of the body.

We live through the body, not the spirit; or, rather, we exist as a spiritualized body awakened to a new sensitivity as all those abstract infinities to which the soul had been projected reemerge on the surface of modern life. The body, which for so long in Western society had been despised, thus comes into a new prominence, not simply through an arbitrary and willful inversion of a traditional mode of valuation but as the new locus of all those human powers and attributes previously separated and infinitized as spirit, soul, knowledge, consciousness, thought, language, and so on.

The animating energies of modern life were conceived as flowing across and through the human body, on whose surface they left, as if on a softened wax tablet or on a photographic plate, an enigmatic trace. Consciousness could no longer be regarded as something separate from the rest of experience; it could not stand apart and observe but could only become flickeringly aware of itself as part of an operation in which it was itself implicated. This was the environment into which "the man without qualities" was born: "whatever still remains to him of his 'own person' seems to him accidental, so completely has he become a passage and reflection of forms and events not his own" (Nietzsche 1973, 115).

Nietzsche inaugurates the important transformation in human self-understanding in the postbourgeois age toward bodily categories and bodily thoughts; in his work metaphysics is transformed into a new language of bodily states and conditions. But rather than glowing with the radiant health of Truth, the sensitive contemporary person can say, with Dostoevsky's antihero, "I am a sick man. . . . But I don't understand the least thing about my illness, and I don't know for certain what part of me is affected" (Dostoevsky 1972, 15). Oppressed by a diseased self-consciousness, the contemporary individual languishes in morbid self-pity, losing this very self-consciousness and individuality in an "expression of the physiological over-excitability pertaining to everything *decadent*" (Nietzsche 1968, 91). Nietzsche characterizes the contemporary world in terms of an overwhelming flood of stimulation: "Sensibility immensely more irritable . . . the abundance of disparate impressions greater than ever: cosmopolitanism in foods, literature, newspapers, forms, tastes, even landscapes. The tempo of this influx *prestissimo;* the impressions erase each other; one instinctively resists taking in anything, taking anything deeply" (Nietzsche 1968, 47).

A hypersensitivity manifests itself particularly in a fascination with touching and being touched; we are interested in the world, "but merely epidermically interested," and cultivate a generally superficial relation to reality.

The "dematerialization" of nature in the physical sciences is felt for an everyday consciousness of the world as a new "sensualism in matters of the spirit." The postmodern is announced as sickness; it is "all body," idealized first as the sensitive and melancholic suffering of consumption, a preparatory hollowing out and bringing to the surface of everything which had been secreted inside the body as the abysmal source of all value. The privileged patients on their Magic Mountain are simultaneously rendered both more spiritual and more sensuous by their illness and isolation from the world; there the body is "exaggerated by disease and rendered twice over body"; and at the same time, as corporeal strength and vigor fade, its image glows with spirit, it is "a soul without a body" (Mann 1960, 229, 100).

The contemporary body is an image of itself; it is a mirror in which is reflected nothing other than the processes from which the mirrored surface is itself constructed. For Nietzsche the contemporary person, "lacking any other pleasure than that provided by knowledge, by 'mirroring', . . . waits until something comes along and then gently spreads himself out, so that not even the lightest footstep and the fluttering of ghostly beings shall be lost on his surface and skin. Whatever still remains of his 'own person' seems to him accidental, often capricious, more often disturbing, so completely has he become a passage and reflection of forms and events not his own" (Nietzsche 1973, 115).

He might have written "she" rather than "he," for in his own terms Nietzsche is describing the "feminization" of the subject, its transformation from a closed, spiritual, individual being into an open, pliant, sensitive, and continuous surface.

All this indicates that already for Nietzsche, as it was to be for Freud, the self is neither an object nor a subject but a loose aggregate of continually changing perspectives. More than that, the domain of experience—the psyche and its world—is detached both from the world of objects (which had been a familiar theme since the rise of Modernity itself) and from the subject or soul. The soul as much as the world of objects lies beyond experience, which occupies a sort of middle ground in some way (which cannot be specified) related to both; or, at least, experience is so constituted that consciousness is necessarily driven to postulate both bodies and souls of an unknown, transcendental sort. In this regard, at least, Freud is quite closely related to the phenomenological school (in spite of his various attempts at reductionism in his earlier writings) and was directly influenced by Brentano, whose lectures he attended while he was a medical student.

Nietzsche's attack on metaphysics is not simply an inversion or transvaluation of classical values, it is a rejection of the notion of Truth as the inner world of the soul; it is the rejection of all "depth." For Nietzsche the perspectivism that is an inevitable consequence of the Copernican Revolution means not only that the ego should not regard itself as a privileged point of view from which to construct a picture of the world and that it must accept the "objectivity" of the world as a projection of its self-certainty, but that this self-certainty is itself no more than a temporary crystallization from the flux of reality. As well as registering itself in this (periodically) structured form, reality also impinges on the human being in terms of continuous bodily transitions, in general sensitivity, nervousness, and irritability. In relation to the immediacy of human experience, the soul remains as unknown as the world of objects. Nietzsche no more than Freud argues that the hidden depths of the soul can be brought to light; rather, he argues with Freud that a proper self-understanding demands that human reality be approached at its own level. This, after all, is hard enough, and the avoidance of mystification does not lead to a simplistic form of understanding. Nietzsche is as determined as Freud to reveal the self-deceptive aspects of human subjectivity and action, and like Freud he views this deceptiveness, rather than originating in some mysterious reticence of the soul, as an inherent aspect of the complexity of human reality.

We cannot avoid living in a world to which an "ego" seems preadapted, but as this ego is itself part of that world, it provides only a partial vision of reality (including itself). The human is never wholly known because knowledge is a partial relation to reality. We are, therefore, continually surprised by ourselves; the Self often appears more disturbingly strange than the Other in which, paradoxically, we recognize ourselves.

The End of Inwardness

Robert Musil, onetime engineer and student of Ernst Mach, has written what is perhaps the most compelling account of the condition of the soul in the contemporary world. His great novel *The Man without Qualities* takes as its starting point the fragmented character of modern urban life as a practical expression of the disintegration of the ego: "But in the city, where experiences come by the thousands, we can no longer relate them to ourselves; and this is of course the beginning of life's notorious turning into abstraction" (Musil 1995, 708). The notion of coherent individuality, of *Bildung* and of a biographical logic of self-development, could no longer be sustained even as a fiction (and it was always as fiction that the "depth" of the soul had been most important). Thus, "to find a secure foothold in the flow of phenomena is like trying to hammer a nail into a fountain jet of water" (Musil 1995, 494). And as a result we become equally indifferent to everything: "Everything that actually happens passes over us like rain and sunshine" (Musil 1995, 744).

The soul, indeed, no longer has any place in the modern world, which, after all, is a product of the engineer, and an engineer builds without regard to the soul's needs or wishes. "A soul—What's that?" asks one of his characters. "It is easy to define negatively: It is simply that which sneaks off at the mention of algebraic series" (Musil 1995, 106). As "children of a nerve racked age," we have "ideas, of course, but no soul" (Musil 1995, 527). For us intelligence serves as "a good imitation of the soul," and "morality replaces the soul with logic" (Musil 1995, 537, 552). Money, "which is both moral and rational," not soul, rules the world. There is a sense that (as Pascal had already noted) what seems most needed "is a strong, healthy delusion" that can restore "life's inherent joy" and overcome the pervasive neurasthenia and frantic directionless activity of the age. Indeed, "one was obliged to surrender oneself to an illusion if one received the grace of having one" (Musil 1995, 987). But the world was now bereft of illusions and, therefore, of any sense of direction in the ceaseless flow of events: "How was anyone at that time to know whether to turn right or left on leaving the door, unless he had a job" (Musil 1995, 987).

In general, "life was becoming more and more homogenous and impersonal. Something mechanical, stereotypical, statistical, and serial was insinuating itself into every entertainment, excitement, recreation, even into the passions. The life will was spreading out and becoming shallow, like a river hesitating before its delta" (Musil 1995, 1189).

But the retreat of the soul, its retrenchment that apparently leaves its contemporary manifestation as "surface ripples of an ocean the immense depths of which are hardly troubled by them," is deceptive. The soul, which had been abandoned to an inward abyss, now flows back into every contemporary and superficial experience of life.

For Musil's characters the illusion of self-consciousness as an inner depth has all but vanished. For them "the outer chain of events and the inward one ran on independently side by side" (Musil 1995, 460), and life could no longer make sense in terms of their interrelation. The novel moves to a depiction of life as a surface on which outer and inner have fused, and the contradictions of Object and Subject, if they are not resolved, then certainly become meaningless. Here, where the body has also been opened to the world, to life as a ceaseless flow of activity, soul and body come together in a new way as indeterminate and ever-changing play of feeling.

Soul and body lose their separateness and mutual antagonism, reviving primordial and infantile modes of experience. "Somehow the outer world did not leave off at his skin, and his inner world did not merely shine out through the window of reflection; but both blended into a single undivided state of separateness and presence" (Musil 1995, 410). This goes beyond the "double consciousness" and "hysteria" of the age. It is "as if the body were no longer part of a world where the sensual self is enclosed in strands of nerves" (Musil 1995, 786). There is a pervasive sense of "dissolving in thin air" (Musil 1995, 806).

The body has acquired soul-like attributes, and the soul has realized itself in the body. In this condensation of time and space, memory becomes contemporaneous with the present, and the past loses its distance. Recollection, indeed, loses the quality of interiority and is assimilated to the "soulless fleeting quality of memory" (Musil, 1995, 932). For an era where "what was counts for nothing and what one does is less important than what one does next," the contemporary flux of phenomena merges with the earliest recollection of primal life anterior to the disjunction of object and subject: "When I remember as far back as I can, I'd say that there was hardly any separation between inside and outside . . . our feelings, our desires, our very selves, were not yet quite inside ourselves" (Musil 1995, 979). And now they have escaped again.

In a remarkable passage Musil invokes the ambiguity of twilight, as Proust had done, not to wrap reality in a shroud of ambiguity but to free it from the illusions of an enlightened age:

> The night embraces all contradictions . . . no word is false and no word true, but each is that incomparable birth of the spirit out of darkness that a person experiences in a new thought (thoughts born of life and body, not ideas). . . .

For in these nights the self holds nothing back; there is no condensation of possession on the self's surface, hardly a memory; the intensified self radiates into an unbounded selflessness. . . . And it is not the mouth that pours out its adoration but the body, which, from head to foot, is stretched taut in exaltation above the darkness of the earth and beneath the light of heaven, oscillating between two stars. (Musil 1995, 1179–80)

The detached realm of the human, formed into a filament of life and, as it were, pressed between infinities into which it can never expand, is continually forced back upon itself. Even the understanding can no longer penetrate these regions beyond the proper domain of experience: "All understanding presupposes a kind of superficiality, a penchant for the surface, which is, moreover, expressed in the root of the word 'comprehend', to lay hold of, and has to do with primordial experiences having been understood not singly but one by the next and thereby unavoidably connected with one another more on the surface than in depth" (Musil 1995, 1184).

Reality is no longer sensed at a distance, vision and hearing are dethroned as the privileged distance senses, and increasingly significance is given to vague and transient states of feeling, feelings that are difficult to locate and that, like primordial realities, continually transform themselves one into another. Feeling is the quality that betrays life's surface, reveals its shape and texture. Emotions register surface phenomena: warm/cold, rough/smooth, soft/hard, and undirected movement, waves engulfing and receding, tidal flows, pulses, tension and relaxation. Feeling is the topologically sophisticated sense, the one that most adequately represents the flux of reality and the one that carries with it the least risk of hypostatizing transient states into metaphysical principles. In an originally unpublished section of the novel, Musil records his hero Ulrich's attempts at constructing a theory of the emotions, a treatise which amounts to a descriptive psychology of the contemporary soul in opposition to either classical bourgeois or Romantic versions of Modernity.

Ulrich regards the specific quality of contemporary reality as emotion, as transient and ill-defined feelings. The issue is complicated in that what we term the "emotions" are no more fixed, historically, than any other aspect of experience or, indeed, its framework. The emotions that Ulrich (and Musil) describes are not conceptualized and given a specific form and label such as anger, fear, or jealousy but exist, rather, as vague tendencies, waves of warmth/coolness, attraction/repulsion, and so forth. Emotions are inherently short-lived; "they are not genuine when they last" (Musil 1995, 1229). And in contemporary terms love (just because it conceives of itself as permanent) has become unemotional and "cold." In the draft of what was intended to become a full-scale treatise, "Naive Description of How an Emotion Originates," Ulrich does not reach down into hidden depths to discover normally concealed sources of energy and meaning. Emotion, rather, begins with "impressive but incomplete experiences," with certain "states of readiness" and small "tendencies" that then "spread" and flow. Emotions "condense" on the surface of life, gathering into rivulets of feeling that flow into one another. Ulrich claims emotion spans any division between "inside and outside"; between the I and the not-I. There is a "double direction" in emotion that "imparts to it the nature of a transitory phenomenon" (Musil 1995, 1264).

Emotion, rather than knowledge, provides a key to a reality in which every differentiation has become transparently arbitrary; it is the most adequate representation of the real flux of experience: "And yet no emotion is unmistakably what it appears to be, and neither self-observation nor the actions to which it gives rise provide any assurance about it" (Musil 1995, 1321). Here too the dreamlike character of self-abandonment is apparent; we become aware of emotions, of the ceaseless flow of feeling, as of something happening to us, something sweeping over us and carrying us away, or, at least, flowing around us; continually enigmatic and ambivalent, never easy to pin down and something which escapes the self, forming a continuous background state of being in distinction to which the ego establishes itself as a specific and seemingly permanent nucleus. But in the contemporary world the self has dissolved into this background and become indistinguishable from its multiplicity of ephemeral states.

Melancholy

The body is a foundational construct of Modernity; it is a spatial category which in modern society becomes historicized. The soul, which is equally central to the development of Modernity, develops out of the experience of time and becomes spatialized. In contemporary society the body loses its weight and substance; it is nothing other than an image or a shadow. At the same time the soul, rising from its depths, becomes entangled in sensuous matter. These curious transformations hint at the radical way in which Modernity involves the dissolution not only of fixed and hierarchical categories of nature and society but also the modalities of intimate self-experience. From being a soul inside and animating a closed body, the human subject in modern society developed toward a physical-psychic surface, an interactive body-soul rather than a dualistic Object/Subject.

What previously has been referred to, somewhat mysteriously, as the "body-shadow" or "bodily presence" may now be described as the "soulful body," as a body image in which there is a preponderance of soul. The surplus of soulful elements remains, as it were, trapped in the body and cannot enter into the marketplace of representations, giving rise to an undifferentiated sense of weight. Paradoxically, as Thomas Mann pointed out, in illness the sense we have of being "all body" is actually a result of being too "soulful". We do not "feel" the body at all; we become aware of its specific form and qualities as moments of the soul. From the perspective of the soul, this characteristically modern imbalance (a kind of indicator of the extent to which the soul has fused itself to and "opened out" the body) has been most generally described as melancholy. Indeed, if "feeling" (rather than knowledge) has become the characteristic modality of experience in contemporary society, melancholy has become its pervasive content.

At first sight this seems a strange outcome. In the context of the decline of feudalism, the intellectual and cultural vitality of both northern humanism and the Italian Renaissance appears contrary to any conception of human wretchedness. Is not Modernity, by virtue of its self-assertive autonomy, the denial of melancholy?

Certainly, the meaning of melancholy, as of everything else, underwent a profound change with the emergence of Modernity. Deeper reflection put a swift end to all such premature optimism. Nature, rather than being a symbolic intermediary, emerged in the new world picture as an insurmountable obstacle between the human and the divine. Whether viewed "atomistically" as a naturally given unity, or "dialectically" as the emergent properties of a specific set of relations, the human individual found himself or herself in a condition of "unprecedented inner loneliness" (Weber 1936, 104).

Long associated with contradictory tendencies, on the one hand, to spiritual elevation and artistic sensitivity and, on the other, to lethargy, indifference to the world, and acedia, melancholy was given a new and coherent meaning with the emergence of Modernity as a sense of cosmic dislocation. The feeling of being alone in a void, of isolation in the face of the double infinity of external and internal space, is at the heart of both Bruno's frenzy and Montaigne's sorrow. What Burton called "sadness without cause" came into its own as the immediate experience of modern life.

The Elizabethan Age was rich in melancholy, and increasingly "heaviness" replaced "darkness" as one of its defining characteristics. Over a long period authors from quite different backgrounds have agreed and were eventually to retrace a diversity of insights back to this common source. Melancholy is to be "overwhelmed with heaviness . . . heaviness without cause" (Timothy Bright), "dolour or hevynesse of minde" (Thomas Elyot), and "unwelcome heaviness" (Goethe). Finding its modern form as "anguish, dullness, heaviness, and vexation of spirit" (Burton), it remains "devitalized existence . . . heavy with daily sorrows" (Kristeva). Inexplicably "a multitude of sorrows" "suddenly weighs one down," and "my frailest memories take on the weight of rocks" (Baudelaire).

By the time Burton wrote his *Anatomy of Melancholy* (first edition 1621), he could afford to make his claims rhetorically: "For who indeed is not a fool, melancholy, mad?" Thomas Nashe and Ben Johnson had already satirized its more self-conscious and affected devotees, while Timothy Bright's *A Treatise of Melancholia* (1586) had established a new medical tradition in its study and treatment. For both literary and medical authors, melancholy represented something fundamental to the modern condition. It could not be treated as a set of purely physical symptoms, nor as an arbitrary and rare derangement of the sensibilities or of the mind. Melancholy had its roots in the inescapable reality of human existence. Burton as both a divine and a physician was, therefore, especially well qualified to be melancholy's anatomist. And, like Michel de Montaigne, whose lapse into melancholy was "enraptured by sadness," he anatomized melancholy to distract himself from its torments, "to ease my mind by writing."

The causes of melancholy are legion, or at least appear to be. Any illness, misfortune, or circumstance of life may be either a cause or a symptom (or both) of melancholy, but it is the imagination that makes it so. Melancholy is a surfeit of soulfulness, an uncontrolled imagination: "This strong conceit or imagination is *astrum hominis* (a man's guiding star), and the rudder of this our ship, which reason should steer, but, overborne by phantasy, cannot manage, and so suffers itself and this whole vessel of ours to be overruled, and often overturned" (Burton 1932, 1:257).

The spectacle of modern life is indeed melancholy, a "vast, infinite ocean of incredible madness and folly" in which all human beings are prey to "melancholy fears without a cause" and are distinguished by being "miraculously vain, various and wavering." Imagination, which is a kind of infinite inward space, has been wrenched free of a fixed cosmological order and places its relentless question mark over every momentarily settled state of being. The modern form of melancholy joins modern cosmology and psychology to the traditional imagery of the Fall. As a divinely cunning punishment for disobedience, God has granted man an inner freedom which, finally realized in the modern world, proves to be a torment which individuals cannot help but impose upon themselves.

While Burton and Montaigne recommend the distraction of writing as a means of coping with melancholy, Pascal recognizes that distraction is, in fact, its most insidious form. Distraction is a paradox; it is continuous movement in the pursuit of absolute rest: "We seek rest . . . [but] rest proves intolerable because of the boredom it produces. We must get away from it and crave excitement." Distraction is an oscillation between energetic ecstasy and lethargic indifference. But these polarities are fundamentally identical. They are merely different forms of boredom. Pascal understands that diversionary activities do not surmount but carry within them the boredom that is their immediate cause. And it is first as boredom, therefore, that melancholy makes its way in the modern world. Pascal, indeed, is the first to define boredom as the central experience of Modernity. Boredom is inherent in the secular individualism that is the only moral foundation of modern (specifically modern capitalist) society. And although it often appears disguised in the particularities of a more specific malady, boredom is the commonest of diseases and reveals a boundless spiritual longing: "Man is so unhappy that he would be bored even if he had no cause for boredom, by the very nature of his temperament, and he is so vain that, though he has a thousand and one reasons for being bored, the slightest thing, like pushing a ball with a billiard cue, will be enough to divert him" (Pascal 1966, 136).

"What else does this craving, and this helplessness proclaim" Pascal asks rhetorically, "but that there was once in man a true happiness, of which all that now remains is the empty print and trace." Immediate self-knowledge is the "unhappy consciousness" of wretchedness and inconsolable cosmic grief. A soul lies within us and stirs to life as the power of reason, but it gives us no joy. Its presence, rather, is a perpetual irritant, a tormenting reminder of how far we have fallen beneath an ideal state of bliss.

"That our age is an age of mental depression, there is no doubt and no question," remarks its closest intimate (Kierkegaard 5:5771). Its ubiquity rests on the consciousness of the modern world as a set of individuated objects isolated in space and set in motion according to universal laws of nature devoid of intention or design and blind to their consequences. The classical language of melancholy and its associated network of moral and psychological ideas have been transformed and adapted to describe the immediate experience of Modernity as the consciousness of "inner loneliness." Both cosmos and society appear as a meaningless and chaotic background to the emergent "ego," which, resting on nothing more substantial than its own image, is swept into the turmoil of civil society or, withdrawing, oscillates between depressed self-absorption and extravagant states of rapture.

Having established itself as melancholy, the modern soul, expanding and fusing to the body, infected every form of sensuousness with a certain morbidity. Thus, for example, Ludwig Tieck writes that "existence and torment are one and the same word" and describes modern life as "an unveiling of the madness, the frenzy of all life," as "sheer nervousness" (Tieck 1831).

Contemporary melancholy, mournful, heavy, and dizzy with infinity, is also charged with the "metaphysical lucidity of depression" (Kristeva 1989, 4). Like the pictures of Caspar David Friedrich and Giorgio di Chirico, the impenetrable objectivity of the modern world presents itself to the detached and aimless spectator as a pure appearance and, thus, with dreamlike clarity.

The pervasiveness of melancholy attests, as does the ubiquity of bodily shadows, to the incompleteness of the project of Modernity. These residual, nonrational and nonrepresentational, contents of experience, at first no more than the undigested debris of premodern forms of life, persist. Impervious to the modern solvents of distraction and imagination, melancholy takes root and nourishes itself on every form of contemporary superficiality. Melancholy drapes itself over the contemporary world, obscuring its cheerful face and weighing down its dancing step.

The full consciousness of the modern age came to itself as a depressive mood that deepened and persisted into a new mournful sensibility. Modernity is universal melancholy. "Melancholy is at the bottom of everything," Amiel confides to his *Journal;* it expresses, though it cannot fully represent, "the obscure self, the pure subjectivity which is incapable of realizing itself in mind, conscience, or reason, in the soul, the heart, the imagination, or the life of the senses, and which makes for itself attributes and conditions out of all these forms of its own life" (Amiel 1906, 58). And, speaking for many, Schelling captures this darker aspect of Modernity: "A veil of sadness is spread over all nature . . . a deep unappeasable melancholy. . . . The darkest and deepest ground in human nature is . . . melancholy" (Price 1963, 45).

THREE

Spirit

*T*HE BODY can be comprehended as an accumulation of historically constructed self-images, intimate spatial representations of distinct epochs whose specifically contemporary form is the open surface. The soul may be understood contextually as a spatial representation of temporal self-images, the contemporary form of which is realized in the depthless extension of immediate experience as a stream or flux of consciousness. It might, therefore, seem unnecessary to inquire about the relation of body and soul, which, whatever their tangled and disentangled histories, give every appearance of coming together in the essential identity of contemporary experience. In every sense contemporary identity—the self-identity of contemporary life—is an indistinguishable mingling of body and soul. Existence has become a surface upon which all the antinomies of bourgeois thought and experience are dissolved. Contemporary self-identity is a universal indifference. Everything is the same because, in the endless process of social differentiation, no difference is experienced as real and essential; no difference makes a difference. Every distinction has become transparently conventional, transitory, and inexpressive, no more than an accident seized and molded into the appearance of necessity.

This, indeed, is now a well-known if not a well-established view. But the thesis of postmodernism—the monism that swallows up the dualities of object and subject in all its guises—for all its aggressive rejection of metaphysics, must nonetheless confront the problem of identity and difference. Indeed, the weakness of the postmodern view is just that it dwells complacently in the contemporary (unexplained and fortuitous) unity of body-soul without grasping in a critical way its preconditions or, which amounts to the same thing, offering any insight into the nature of this unity. From a postmodern perspective all categorical distinctions are dissolved in a symptomatic ahistorical discourse, and every social relation is reduced to a common and empty identity.

But simply to reject the postmodern perspective and to seek to grasp the present wholly in terms of the past and concepts rooted in the past is to obscure rather than illuminate the distinctive character of contemporary life. To seek, for example, a causal explanation for the emergence of a specifically contemporary body-soul image would be to invite a contradiction. Causality belongs to the classical language of the bourgeois body image, to a normative conception of reality reducible to the inertial point-mass. Equally, to make sense of modern sensitivity in terms of the meaningful expression of an interior soul is to invoke a mode of self-understanding rooted in earlier conditions of experience. The soul has lost its depth and expressive power; body and soul have opened and intermingled, conjoined as the active surface of contemporary life. But this has not resolved the difficulties of Modernity; Subject-Object distinctions have neither been wholly transcended nor resolved. They reappear unpredictably on the contemporary surface of life, which, accommodating the entire range of past constructions and interrelations of body image and soul, is tolerant of the most glaring contradictions. The contemporary fascination with paradox, irony, and the inauthentic, indeed, is only possible because of the persistence of at least an intermittent meaningful commitment to directness and authenticity.

It would be unhelpful to sink into some premodern idea of the body-soul interaction as a refuge from the inconsequential relationalism of postmodernity. It is the strength of the postmodern claim that it can continually resituate itself, and every other position, in such a way as to expose the limitation and partiality of every "substantial" view of the present. Increasingly desperate efforts to revive and even complete the project of Enlightenment and to discover (magically) that, after all, there are universal moral values (human rights), norms of reason, beauty, and so forth, carry little conviction and make sense only in the context of an older conceptualization of spirit. This is not to claim that such efforts are without significance but, rather, that their significance is self-limiting.

Yet in spite of the success of the postmodern claim, it still seems unavoidable (if not valid) to ask if there is not a difference that makes a difference, a necessary difference from which human consciousness and experience can emerge and upon which they can be founded in a nonarbitrary way, a difference in which real presence and authenticity can take root. And here, even more clearly than could be revealed in discussing the body or the soul, the significance of an older vocabulary becomes evident. What the postmodern condition posits, above anything else, is a spiritless world. So the critical task becomes that of establishing the possibility or otherwise of spirit for contemporary experience.

"Spirit" is the absent term in Descartes's understanding of the world as Subject and Object; it seems it has become redundant. Equally, spirit lies outside the distinctions of Self and Other or Ego and World. All agree to the characterization of the present as spiritless, not only in the Enlightenment sense of witnessing the final triumph of secularized intellectual understanding of the world but, more generally, as a radical "disenchantment" of that world in terms of its human content. Spirit, whether conceived strictly in terms of human immanence or in terms of an irreducible transcendence, seems equally irrelevant to the understanding of contemporary life.

The coupling of Modernity and "spirit," then, is problematic. Whatever they might signify as representations, the phenomenal actuality, if not the substantial presence, of body or soul can hardly be challenged; but spirit invokes a more radically contested reality. The very notion of Modernity might be construed as a process of despiritualization or of enlightenment (depending on one's point of view); a development, that is, in which the genuinely human relation of historical and personal transcendence is swallowed up in the dehumanizing mechanism of civil society, or which (again depending on the point of view) sweeps aside all those prejudices, superstitions, and errors that constrained people in modern society to abandon their freedom to misunderstood aspects of their own activity. The notion of spirit, that is to say, is intimately bound up with the ideological struggle over Modernity itself.

Yet the term at least survives. And we commonly refer to "spirit" in a noncontroversial way to designate the general cultural assumptions of a period or group, as in the "spirit of the times," and so on. We might thus distinguish between the spirit of Modernity (descriptive typifications of modern culture) and spirit in Modernity (which invokes the struggle over secularization and enlightenment). Indeed, what is distinctive in contemporary culture is just that, as body and soul have come together in a new way as the surface of life—the surface that is life—so the spirit of Modernity and spirit in Modernity have become identical. Thus, characteristically, the most secular of modern writers have most clearly expressed the contemporary nature of spirit, while at the same time the most persuasive modern defense of a religious conception of spirit has been productive of the most subtle secular analysis of the culture of Modernity.

SPIRIT AS SYNTHESIS

What is spirit? In a preliminary way the notion of spirit can be linked to those of body and soul. In a challenging text Søren Kierkegaard articulates the insights fundamental to an understanding of spirit and to the spiritless character of Modernity: "A human being is spirit. But what is spirit? Spirit is the self. But what is the self? The self is a relation that relates itself to itself or is the relation's relating itself to itself in the relation; the self is not the relation but is the relation's relating itself to itself. A human being is a synthesis of the infinite and the finite, of the temporal and the eternal, of freedom and necessity, in short, a synthesis. A synthesis is a relation between two. Considered in this way a human being is still not a self" (Kierkegaard 1980, 13).

The synthesis of spirit has as its precondition the union of body and soul. The psychophysical unity of the self requires the one as much as the other. Commonly, Modernity has been viewed as overly "material," as an imbalance of body over soul. The human is viewed (and misunderstood) exclusively under the category of nature; it is all finitude, temporality, and necessity. Kierkegaard, however, attacks the Romantics for the contrasting imbalance, for conceiving the human exclusively in terms of the inner soul, as "authentically" infinite, eternal, and free. Romanticism and idealism were representative, in his view, of the completely fantastic, nonspiritual egoism implicit in the conditions of modern life. And, though establishing his own position through an impressive critique of Hegel's philosophy, he is at one with the latter's rejection of Romanticism. The "beautiful soul" is an illusory ideal which reflects the most superficial aspects of what Kierkegaard referred to as the Present Age.

The self is neither an inherent tendency to bodily integration in relation to which the soul is formed as its natural representation, nor is it a purely soulful interiority in relation to which the body functions as an expressive medium; it is, rather, an emergent reality which conditions the proper interrelation of body and soul. The synthesis of the self, to be a synthesis, requires that both body and soul play a conditioning part. The resulting unity, however, is not itself spirit, only the possibility of spirit. This synthesis is no fixed, indwelling unity but a dynamic interactive relation which itself has a history and takes shape through a variety of changing forms: "In the relation between the two, the relation is the third as a negative unity, and the two relate to the relation and in the relation to the relation; thus under the qualification of the psychical the relation between the psychical and the physical is a relation. If, however, the relation relates itself to itself, this relation is the positive third, and this is the self" (Kierkegaard 1980, 13–14).

For Kierkegaard, Modernity was characterized by a fatal division between body and soul; so much had been clear since Descartes's writings. Indeed the spiritless disintegration of modern life meant that neither sensuous pleasure (the highest conception of life within the body perspective) nor inner freedom and unity (the epitome of the soul) could be fully realized. Life was composed, in fact, of superficial and stereotypical responses to undemanding and routinized situations. Any conception of selfhood was dissipated in continuous adjustments to public opinion; selfhood was nothing more substantial than the fashion of the day. As a result, both body and soul, irrevocably divided from each other, themselves dissolved in fragmentary experiences from which neither physical nor soulful coherence could be recovered.

Spirit should not be reduced to body or soul; neither should it be reduced to the simple unity or interaction of soul and body. Spirit is not soul or body, nor is it both soul and body. It is sui generis and thus requires an appropriate language of terms adequate to its description. For the most part, this language was provided for Kierkegaard by Hegel, whose *Phenomenology of Spirit* was (and indeed remains) the most significant attempt to make spirit central to the conceptualization of Modernity (Habermas 1987). Indeed, Hegel defines Modernity in terms of spirit; in a well-known passage he sums up the restlessness of the age as follows: "Spirit has broken with the world it has hitherto inhabited and imagined, and it is of a mind to submerge it in the past, and in the labor of its own transformation. . . . The frivolity and boredom which unsettle the established order, the vague foreboding of something unknown, these are the heralds of approaching change" (Hegel 1977, 6–7).

Yet, Kierkegaard argues, Hegel, having grasped the essentially historical nature of spirit, goes on to assimilate spirit to soul and describes the self-unfolding of spirit as a process akin to intellectual growth and self-development. Self-consciousness and absolute knowledge of itself become the telos of spirit. In fact this criticism of Kierkegaard's was hardly fair. Hegel was far from being a Romantic rationalist; and in the Preface to the *Phenomenology*, he expresses a view of spirit, the spiritlessness of the present, and of philosophy's task in relation to both with which Kierkegaard could have concurred: "Spirit has not only lost its essential life; it is also conscious of this loss, and the finitude that is its own content. Turning away from its empty husks, and confessing that it lies in wickedness, it reviles itself for doing so, and now demands from philosophy, not so much *knowledge* of what it *is*, as the recovery through its agency of that lost sense of solid and substantial being. Philosophy is to meet this need . . . by running together what thought has put asunder, by suppressing the differentiations of the Notion and restoring the *feeling* of essential being: in short, by providing edification rather than insight" (Hegel 1977, 4–5).

But the wholly abstract version of Hegel's philosophy with which Kierkegaard became familiar in Denmark justifiably attracted condemnation as arid, formal, and conservative.

In opposition to both (the later) Hegel and the Romantics, Kierkegaard offered a comprehensive, critical description of the life possibilities of Modernity, demonstrating in each case the inherent tendency of the "modern spirit" to fragment and "misrelate" the elements of selfhood, body and soul. In a paradoxical manner modern spirit seemed to undo itself and literally fall apart into its elementary, nonspiritual elements. Modernity, in this view, was not merely an infatuation with science as an intellectual system for analyzing nature, it was a social mechanism for the practical analysis (destruction) of humanity.

Despair of the Present Age

During the 1840s Søren Kierkegaard, writing under a series of fanciful pseudonyms, not only anticipated all the central elements of the contemporary postmodernity thesis, he found compelling grounds for its rejection. What is particularly striking about these writings, quite apart, that is, from their literary brilliance, is that by that time neither the description of contemporary life nor its rejection formed part of well-established canons of modern philosophical argument or social, political, and psychological analysis. Yet Kierkegaard's writings are integral to the discourse of Modernity conceived in the broadest possible fashion. His marginal position in Danish academic life and that of Denmark in the emergence and growth of modern European societies allowed him to adopt a perspective outside both the mainstream of modern development toward scientific rationalism, positivism, and utilitarianism (Body) and its main rivals, Romanticism and idealist philosophy (Soul). It is only quite recently, when both of these tendencies can be viewed as different aspects of the development of Modernity as a whole, rather than as competing and mutually exclusive worldviews, that Kierkegaard's works have become significant as a major anticipation of contemporary intellectual and cultural themes and as a source of new forms of self-understanding in contemporary society (Matuštík and Westphal 1995).

In two works in particular, the *Either* of *Either/Or* and the literary review *Two Ages*, Kierkegaard provides a description of the leading characteristics of contemporary experience, the experience of Modernity as spirit.

In 1846, having completed a major work whose title, *Concluding Unscientific Postscript*, hinted that it was to be his last, Kierkegaard wrote a long review of a novel, *Two Ages*, that he wrongly believed to have been written by J. L. Heiberg, Denmark's leading literary critic and aesthetician. In this review Kierkegaard claims the Present Age to be spiritless not just in the sense that it is bereft of all religious sentiment (which in itself would be no bad thing), but in that it lacks passion in comparison with the secular Age of Revolution that preceded it. He characterizes the Present Age in terms of the dominance of bourgeois values and the bourgeois style of life. It is governed by the demands for respectability and the appearance of busyness. It is a society in which public opinion is everything.

His review turned into a general comparison between the contrasting cultures of an Age of Revolution, which "is essentially passionate, and therefore it essentially has *form*" (Kierkegaard 1978, 61), and of the Present Age, which "is essentially a *sensible, reflecting age*" (Kierkegaard 1978, 68). There is, in fact, nothing particularly historical in this contrast. He does not refer to any particular period as an Age of Revolution; and when, two years later, Denmark's belated bourgeois revolution did take place, he did not feel compelled to alter his judgment of the conservative tendencies of the present. The European-wide social upheavals of 1848, indeed, were typical of the age—which contained, rather than being transformed by, them—"flaring up in superficial short-lived enthusiasms and prudentially relaxing in indolence" (Kierkegaard 1978, 68).

The Present Age has become an age of publicity, in which nothing real happens, an age of ceaseless chatter and exhibitionism in which members of the public are caught up in perpetually renewed and quite meaningless anticipation of events that never actually occur. In terms reminiscent of his celebrated contemporary Alexis de Tocqueville, he draws attention to the leveling tendencies of the Present Age, which result in a general social and cultural indifference and lack of distinction (Tocqueville 1968, vol. 2). It is, above all, an age of abstraction, in which medium the "single individual" cannot live; he "has not fomented enough passion in himself to tear himself out of the web of reflection and the seductive ambiguity of reflection" (Kierkegaard 1978, 69). It is clear from Kierkegaard's admittedly rather general discussion that he conceives his ideal "single individual" as in some way "defined" through passion: "So also in the world of individuals. If the essential passion is taken away, the one motivation, and everything becomes meaningless externality, devoid of character, then the spring of ideality stops flowing and life together becomes stagnant water—this is crudeness" (Kierkegaard 1978, 62).

It is equally clear that his notion of passion is quite distinct from either the English empiricist or the Continental metaphysical traditions in modern psychology. Whereas, for the former, passion was viewed almost exclusively as a disturbing element within a rationally conceived and intentional ego, and for the latter passion was conceived in terms of an absence within the ego—and thus as a stimulating desire to possess something that would complete and express the self—Kierkegaard regards passion as the multiplicity of differences that give structure and form to human experience. But in the Present Age, we might say, no distinctions can withstand the dissolving tendencies of abstraction. The inner tension and color are drained from individual experience and, therefore, from social relations: "The coiled springs of life-relationships, which are what they are only because of qualitatively distinguishing passion, lose their resilience; the qualitative expression of difference between opposites is no longer the law for the relation of inwardness to each other in the relation. Inwardness is lacking, and to that extent the relation does not exist or the relation is an inert cohesion" (Kierkegaard 1978, 78).

The citizen of the Present Age "does not relate himself in the relation but is a spectator." Everything in consequence is trivialized: "Not even a suicide these days does away with himself in desperation but deliberates on this step so long and so sensibly that he is strangled by calculation" (Kierkegaard 1978, 69). Whereas a passionate age is united through "enthusiasm," "*envy* becomes the *negatively unifying principle* in a passionless and very reflective age" (Kierkegaard 1978, 81). Envy, indeed, is a novel and ingenious means of preserving order: "Reflection's envy holds the will and energy in a kind of captivity." But in "holding the individual and the age in a prison," reflective envy is a self-suppression which has no need of "tyrants and secret police, nor the clergy and aristocracy" (Kierkegaard 1978, 81–82).

The Present Age annuls passion and the contradictions essential to passion. It is preoccupied with "chatter," which is the annulled passionate distinction between being silent and speaking (Fenves 1993). Where silence and speaking are linked in their essential relation to the person, "chatter-ing gets ahead of essential speaking" and merely "reflects" inconsequential events; it is nothing but "the caricaturing externalization of inwardness" (Kierkegaard 1978, 98–99). And, typically, the modern thinker, in hastily announcing a new philosophy, too easily elides the distinction between subjectivity and objectivity and is productive of nothing but empty "lo-quacity." By the same token it is an age of "principle," annulling the dis-tinction between form and content in a high-minded insistence on acting ethically. But "one can do anything and everything on principle," because the principle lies outside the person, who may "personally be a non-hu-man nonentity" (Kierkegaard 1978, 101–2). It is specifically an age of "su-perficiality," which, as the annulled passionate distinction between hid-denness and revelation, is "a revelation of emptiness." This superficiality manifests itself most clearly in an "exhibitionist tendency" which is caught up in "the self-infatuation of the conceit of reflection" (Kierkegaard 1978, 102). The extensive and ever-changing surface of modern life is nothing but a kaleidoscope of reflections, "and eventually human speech will be-come just like the public: pure abstraction—there will no longer be anyone who speaks, but objective reflection will gradually deposit a kind of atmos-phere, an abstract noise that will render human speech superfluous, just as machines make workers superfluous" (Kierkegaard 1978, 104).

The Present Age has no "depth." From *Two Ages* to *The Book on Adler*, Kierkegaard traces a series of connections linking together apparently iso-lated aspects of modern culture as equivalent reflections on the surface of life. And through the medium of reflection, the most disparate of human contents, from the conventions of everyday behavior to the latest philo-sophical craze, are reduced to a characterless flux of essentially identical elements.

Many of these remarks now seem astonishingly prescient and make yet more remarkable the enigma of Kierkegaard's authorship, one of the least likely writers, perhaps, in whose works to have discovered a premature "critique of postmodernism." In order to understand more clearly the sig-nificance of this critique, it should be placed in the context of the pre-viously composed pseudonymous works devoted to an exploration of the "aesthetic sphere of existence."

The Present Age is not without cultivation. The author of *Either* (a fictionalized pseudonym) represents an advanced figure from the contemporary world, a young man, superbly educated, highly gifted, acutely sensitive, and disillusioned. It is a figure more or less recognizable in the youthful hero of Romantic literature, such as Pushkin's Onegin or Lermontov's Pechorin. Given the conditions of the Present Age, how is the young man of *Either* to live? The answer is provided in the form of lived examples rather than in terms of an analytic description made from the vantage point of some position other than that of the young man himself. This results in an extraordinary display of literary pyrotechnics, a loose collection of essays of varying length and subject matter all more or less indicative of the restless mood of contemporary existence. Given the spiritlessness of the Present Age, the young man loses himself in the continuous flux of immediacy.

He conceives his life as directed by the secular pursuit of pleasure, not indeed by unrefined or coarse forms of gratification but by the most exquisite aestheticism. The young man lives immediately; he is dominated by the urge to experience reality in terms of its sensuous, and therefore transitory, fullness. A more recent critic of Romanticism succinctly describes the point of view: "The romantic wants to do nothing except experience and paraphrase his experience in an emotionally impressive fashion" (Schmitt 1986, 100).

Inasmuch as spirit has emptied itself into the forms of immediacy (indeed these forms exist only to the extent that it has), the young man seeks above all the transfiguring experience of love. The *Either,* thus, gains a certain coherence in being so many separate approaches to the phenomenon of erotic love as the crystallization, so to speak, of spirit on the surface of modern life.

But as a wholly modern, advanced, and disillusioned individual, the young man cannot grasp spirit in love; he can find in it only the possibility of erotic and sentimental pleasure. And just because he seeks it only in terms of the pleasure it might afford (in terms, that is, of his own ego), it affords him no pleasure at all, or rather, pleasure remains part of a world which he can enter into and experience only by chance; it cannot be determined by himself or by his relation to another.

His various experiments end in disappointment; rather than being propelled from pleasure to pleasure, he is in fact sunk deeper and deeper into melancholy, in the boredom that seizes him consciously between, and unconsciously within, increasingly desperate bouts of enthusiasm. The more determined he becomes, the more savagely he hurls himself at reality, the less able is he to enter into its possibilities. Reality repels him; indeed, it disgusts him. The determination to live in immediacy results in its very opposite; an aesthetic distancing of reality for which "religious, moral, political, and scientific matters appear in fantastical draperies and in strange colors and hues" is no more than "an occasion and an opportunity for romantic productivity" (Schmitt 1986, 16, 17).

The real nature of this melancholy—a melancholy which had afflicted every young hero of the Romantic age—becomes the subject matter of *Or*, which purports to be a series of long letters in which an older friend offers the young man friendly advice.

According to Judge William (the putative author of *Or*), the young man's boredom is a direct consequence of his absorption in the moment. In living immediately he becomes identical with the chaotic flux of activity that characterizes the Present Age. The fragmentation of personal identity is not the consequence of a perverse modern spirit in the sense of an attitude of some sort; it is inherent in the conditions of contemporary life. Pleasure escapes the young man because, like Musil's man without qualities, he experiences himself in the evanescent trace of a multitude of diverse experiences: there is no "self" to enjoy the pleasure that occasionally and arbitrarily flows through him, no "self" to fashion these diverse moments into a continuous history of the soul.

Judge William presents an alternative view of life, one based on ethical decision, on the conception of action under the determinants of good and evil. The fundamental quality of such a form of life is not so much to seek the good as to continually have before oneself the duality of good and evil. The critical point for the Judge's perspective, therefore, is not the specific character of goodness but the choice of the self as a being for whom the distinction of good and evil is continuously and essentially present. It is through this choice, indeed, that the self in a more mature and stable form is born.

Now "choice" here cannot be the same as making a "decision" among alternatives. Decision is part of a rational language which only makes sense once the self has formed itself into a decision-making being. The problem, conceptually and existentially, is how such a being is formed in the first place. The Judge argues that the young man's boredom is a clue; this lack of sustained interest in anything, his lassitude and sense of worthlessness, are commonplace in modern life (as Pascal and later Hegel had already made clear) and indicate a deeper dissatisfaction, the first stirring of the self as an ethical being, a being for whom contemporary fragmentation of experience is to be rejected. He advises the young man to "choose despair"; to despair "seriously," because in that choice lies the opportunity of opening up another form of existence rich in life-giving possibilities.

As it is usually read, Kierkegaard's text, though not presented as an argument, is viewed not only as a clear statement of his own views but as a convincing refutation of what would nowadays be called a postmodern thesis. The Judge's views are presented without editorial comment after the young man's essays, as an unanswered analysis and commentary. At first sight, certainly, this commentary appears authoritative. Yet, as much as *Either*, it lacks authorial directness. Kierkegaard himself hides so completely behind his creations that *Or* as well as *Either* should be read as a novel for which the author absolves himself of any responsibility. Indeed, such are the convolutions and refinements of his forms of indirect expression that as a literary innovator Kierkegaard is in the vanguard of postmodernism. If the point of *Either/Or* is to reject postmodernism and urge its rejection on others, he has chosen a radically ironic way of expressing this.

It seems more plausible, thus, to read the work as an initial encounter which remains unresolved at the end of the book. We can imagine the young man answering back; someone so intellectually gifted is hardly likely to surrender at once to the Judge's conventional views of marriage and ethical responsibility. The young man would surely regard his older companion's psychology as naive and out of touch with the conditions of modern life.

In fact the confrontation continues in a series of pseudonymous works that quickly followed this initial encounter. The young man, variously incarnated, is not swayed by argument and is not attracted by the vision of an ethical life. Such an existence is wholly lacking in the spirit that he feels is active in the world, but that he cannot grasp. In his view it is the Judge who is living in a fantastic and unreal world, a world which made sense, if it ever did, only in the past. This mode of self-fashioning denies the very quality of existence to which, in spite of everything, the young man clings. The ethical, just because it depends on the denial of immediacy, should not be judged a "higher" stage than the aesthetic; it is, rather, an illusory realm filled with nostalgia for the premodern world and its presumed certainties. True, it has adapted to the language of Modernity; its certainties are translated into the moral language of the self, of the ego as a central perspective. But this is nothing more than a halfhearted attempt to preserve an outmoded worldview.

The young man's boredom is not cured by the presumed transformation into ethical categories; it is taken up and magnified as guilt, which is the ethical form of despair. In guilt the self-deception of the ethical becomes clear; the choice of the ethical implies the choice of the good, but evil continually flows from actions whose precise outcomes can never be known. Yet the self-determining view of the ethical requires that the self accept responsibility for all the consequences of its actions. Psychologically this cannot be accomplished; guilt is a kind of compromise between acceptance and rejection of responsibility and a method of distancing the self from reality. Melancholy, then, is another version of aestheticism that holds the world at a distance but, as this world is false and distorted, does so as a justifiable form of self-protection.

This perverse melancholy also holds the key to its own transformation. The rejection of a false reality may be the initial stage of accepting a more fundamental truth. Thus, in the theory of the stages that unfold in the pseudonymous works, it is possible to view the religious as a "higher" resolution of the despair of both the aesthetic and the ethical "spheres of life." Melancholy as "sadness without cause" develops continuously with Modernity as its counterimage and anticipation of its passing. It is at the same time the spiritless character of the Present Age and the spirit concealed in the broken heart of Modernity.

SPIRIT AS COMMODITY

Hegel's language of spirit was adopted by his foremost critics, including the young Karl Marx who, at the same time as Kierkegaard's pseudonyms, set himself the task of demystifying idealist philosophy. And, like them, he presented an alternative, critical view of spirit in Modernity, rather than a wholly spiritless view of the present.

Striking similarities between the young Marx's spiritual radicalism and Kierkegaard's contemporaneous critique of Hegel have been pointed out (Löwith 1964; Westphal 1987). Neither was content with a merely intellectual refutation of Hegel's thought, insisting, rather, on a genuine critique which exposed the real conditions of life which made that thought possible and, in a sense, valid. Hegel's philosophy is important for them both just because it so accurately captured the historical character of modern experience. Indeed, the Hegel of the *Phenomenology of Spirit* is sensitive to the claims of actuality over all abstract reasoning, and it is as much in its name, as in terms of original insights of their own, that Kierkegaard and Marx rejected the later development of his thought away from its existential origin toward the scholastic systematization of the *Logic*.

This rejection amounted, in fact, to a renunciation of the whole tendency of Modernity. Yet it is just in this tendency toward abstraction that the young Marx is at one with the pseudonyms in detecting Hegel's most compelling, if obscured, realism. They claim that the actuality of modern life is itself a distorted and illusory social form, so that the increasing detachment of Hegel's philosophy from the human content of experience is, indeed, indicative of the most pervasive and important of real social processes. It is the Present Age that is the real foundation of Hegel's philosophy, and the inhuman abstraction of that philosophy proclaims, in its very unreality, the real need to transform the conditions of the age rather than to realize its demonic vision of Reason. The demand for a new philosophy is simultaneously, therefore, a revolutionary call for a new way of life.

In this context both Marx and Kierkegaard mount powerful attacks on religion in modern society. For both men religious institutions have come to represent a spiritless and rational theology, allied to an equally spiritless morality, in defense of the empty conventionality of the Present Age. Yet religion is no crude error; it is an *"inverted consciousness of the world,"* because the Present Age and its institutions are an *"inverted world"* (Marx 1975, 244). Illusory and distorted, modern religiosity remains, nonetheless, "the heart of a heartless world."

At this point Marx parts company from his unacknowledged companions. For Marx the struggle over religion becomes "a struggle against *that world* whose spiritual *aroma* is religion" (Marx 1975, 244). The critique of the spiritless conditions of modern life is sharpened into an analysis of its specifically "objective" form, the commodity, while for Kierkegaard the "objectless" character of melancholy is pursued, so to speak, for its own sake. It is important to note, however, that Marx's analysis of the commodity as the conceptual and historical foundation of his "critique of political economy" is continuous with his earlier critique of religion. And, interestingly, he chooses to characterize the alienated and illusory character of the commodity by a term introduced by Charles de Brosses in 1760 to described the distinctive feature of what was taken to be the most primitive of religious beliefs: "fetishism."

In *Capital* Marx places his analysis of the commodity before everything else. It is the key to his understanding of Modernity as the capitalist mode of production, and it is clear from the outset that the commodity is a "spiritual" entity. It is the material form in which spirit enters the modern world. And it is no less spiritual in being thus actualized, as the fruit rather than the aroma of spirit. It is in, and through, the novel form of the commodity, in fact, that in modern society body and soul are effectively synthesized. The commodity is a special kind of thing. It is a useful thing which is not only capable of being exchanged for another useful thing; it comes into existence in order that it might be exchanged. The exchangeability of the commodity defines its value, and this value, or capacity to be exchanged, is the direct result of its being produced, of its being a product of human labor. The commodity, in other words, is a meaningful thing, a thing which is a bearer of value to the extent to which it is the externalized and crystallized form of human labor.

But this simplicity is deceptive. On closer inspection what is "at first sight an extremely obvious, trivial thing" emerges as "a very strange thing, abounding in metaphysical subtleties and theological niceties" (Marx

1976, 163). The commodity is "a thing which transcends sensuousness." The thing itself takes on the characteristics of the social relation through which it was produced. The relative values of commodities in exchange are divorced from the labor process that is the source of this value and is viewed, instead, as inherent in the thing itself. And, because of this, the relationship between the producers "takes on the form of a social relation between the products of labor" (Marx 1976, 164). That is to say, "the commodity reflects the social characteristics of men's own labor as objective characteristics of the products of labor themselves," and "it is nothing but the definite social relation between men themselves which assumes here, for them, the fantastic form of a relation between things" (Marx 1976, 165). Transformed into an oppressive and strange world of pure objectivity, commodities reflect upon their creators a melancholic self-image.

Two particularly interesting consequences flow from Marx's insight. The first is the indifference of exchange value to the specific characteristics of the commodity. Marx often refers to "the commodity" as if it were a generalized product, a universal object, the sole thing of modern society. Commodities are produced by labor power itself entering into the general process of exchange; and this is possible only because human labor, however differentiated and specialized, can, in the conditions of modern machine production at least, be regarded as a universal and undifferentiated capacity or power. What this power produces, similarly, is "all of a piece" with its human creator, and however differentiated and split up its products become, they remain interchangeable because they are all viewed as the products of this power. This view of labor power is, however, a consequence of a generalized process of exchange, rather than the generalization of exchange being predicated upon the assumption of the universality of labor: "Men do not therefore bring the products of their labor into relation with each other as values because they see these objects merely as the material integuments of homogeneous human labor. The reverse is true: by equating their different products to each other in exchange as values, they equate their different kinds of labor as human labor. They do this without being aware of it. Value, therefore, does not have its description branded on its forehead; it rather transforms every product of labor into a social hieroglyphic" (Marx 1976, 175–76).

The "mystical character of the commodity" is simply the result of the fact that "the commodity form reflects the social characteristics of men's own labor as objective characteristics of the products of labor themselves, as the socio-natural properties of these things" (Marx 1976, 164–65).

Second, Marx argues that in entering into the process of exchange, labor power is alienated from its personal possessor. In becoming the property of another, and used according to another's needs and wishes, the entire labor process ends in creating a world of things which stands over against its creators as an estranged and oppressive objectivity; "the object that labor produces, its product, stands opposed to it as *something alien*, as a *power independent* of the producer" (Marx 1975, 324). Hence, "the worker is related to the *product of his labor* as to an *alien* object." The worker, thus, "becomes a slave of his object," and "the more the worker exerts himself in his work the more powerful the alien, objective world becomes which he brings into being over against himself, the poorer he and his inner world become, and the less they belong to him" (Marx 1975, 325). Human labor power, in itself becoming a commodity, forces people into the midst of this alien world, and inversely, its oppressive otherness penetrates their very being. The modern world is estranged but irresistible; it is fascinating.

The commodity form, not religious ideology, becomes a "veil of illusion" placed between the human subject and its authentic world. And just as the personal experience of melancholy may transform itself inwardly into a revolutionary and free spirituality, so for Marx the most materialistic and inhuman aspect of modern capitalism is also its distinctive and potent form of spirit, the locus of both its oppressive power and its eventual transformation. Alienated labor is modern spirit, the negation in which is preserved the possibility of a new human reality.

SPIRIT AS VALUE

Max Weber, among the founders of sociology, provides the most comprehensive and compelling account of the paradoxical character of modern spiritlessness; and like Kierkegaard and Marx, he discovers the real spiritual essence of this spiritlessness.

The foundation of Weber's view of Modernity is to be found in his conception of spirit as value, and value as the source of meaning in the context of social action. Weber's well-known methodological principle defines social action as behavior that is "subjectively meaningful"; and in a variety of historical and comparative works, he schematizes the most pervasive and significant forms of subjective meaning in terms of the "values" that they presuppose.

"Meaning" should not here be confused with intellectual understanding, nor should "value" be confused with a specific content of the soul. While Weber discusses—and frequently intuits in a brilliant fashion—the meaning of social action in terms of the beliefs and worldviews of those involved, he makes it plain that this is by no means an essential relation. "Meaning" often refers to vague motives, intentions, and feelings and to the actualization of specific states of being such as pleasure or salvation that rarely correspond to any clear idea or system of beliefs. More importantly, meaning is not construed, in the Romantic fashion, as the realization of an individuated interior longing or desire. Meaning, however subjective it appears in content, is something essentially external to the individual. Furthermore, the link between meaning and value, as the higher-level organizing principle and source of significance for everyday actions, is something strictly extraterritorial in the sense that it has no necessary connection to the flow of events itself: "The *meaning* we ascribe to a phenomenon—that is, the relations which we establish between these phenomena and 'values'—is a logically incongruous and heterogeneous factor which cannot be 'deduced' from the 'constitutive elements' of the events in question" (Weber 1975, 108).

It is not just in our capacity as sociologists or historians that we make these deductions. We cannot avoid interpreting many human events (including actions of our own) as "actions" in the strong sense of bodying forth meanings that stand in some definite relation to a relatively small number of possible ultimate values as their source and telos. Weber would have agreed with Nietzsche when, through Zarathustra, he declares that "Man first implanted value into things to maintain himself—he created the meaning of things, a human meaning! Therefore he calls himself: 'Man', that is; the evaluator. . . . Evaluation is creation" (Nietzsche 1961, 85).

Not all actions are to be regarded as meaningful in this sense; actions may be interpreted as springing automatically from particular states of emotion, such as anger or fear, or may be viewed in terms of the continuous reenactment of an immemorial tradition. Modernity, in this perspective, can be seen in its most general sense as bringing almost the entire realm of human action under the sway of values. In the context of the present discussion, that is to say, the human world must be regarded as spirit. Values are spirit in just the sense described by Kierkegaard; they provide the synthesis that not only relates body and soul but "relates itself to itself." Values are wholly human and, therefore, the product of human activity; but they are values only to the extent that they are experienced as "given" and exterior to the immediate body-soul unity of the individual. Societies, epochs, and different social groups can thus be understood from the perspective of the value or spirit that confers meaning upon their characteristic forms of activity.

This starting point makes Weber's understanding of the peculiar character of Modernity all the more challenging. On the one hand, he argues that Modernity can be understood in terms of a specific value or set of values which he typifies as the "spirit of capitalism"; while, on the other hand, he argues that Modernity is characterized above all by the "disenchantment of the world," the annihilation of value as such. Not only are these two very different conceptions, but the notion of disenchantment seems to contradict his philosophical-methodological premise that all human activity is inherently spiritual. A brief consideration of these apparent inconsistencies, however, rather than expose analytical shortcomings in Weber's work, will illustrate the irreducible duality and strangeness of spirit in Modernity.

Asceticism as the Spirit
of Modernity

What Weber calls the spirit of capitalism is both a general set of values associated with the development of modern society and, significantly, the transformation of a historic form of religious spirituality. Thus, just as for Hegel, Modernity "is only the manifestation of religion as human reason, the production of the religious principle under the form of secular freedom" (Löwith 1949, 45). In discovering the religious roots of modern secularism, Weber is pointing to the continuity of spirit-as-spirit through this transformation.

The significance of Weber's thesis has already been noted in the context of the development of a particular, individuated, and interiorized conception of the soul; but it is also significant as a description of spirit. Here the continuity with premodern religiosity seems evident. In the West asceticism has been a more or less continuous feature of religious values, though, it should be added, in extreme and individualistic forms it has also been the most persistent and dangerous form of heresy. For Christianity the world is God's creation and, though spoiled by human disobedience, is not in itself evil; the enjoyment of nature and the satisfaction of natural needs, therefore, does not necessarily lead us away from God.

According to Weber, however, asceticism in its modern form has a specifically novel meaning as a technique for the building and maintaining of the inner certainty of faith. It is as a means of coping with the "unprecedented inner loneliness" inherent in the Reformation, and particularly in Calvin's conception of the absolute transcendence of God and humanity's complete dependence upon his freely given gift of grace for salvation, that modern asceticism has developed. An ascetic way of life—a rigorous and systematic form of self-restraint, formed into a secular vocation—was recommended as an antidote to religious doubt and anxiety. In terms of religious value there was no inherent connection between asceticism and salvation; ultimately, because God is wholly transcendent there could not be any meaningful connection between human activity and the divine will and, therefore, no means of influencing his decision or discovering its implication for an individual. However, Weber argues, the "extreme inhumanity of this doctrine" encouraged the assumption that the inner sense of faith was, in fact, a gift of grace and a certain sign of election. Furthermore, as worldly activity, in the specific historical conditions in which Puritanism arose in Western Europe, resulted in the accumulation of wealth and increasing social differences, those consequences themselves became suffused with religious meaning.

Weber, of course, does not imagine that the specifically religious form in which the spirit of capitalism first triumphantly made its entry in the modern world remains necessary to the successful development of capitalism itself, or even that in a more diffuse sense it persists as its "aroma." Modern capitalism is a self-sustaining and wholly secular business: "The Puritan wanted to work in a calling; we are forced to do so. For when asceticism was carried out of monastic cells into everyday life, and began to dominate worldly morality, it did its part in building the tremendous cosmos of the modern economic order. This order is now bound to the technical and economic conditions of machine production which to-day determine the lives of all the individuals who are born into this mechanism, not only those directly concerned with economic acquisition, with irresistible force" (Weber 1976, 181).

Modern rational capitalism is sustained less by passionate commitment, whether in the form of "secular passions" or the "sport of money making," than by the sheer inertia of its mechanism: by a kind of spiritual atrophy.

But in an interesting way Weber hints at a new form in which spirit, which first took possession of modern society as dynamic capitalism, remained an active and essential part of everyday life. At the close of his famous essay, he remarks: "Since asceticism undertook to remodel the world and to work out its ideals in the world, material goods have gained an increasing and finally an inexorable power over the lives of men as at no previous period in history. To-day the spirit of religious asceticism—whether finally, who knows?—has escaped from the cage. But victorious capitalism, since it rests on mechanical foundations, needs its support no longer . . . the idea of duty in one's calling prowls about in our lives like the ghost of dead religious beliefs" (Weber 1976, 181–82).

And though he had arrived at this conclusion by a very different path than that followed by Marx, it nonetheless echoes, in its conceptualization of material goods as spiritual powers, the opening sections of *Capital*. Indeed, the impression of agreement here is enhanced by Weber's insistence that whatever the origin of this peculiarity, the dominance of things was now "inexorable."

There is a sense in which Weber's statements express a truism. Whether as "material goods" or as "commodities," modern life is lived in the continuous presence of things, and the inner life of the human individual is largely conceived, we might almost say only becomes possible, in relation to these things. There seems nothing more evident than this. We cannot readily imagine living in a world bereft of things or even, perhaps, a world in which, for all practical purposes of an individual viewpoint, there is not a boundless extension and an infinite variety of things. The entire character of modern life, it seems, is colored by both the strangeness of things and by our dependence upon, and intimacy with, things. There is at once something absolutely alien, and something uncannily familiar, with this world. That is to say, things do not simply exist; in their teeming variety they seem to form relations with each other, as well as, or in preference to, us; to constitute, in other words, an entire and self-sufficient world, a world into which we are occasionally invited as spectators.

The entire process of investing value in things engenders a series of disturbing paradoxes for the classical modern, as well as premodern, conceptualizations of spirit. The curious inversion that Marx pointed to—the illusory character of the commodity—is here understood as a "materialization" rather than as a secularization of religious values. An obligatory character marks the material thing as a value: its exteriority, its being a source of life and goodness, its magnetic effect on the individual's orientation to the world. The human being naturally turns toward values and seeks them, and in modern society values are consecrated as things. Understandable, too, becomes the process by which spirit, appearing initially as the value of asceticism, at first tentatively but then with increasing determination divested itself of its specific obligations of constraint and self-control. Inasmuch as value was transferred to things themselves, the acquisition and consumption of these things, rather than being a dangerous pleasure, became a duty. Hence the increasing ritualization of social action, the compulsive renewal of wants, the continuing and restless quest carried over from every partial and unsuccessful act of consumption to the next; nothing less, we might suppose from the context of Weber's brief hint, is involved in this, the most characteristic and banal feature of contemporary social life, than a renewed and reinvigorated quest for salvation.

Disenchantment

But if, in the particulars of his historical argument, Weber ends on this ambiguous note, in more general discussions of contemporary society he seems decisive and single-minded. The long-term implication of Modernity is the "disenchantment of the world." This is viewed as the outcome of the process of rationalization that is both a central feature of the development of Western society and a key characteristic of Modernity.

Weber defines rationalization in terms of two inseparably linked processes: first, "an increasing theoretical mastery of reality by means of increasingly precise and abstract concepts" and, second, "methodical attainment of a definitely given and practical end by means of an increasingly precise calculation of adequate means" (Weber 1948, 293). In this process the magical unity of the primitive world is sundered into two radically distinct realms: "into rational cognition and mastery of nature, on the one hand, and into 'mystic' experience, on the other" (Weber 1948, 282). And its most general result is that religion, which is the active source of the demand that the world should be meaningful in its totality as a cosmos, is "shifted into the realm of the irrational."

The dominance of science in the modern world rests on its technical superiority in the calculation of human means, but this superiority does not imply a greater practical grasp of the conditions of life for the average member of society. Rather, the acceptance in general that such conditions have been explained, or are explicable, by someone is sufficient to sustain the conviction that all such conditions can be rationally understood: "The savage knows what he does in order to get his daily food and which institutions serve him in this pursuit. The increasing intellectualization and rationalization do *not*, therefore, indicate an increased and general knowledge of the conditions under which we live. It means something else, namely, the knowledge or belief that if one wished one *could* learn it at any time. Hence, it means that principally there are no mysterious incalculable forces that come into play, but rather that one can, in principle, master all things by calculation" (Weber 1948, 139).

For the modern world knowledge has become "detached" from all other values and is validated in terms of procedures immanent to the sphere of knowledge itself; it does not require any external authority. As practical life has increasingly come under the sway of scientifically validated means, this has the result of ridding mundane activities of the taint of any magical or religious residue. But it does not mean that modern individuals are unconcerned about the "meaning" of nature or of their own existence. Far from it; it implies only that they cannot appeal to accepted standards of natural knowledge to sustain any specific meaning discovered within their experience. Indeed, "we live as did the ancients when their world was not yet disenchanted of its gods and demons, only we live in a different sense. As Hellenic man at times sacrificed to Aphrodite and at other time to Apollo, and, above all, as everybody sacrificed to the gods of his city, so do we still nowadays, only the bearing of man has been disenchanted and denuded of its mystical but inwardly genuine plasticity" (Weber 1948, 148).

Modernity can be viewed as a gradual process of extending the sphere of rationalization in the specific sense of subsuming ever more extensive areas of human action under the means-end schema. All judgments of action become judgments of the appropriateness of means to specific ends and are subject to continuous revision in the light of developing knowledge and technique. The ends of action—values—are in principle excluded from this process as they bear no systematic relation to the methodical improvement of purely technical means of world mastery.

The long-term process of secularization in the West involved a radical rationalization (in Weber's first sense) of the religious sphere itself. The specific character of religious value was clarified in a systematic way in relation to primitive assumptions about the nature of God and his relation to the human world and through the eradication of all magical means of salvation. More significantly, however, the completion of this process in Calvin's Reformation gave rise to particular psychological forms of adjustment (Puritanism) that in turn resulted in the establishment of an ethical system (the Protestant ethic) in which salvation became subject to the calculus of means-ends relations. Asceticism and worldly success became a new means for obtaining the ultimate satisfaction of faith (a rationalization of religion in Weber's second sense). The attempted incorporation of religious value within the sphere of rational calculation indicates the most radical and distinctively modern form of secularization.

The peculiar character of Modernity lies not simply in the rationalization of all means but in the radical relativization of the specific meaning of any action in terms of the values that might be imputed to it. The extralogical relation of value to the world of action becomes transparent, rendering all meaning the result of a fundamentally arbitrary act of will. Weber expresses this insight directly in terms of the "infinitude" of any empirical reality: "Now, as soon as we attempt to reflect about the way in which life confronts us in immediate concrete situations, it presents an infinite multiplicity of successively and coexistently emerging and disappearing events, both 'within' and 'outside' ourselves. The absolute infinitude of this multiplicity is seen to remain undiminished even when our attention is focused on a single 'object'" (Weber 1949, 72).

Given the recognition of the impossibility, in principle, of applying scientific means to issues of meaning, together with the historic example, in practice, of the Protestant ethic as a means of both salvation and secular advancement, Modernity has irresistibly developed toward the assimilation of all ends (so far as they are foci of collective action) to the single demand for continuously improving means. Ends, and the values that define them, are now considered exclusively as empirical states of affairs toward which all action is directed as a given aspect of reality. The resulting "iron cage" of Modernity implies the exclusion of all irrational values from the public discussion of the appropriateness or otherwise of any existing or proposed sequence of action.

But in spite of the general disenchantment of the world, we cannot help but attribute meaning to human action; and inasmuch as human action is bound up with the world of things, we also impute a meaning to these things. We do so primarily, however, as private individuals who, withdrawing from the rationalized public space of the market, office, and factory, indulge in what are essentially premodern modes of apprehension. It is also worth noting that in Weber's view the stability of modern rational capitalism is a consequence of this duality, a hidden complicity between, on the one hand, a wholly rationalized and meaningless system of production and public life and, on the other, a retreat into private, nonrational modes of valuation. For modern society, "many old gods ascend from their graves; they are disenchanted and hence take the form of impersonal forces. They strive to gain power over our lives and again they resume their eternal struggle with one another" (Weber 1948, 149). It remains the case that "so long as life remains immanent and is interpreted in its own terms, it knows only of an unceasing struggle of these gods with one another. Or, speaking directly, the ultimately possible attitude towards life are irreconcilable, and hence their struggle can never be brought to a final conclusion" (Weber 1948, 152). And this, for Weber, is an intolerable situation. He is driven to the uncompromising conclusion that "it is necessary to make a decisive choice."

The modern world becomes wholly disenchanted; nothing lies beyond the immediate actuality of the things and events that ceaselessly propel it into the future. There is no longer any mystery in being. At the same time, just because every thing is a transient means to another still indefinite and incomplete action, nothing can lay claim to the privilege of an incontestable reality. Not only do things appear and disappear, emerging and returning to the "flux" of nothingness, each thing while it enjoys its moment of actualization does so within a realm which has in some sense been devalued. The impermanence of things becomes a token of the fragility and fragmentation of being itself, rather as, for an earlier age, their apparent stability and permanence had symbolized its unity and coherence. As a result we become spectators within the world of objects and events, as if watching a monumental and baffling theatrical production whose plot, which was originally expressive of our own will and purpose, has become incomprehensible: "The fate of our times is characterized by rationalization and intellectualization and, above all, by the 'disenchantment of the world.' Precisely the ultimate and most sublime values have retreated from public life either into the transcendental realm of mystic life or into the brotherliness of direct and personal human relations" (Weber 1948, 155).

The Reenchantment of the World

There is a series of evident contradictions between the process of rationalization and the disenchantment of the world. First, the total rationalization of the world is inherently irrational. Second, the "meaning" of action in this process is not eradicated but individuated and interiorized. Third, and

most importantly, the given of economic value is also irrational and therefore meaningful; the reduction of economic action to technical efficiency
in a strict sense, therefore, is not possible because its meaning as "economic" remains firmly in the realm of irrational value. It is a "symptom"
(both result and sign) of these contradictions that material forces have
come to dominate contemporary social life and have taken on a specific
character as spirit.

For Modernity all social action becomes subject to rational calculation
in terms of the relations of means to ends. But ends are systematically removed from the sphere of rational reflection, so all calculation becomes
the mediation of means to means. The entire process ends in a supremely
irrational and ultimately meaningless condition, and one which, it might
be added, corresponds to the breakdown of mechanical causality in the scientific view of nature. However, quite apart from the polemical interest
that might account for an element of exaggeration in Weber's formulation
of these issues (Hennis 1988; Schluchter 1996), he is far from concluding
that, for Modernity, human action in general has become meaningless.
One commentator rightly points out that "the disenchantment of the
world, too, poses a problem of meaning" (Roth and Schluchter 1979, 71), a
problem which, in a host of practical ways, we cannot help but try to solve.

In this context Weber briefly describes, as a counterpoint to the process
of rationalization and disenchantment, the corresponding differentiation
and articulation of specific "value spheres" that continue to confer meaning on human action and, indeed, in modern society frequently become of
far greater significance than hitherto. Without justifying his classification
he takes as given a modern separation not only of the economic but the political, aesthetic, erotic, and intellectual modes of valuation from the religious and from each other. The long-term rationalization of Western culture can be understood, in this perspective, as a tendency toward the
differentiation of value spheres rather than, more simply, as the gradual
emergence and ultimate dominance of an intellectual conception of rational action.

The character of spirit—as value—is revealed primarily in its enigmatic
givenness; it exists as something outside of the voluntaristic sphere of action of individuals and groups. It imposes itself as a given reality, indeed,

as a defining quality of reality as real. In contemporary society this characteristic of spirit has been ceded to the commodity and has, consequently, become thinglike. The power of things over us, the "material" character of contemporary culture, exists precisely in this absorption of spirit. Spirit, thus, exists as something absolutely concrete. This is one significant meaning of "disenchantment," in fact an ironic statement of the real "enchantment" of the present and a definition of its distinctive aura. The power of things over us does not lie in their pure facticity or objectivity—in themselves they remain nothing—but rests on their qualities as bearers of value, of spirit.

At the same time the characteristic "thingness" of objects, including commodities, changes during the development of Modernity. Classical bourgeois Modernity, which so preoccupied Weber, emerges as the "closed body." Objects appear as independent, bounded, and unresponsive objects. A personal relation to objects is primarily one of ownership; objects are reduced to being property. This is a limitation against which the Romantics rebelled and which, in contemporary society, has been fundamentally altered by a new "open" body-soul relation. Corresponding to the "open body," objects lose their exclusivity and passivity. Commodities in general (and not just works of art) dissolve into fluid images, extend an "aura," and make an impression which cannot be characterized in terms of legal rights of ownership. Objects are penetrated by spirit, establishing the possibility of a variety of new and distinctive relations between persons and things (Benjamin 1973). Increasingly, therefore, sociologists are turning to aesthetics to gain insights appropriate to the understanding of contemporary "material" life (Bourdieu 1986).

This is in sharp contrast to the conventional understanding of Modernity for which quality is replaced by quantity, and objects become indistinguishably identical as quantities of matter. The differentiation of things, in that view, is wholly arbitrary. The modern economy becomes increasingly impersonal and universal and operates according to the interplay of interests on a market. But the drive toward moneymaking and the enjoyment of commodities in consumption are not natural phenomena but, rather, meaningful action in terms of the ultimate value of economic goods as the embodiment of spirit.

What is peculiar about the value of Modernity is not that individuals feel it as a compulsive and urgent demand in some way imposed upon them from the outside (this is true of all values), but that this compulsion persists irrespective of the "beliefs" of the individual. Whereas in premodern societies the surrender to an ultimate value was tied to an entire subjective cosmos for which such a value made sense and appeared to be its founding assumption, Modernity has broken free of any dependence upon beliefs as such; its ultimate value is realized as compulsive action that gives rise to things—to commodities that satisfy appetites and needs that have sources other than this value itself—and it thereby gains a life of its own independent of the human life contents that are alone meaningful.

This is the source of the "magical" character of modern life, the mysterious power that things exercise over us. The givenness of value in modern society, thus, is of a double sort. It is given as a value, and this value is realized as a thing, rather than as a subjective disposition. The entire structure of rational action is predicated on this "magical" relation. And our surrender to things, it should be noted, succeeds in stabilizing modern capitalism far more effectively than any ideological gloss upon the process of production.

SPIRIT AS THE SACRED

In a general and often casual and unsystematic fashion, both the domain and source of human value are acknowledged in the terminology of the "sacred," which is treated as an unproblematic intellectual category through which spirit may be thought. But immediately two ways of thinking and two distinctive sets of oppositions are disclosed; the sacred may be defined in relation either to the "secular" or to the "profane." Whereas Weber's monumental comparative historical sociology of Western society is concerned in one of its central dimensions with the contrast between the sacred and the secular and with an exploration of the ambiguities and paradoxes of the process of secularization, Emile Durkheim sought to clarify the character of Modernity in terms of the distinction of the sacred from the profane.

The Sacred and the Profane

To understand the importance of the distinction between the sacred and the profane for Durkheim, it is necessary briefly to recapitulate the context of his general sociological account of the nature of modern society. It is essential, in fact, to recall that he began with an analysis of modern society, and that his understanding of primitive society, and of the religious character of primitive society, is deduced from his existing theory of modern society. Though he would like to give the impression of moving from the simple, primitive, and archaic toward the complex, civilized, and modern, in fact, as was commonly the case throughout the latter part of the nineteenth and early part of the twentieth century, he proceeds the other way about.

For Durkheim modern society is characterized primarily by complexity. It is the sheer interrelated dynamism of modern society that is its fundamental and most significant feature. Modern society is highly differentiated, and like an organism its unity is an emergent property of the interrelated differences among its parts. It is not difficult to understand, on this basis, the powerful forces that tend toward continuity, stability, and even inertia in modern social life. Individuals, groups, and institutions are confronted by a vast array of interrelated parts to which they must adjust not only as a given reality but as one which exerts a powerful coercive and self-renewing force. It is the specifically moral character of the compulsion generated by the organic interdependence of modern society that, in fact, guarantees its stability. At once a critic of utilitarianism and its psychological heirs in France and Britain and of Romanticism in both its idealist philosophical and popular mystical varieties, Durkheim championed the cause of what he took to be a properly sociological understanding of modern society in terms of mutual interdependence, which implied neither harmony nor conflict but a frank realization of the existing states of things as if they were the result of autonomous and impersonal forces.

The real intellectual puzzle for Durkheim lay in the difficulty of grasping the nature of simple societies. Imagine an undifferentiated society, a society without a high level of dynamic density, mutual interdependence, and differentiation. How could such a "social protoplasm" constitute a society; how could it persist as a complex of relations which might be said to exist as something over and beyond the merely day-to-day activities of its individual members? Indeed, in what sense could such an undifferentiated state be conceived as the context of individual existence at all?

Of course Durkheim can only imagine such a condition and cannot directly observe, or rely on the direct observation of others, for an account of such a simple social body. But he feels justified in extending backwards, toward an ever more remote and archaic past, the process of deindividuation and dedifferentiation through which (by deduction from his understanding of complex societies) he arrives at descriptions of extant primitive societies.

He calls the cohesive force of simple society "mechanical solidarity," unlike the "organic solidarity" that is generated from the complex network of interaction in modern society, this is created and sustained only by recourse to an essentially artificial device. The mechanism for generating solidarity is indeed the same in both cases; it depends on nothing else but the repetition of social relations; once entered into, every relation has a tendency toward repetition which is recognized as a certain obligation, a moral compulsion to maintain and repeat. The difficulty is that in simple societies, in which small groups are more or less completely self-sufficient, there is no necessity for such interaction. The occasion for social interaction has to be created, as ritual. In the case of elementary, simple societies, however, this is very difficult to understand because social interaction seems to presuppose itself. Ritual is regarded as both the consequence and cause of social cohesion and solidarity. It seems that society must precede itself, that its foundation depends upon its having already come into existence. Indeed, it is this essential contradiction which Durkheim tries to resolve in *The Elementary Forms of Religious Life*.

For Durkheim the foundation of society is discovered in religion. But how is this to be understood? On the one hand, he seems to claim that religion provides the only means of generating the cohesion of primitive societies; that without it there would be no occasion for social interaction and thus no society. On the other hand, he seems to say that religion is preeminently a social phenomenon, comprehensible only as an aspect of social life. Quite typically with Durkheim, and he has often been reproached for this, his argument appears to be hopelessly circular; he seems to assume what he set out to demonstrate, and the reader is frustrated by the whole attempt.

Efforts to recover from what appears to be the logical wreckage of Durkheim's sociology insights that are nonetheless vital to the entire sociological enterprise have tended in two quite different directions. First, the functionalist tradition, which is primarily British and American, has taken Durkheim's fundamental point to be found in his view of the consequences of religious practices for the maintenance of social life. Here religion can be viewed as foundational in the sense that it creates the conditions under which the moral force of society is generated as if it were an autonomous force. Here the religious is sacred because society is greater than any of its members, or even of the sum of its parts. Second, the structuralist tradition, which has been more influential among French writers, conceives Durkheim's fundamental argument to be that religion is what might be termed the "natural" foundation of society in the sense that what is essential to religion provides social life with its inescapable point of origin. This view is somewhat lass obvious but introduces in a convenient fashion the central theme—the distinction between the sacred and the profane.

Durkheim begins his account of primitive society with an attempt to define, in its simplest form, the nature of primitive religion because it is here that the social as such becomes visible. He dismisses a variety of what he claims to be empirically unsubstantiated and logically flawed designations of the religious. It is not, thus, to be confused with ideas about the supernatural, with the notion of a god, or, though it also is primitive and widespread, the practice of magic. Durkheim arrives instead at a formulation which has the attractive feature of being completely general. Religion is defined as "a unified system of beliefs and practices relative to sacred things, that is to say, things set apart and forbidden—beliefs and practices which unite into one single moral community called a Church, all those who adhere to them" (Durkheim 1995, 44).

This division of the world into two domains, the one containing all that is sacred and the other all that is profane, is the distinctive trait of religious thought and practice. The centrality of the sacred to this definition is clear enough. Now the sacred can only be defined relationally, that is to say, "the religious phenomenon is such that it always assumes a bipartite division of the universe, known and knowable, into two genera that includes all that exists but radically excludes one another." And again, "Whether simple or complex, all known religious beliefs display a common feature: They presuppose a classification of the real or ideal things that men conceive of into two classes—two opposite genera—that are widely designated by two distinct terms, which the words *profane* and *sacred* translate fairly well" (Durkheim 1995, 34).

Furthermore, the nature of the sacred does not lie in any definite characteristics of a thing, idea, or action but resides wholly in the conventional designation within a community of believers; anything may be sacred. Indeed, "nothing but their heterogeneity is left to define the relation between the sacred and the profane." But, as this heterogeneity is absolute, the pure conventionality of the distinction remains impervious to critical reflection and is regarded as given in as self-evident a fashion as any presumed discontinuity in nature. "In the history of human thought," Durkheim claims, "there is no other example of two categories of things as radically opposed to one another." More than two distinct classes, they are "two worlds with nothing in common. The energies at play in one are not merely those encountered in the other, but raised to a higher degree: they are of different in kind" (Durkheim 1995, 36). Any movement from the one realm to the other, therefore, is "a true metamorphosis," a definite break in continuity which is generally represented spatially: "The sacred thing is *par excellence* that which the profane should not touch, and cannot touch with impunity."

There is some confusion here as to whether religion is defined in terms of substantive beliefs and practices "in relation to sacred things," or whether it should be construed formally as the division between the sacred and profane. Perhaps, as the sacred can be defined only in opposition to the profane, the two may be regarded as equivalent. More seriously, it is unclear if the sacred is to be viewed as a differentiated segment of an originally profane world, if the profane should be regarded as a subsequent differentiation within a primordially sacred world, or whether both are to be understood as simultaneously given in relation to each other.

These apparently insignificant details are in fact the source of the most

far-reaching disagreements in the interpretative traditions of Durkhei-
mian sociology. For the functionalist view the profane is identical with the
"everyday" out of which the sacred is created by a process of exclusion,
while in the structuralist perspective the two are simultaneously the creation of, and constitutive of, social life. For the growing field of religious
studies, it might be added, Durkheim is interpreted as supporting the thesis of primordial sacredness as the "original" human condition (Caillois
1939; Eliade 1959; Bataille 1989).

The Original Rule

A further aspect of the structuralist approach to Durkheim is worth pursu-
ing here. The significant point is that conventional social rules are stable
just because they are arbitrary. Like a language, the rules governing social
life must be learned, and having been learned, they take on the appearance
of effortless naturalism. Social rules tend to be stable because their conventional character often goes unnoticed, and consequently they are rarely
"thought away." Religion is foundational for society because, as a system
of rules and meanings, the religious is pure conventionality. The division
between the sacred and profane has no practical value to social life; it is not
"about" anything. And it is just its superfluous character that makes religion necessary as the general precondition of social life. The religious establishes the domain of convention; it is a "pure" rule—and nothing more.
The religious is, thus, logically prior to any particular social institution or
practice. However vital, however "functionally necessary" some particular
conventionalization—such as kinship relations or economic exchange—
might be for meeting the practical needs of a society, what remains true of
every society and of every occasion upon which human needs are satisfied
is that they can be satisfied only through the establishment and following
of conventions that define for the members of a society an appropriate system of action.

Before society can emerge in actuality, we might say, its possibility must
be realized at the most general level of universality. In the language of Romanticism, religion is the most general positing of society. Religion has no
positive content essential to the development of social life; it is, rather, the
most general expression of society as such. Through religion an inessen-

tial but necessary distinction is established, and from that foundation essential but contingent conventions, in which the particularities of social life exist, may be formed. Religion, thus, is universal; and the distinction between the sacred and profane is held to be general to society not as an empirical generalization but as a more basic matter of principle. Bergson later expressed Durkheim's insight in an arresting formula: "In Nature each rule is laid down by nature, and is necessary: whereas in Society only one thing is natural, the necessity of a rule" (Bergson 1935, 18). And religion is the peculiar form of this foundational rule, an otherwise empty convention which requires only that everything must be done according to some particular rule.

The Religion of Totemism

Durkheim tries to establish his view through a consideration of what was commonly taken to be the most primitive, that is, the simplest and, therefore (*sic*), the most archaic social forms, those of central Australia. A considerable literature on totemism had developed in late nineteenth-century British anthropology. Discussions by Morgan, McLennan, Frazer, Robertson Smith, and others had been cast in the dominant evolutionary mode of thought. But Durkheim's real interest lay in analyzing the structural features of totemism, in its operation as a system of conventions, which had become clearer through the detailed ethnographies of Spencer and Gillen.

The basic features of totemic systems were quite simple. Typically a specific group within the society, a clan, "united by a bond of kinship," refers to itself in terms of a name which is also "the name of a determined species of material thing with which it believes that it has very particular relations." Each clan maintains an exclusive relation to its own totem. Totemic relations are inherited, commonly through the mother. The totem is both a name (distinguishing the clan from any other) and an emblem (representing its unity and cohesiveness), and as an emblematic device the totemic mark is frequently inscribed on the members of the clan to make public their membership in the group. It is its emblematic character that particularly interests Durkheim, for "while the totem is a collective label, it also has a religious character. . . . It is the very type of sacred thing."

As the "figured representation of the totem," the species and the clan are considered sacred in varying (descending) degrees. Durkheim argues that totemism is not a religion of animals or plants "but of an anonymous and impersonal *force* that is identifiable in each of these beings but identical to none of them":

> None possesses it entirely, and all participate in it. Such is its independence from the particular subjects in which it is incarnated that it both precedes and outlives them. The individuals die; the generations pass and are replaced by others; but this force remains always present, alive, and the same. It animates the generations of today as it animated those of yesterday and will animate those of tomorrow. Taking the word "god" in a very broad sense, one could say that it is the god that each totemic cult worships. But it is an impersonal god, without name, without history, immanent in the world, diffused in a numberless multitude of things (Durkheim 1995, 191).

The totem is "the tangible form in which that intangible substance is represented in the imagination; diffused through all sorts of disparate beings, that energy alone is the real object of the cult." Durkheim insists that this is a real force, experienced as the external pressure that is "the source of the clan's moral life." And in this, totemism is not distinct but shares with the more "developed" religions a fundamentally common character, for what is at the basis of all religious representations is not determined images but "indefinite powers, anonymous forces."

The sacred, that is to say, is a specific representation of impersonal forces, which, it is inescapably suggested to the primitive, shape the world in which they live. Thus "the totem is before all a symbol, a material expression of something else." Durkheim coyly and quite rhetorically asks, "Of what else?" It is clear from the beginning that the answer to this question will be "society." The totem is simply the "outward and visible form" of the group.

Durkheim's argument now slides back into the form that he had previously criticized among those who had attempted to account for the generality (if not the origin) of religion on some other basis. Thus of Tylor and Frazer, who held that religion was founded on the representation of nature (of which it was a crude version), Durkheim complains that not only does this rob religion of any reality and stigmatize the primitive as unintelligent, it misrepresents both nature and religion. Nature is not, in fact, a "fit object" for worship. The impressiveness of nature is rather of a dull regularity than of a living and forceful will. But Durkheim does not seem to think it inappropriate to argue that society, unlike nature, is just such a worthy object of reverence.

Echoing Schleiermacher's understanding of God, Durkheim claims that society is God in the sense that it alone "gives us the sensation of a perpetual dependence" (Durkheim 1995, 206). It is society that exercises moral control over us and that forces from us acknowledgment of its own supremacy and superiority.

Furthermore, a god "is not an authority to which we are subject but also a force that buttresses our own." Religious ritual vivifies sentiments through which society can maintain this superiority and provide this strength: "In the midst of an assembly that becomes worked up, we become capable of feelings and conduct of which we are incapable when left to our individual resources" (Durkheim 1995, 211–12). A general effervescence which is a strengthening influence of society makes itself felt through the cult.

But if the totem represents the collective force of the group—its superiority and independence from the individual—what does the profane represent? The difficulty here is that Durkheim had already argued cogently that modern society is increasingly made up of individual representations and that these are, as much as collective representations, social conventions in which must be incarnated the powers of social life. He had also argued that in primitive societies there are very few individual representations; that social life there is more "of a piece" than it is in modern society. So, for primitive society the profane must also represent the totality of society to its members; it could hardly be otherwise. Hence the difficulty; what is the meaning of the profane? And how can the whole basis of Durkheim's argument be sustained if the distinction upon which everything is erected has an unfortunate tendency to break down? Or, to put it otherwise, if the profane is also a religious (spiritual) category.

Relative and Absolute Difference

The difficulty into which Durkheim has drawn us might be expressed in the following way. Either the distinction between the sacred and profane is universal and given with the possibility of society itself, in which case this possibility is represented by the difference between the two domains; or the sacred represents the social as such, in which case it exists "in itself" rather than in relation to the profane.

These alternatives in fact represent in embryonic form the structuralist and functionalist interpretations of Durkheim's work as a whole. Is there a point of view from which these very different perspectives might be related? Certainly there does not seem to be within the context of Durkheim's declared aim of exploring the nature of primitive religion. The whole situation is a little odd. After all, Durkheim taught philosophy as well as sociology and presumably was aware of the criticisms to which he was leaving himself open by alternating within his text, often without warning, between these distinct and apparently incompatible notions of religion and, thus, of the social.

The situation becomes a little clearer if the discussion is related directly to what is implicit in *The Elementary Forms* but quite explicit in the rest of Durkheim's work; namely, that it is the character of modern society which is his central preoccupation. His study of primitive religion, indeed, is only an exercise in conceptual clarification, an exercise which has signally failed. But considered as a meditation inspired by his experience of Modernity, rather than by his imaginary confrontation with the primitive, it makes more sense.

Now in his other works Durkheim had argued quite strenuously for the view that individualism is both the subjective form of the advanced division of labor and the foundation of organic solidarity. The individual, that is to say, is a formal creation of modern society, and the stability of the latter is by no means threatened by the normal development of the former. Thus we might at once invert the conventional categorization of sacred and profane that was too hastily taken from his description of primitive society. In modern society it is individual representations that are preeminently religious or sacred in character, and the conscience collective of modern society is best seen as being crystallized in the form of individuality. Efforts, thus, to rediscover the sacred in collective rituals of modern life have been singularly unconvincing, and Durkheim himself provides the best arguments against such a misapplication of his analysis of primitive religion.

But this hardly solves our difficulty. It merely draws the distinction between the sacred and the profane in a new way. It still appears to be drawing a line on a blank piece of paper, a rectilinear division as if between right and left. This is just the form, in fact, in which Robert Hertz extended Durkheim's notion, and since then a lively anthropology of formal classificatory schemes has ensued (Needham 1973).

The boundary between the sacred and the profane might be viewed differently. First of all, it should be clear that the dividing line left/right model can only be made from outside the actual field of vision being divided. The ethnographer sees both sacred and profane, but in terms of the native experience it must be either sacred or profane. Furthermore, as the profane is also a religious category, it might be seen as derived from the sacred; as distinct, for example, to an "everyday" or mundane world to which both sacred and profane are opposed. The sacred/profane dichotomy seems, in practice, to imply a triangular relation of sacred/profane/mundane.

More significantly, and in line with problems that are conspicuously modern, Durkheim is at least alluding to the difficulty of drawing distinctions from within a particular domain. The distinction between the sacred and the profane might then be likened to a series of other distinctions that have provoked similar analytical difficulties. Consider, for example, the experience of being in pain. Philosophers have discussed this at some length. The central point for the moment is simply to note the peculiar character of pain. As an irritation it can coexist with our normal experience of life, but if it is intensified, it not only becomes ever present but destroys the normal (painless) experiential world. The all-consuming character of intense pain, its destruction of memory, of duration, of the normal experience of space, and so on, has a good deal of what is conventionally described as the sacred about it (Scarry 1985). Then, when the intense pain is relieved, the experience seems, as it were, to shrink in memory and decisively change in character.

The peculiar nature of this relationship has also been widely discussed with reference to the distinction between dreams and waking experience. The subject of dreaming, as was noted at the outset, was significant in the emergence of Modernity and not only figures in crucial texts of Descartes and Hobbes but also forms the central motif of Spanish Golden Age literature. The difficulty of knowing whether we are asleep and dreaming, or whether our experience is a waking perception, remained an unresolved (and ignored) difficulty which reemerged as a critical issue in fin-de-siècle culture. Indeed, whereas Tylor and Frazer had used what they claimed to be the primitive's inability to distinguish waking from dreaming experience as a mark of the primitive's undeveloped state and the mechanism through which the illusions of primitive religion were formed, they were in fact renewing a theme which had been far more significantly and decisively applied to modern developed and civilized peoples.

In this context we might suggest that Durkheim's criticisms of Tylor are actually attempts to establish clear-cut distinctions for modern experience. The difficulty was not that the primitive could not tell them apart, but that we could not. And if this distinction proved groundless, were we not in danger of slipping into a kind of indifference in which nothing would make sense?

Thus, although Durkheim began *The Elementary Forms of the Religious Life* with what appeared to be the unambiguous difference between the sacred and the profane, as the work developed the boundary between these domains became progressively eroded. Not only, from the outside and in terms of his own theory, was there a tendency to slide into a monism of the sacred; but, in terms of a more immediate, phenomenological understanding, his distinction became difficult to sustain.

The difference between the sacred and the profane is so radical that, in fact, it tends to disappear. An absolute boundary is a limit rather than a division. This becomes evident in Durkheim's discussion of the origin of totemic beliefs. The effervescence of the group has a transforming power over experience: "This exceptional increase of force is something very real." It is clear that Durkheim is actually talking about a wholly modern situation, as, for example, a speaker addressing a large crowd, in which "he has achieved communion with it." Durkheim refers to "the demon of oratorical inspiration": "His language becomes high-flown in a way that would be ridiculous in ordinary circumstances; his gestures take on an overbearing quality; his very thought becomes impatient of limits and slips easily into every kind of extreme. This is because he feels filled to overflowing, as though with a phenomenal oversupply of forces that spill over and tend to spread around him. Sometimes he even feels possessed by a moral force greater than he, of which he is only the interpreter" (Durkheim 1995, 212).

However, it is not only in exceptional circumstances that we feel this force; "there is not, so to speak, a moment in our lives when some current of energy does not come to us from without." The peculiarity of the sacred is dispersed throughout the modern world such that, as efficacious as ever, it has in fact become invisible.

In the case of aboriginal society, on the other hand, Durkheim claims that the entire society alternates between profane and sacred states. The profane is dominated by economic activity and "is generally of rather low intensity. . . . The dispersed state in which the society finds itself makes life monotonous, slack, and humdrum." But during its sacred rituals concentrated interaction acts as a powerful stimulant; "a sort of electricity is generated by their closeness and quickly launches them to an extraordinary height of exaltation." Social excitation releases individuals from moral constraint: "The effervescence often becomes so intense that it leads to outlandish behavior; the passions unleashed are so torrential that nothing can hold them. People are so far outside the ordinary conditions of life, and so conscious of the fact, that they feel a certain need to set themselves above and beyond ordinary morality" (Durkheim 1995, 218).

This transformation is complete:

It is not difficult to imagine that a man in such a state of exaltation should no longer know himself. Feeling possessed and led on by some sort of external power that makes him think and act differently than he normally does, he naturally feels he is no longer himself. It seems to him that he has become a new being. . . . And because his companions feel transformed in the same way at the same moment, and express this feeling by their shouts, movements, and bearing, it is as if he was in reality transported into a special world entirely different from the one in which he ordinarily lives, a special world inhabited by exceptionally intense forces that invade and transform him. (Durkheim 1995, 220)

But if these worlds are so radically distinct, entering the sacred effectively abolishes the profane and becomes itself an all-inclusive reality. Like a dream, for which the waking world does not exist, the sacred is a division within the profane which, paradoxically, includes everything within itself.

The Profane in Modern Society

Modern society, thus, rather than being seen in terms of a process of secularization for which the sacred can exist only as a memory or as a theoretical but ineffective possibility, is so steeped in the sacred that we imagine it to be wholly secular! Our absorption in the sacred means that we imagine ourselves to be living within a secular world, whereas, in fact, we have fallen so completely under the spell of the sacred that we cannot any longer recollect a profane existence.

The frenzy of modern life, the continuous overstimulation and heightened dynamic density, the sense of being carried along and carried away by mysterious external forces, all of this is Durkheim's way of characterizing modern society in general rather than the periodic intensification of life in the sacred rituals of the aboriginal.

This has the nice consequence of turning everything on its head. Modern society is a sacred realm, not because it has preserved within it a corner of the sacred to which religious beliefs and practices cling, but, rather, because the sacred has so diffused itself throughout its complex network of relations and so effortlessly renews itself and invigorates itself in collective experience that it ceases to be visible. The consequential transvaluation of values means that everything we thought to be tokens of the retreat of religion into illusory abstraction in fact represents its pervasive and growing strength. The desire for goods, the frenzy of consumption, the longing for objects that are in themselves useless, are the elements of a totemic religion of Modernity. Modernity was from the very beginning associated with new forms of consumerism (Braudel 1983) that renewed themselves at the very moments of its greatest cultural transformations, during the eighteenth century (Brewer and Porter 1996) and toward the end of the nineteenth century (Miller 1981, 1987, 1997; Williams 1982). We have suppressed the profane reserve of an earlier period and consume with the artificial energy of a continuous and ever-present ritual. The dominance of economic life is not, here, the self-assertion of the profane world over the sacred but, rather, the transformation into material form of the religious spirit of Western society.

The ubiquity and banality of the sacred in contemporary postmodern culture render it indifferent, indistinguishable from the profane or the secular. We have returned, in one sense, to a particular characteristic of primitive society. It is not only the primitive that "tends to live as much as possible *in* the sacred" (Eliade 1959); indeed, this characterization of the primitive seems convincing only because, projecting our own experience into an imagined distant past where it comes more clearly into focus, it is the way we understand ourselves.

SPIRIT AS HAPPINESS
AND UNHAPPINESS

Everything which is taken as proof of the spiritlessness of Modernity at the same time loudly proclaims its spirit. Materialism, rationalization, consumerism, worldliness, and the profane character of everyday life come into prominence as the apotheosis, rather than the negation, of spirit in Modernity. This view—what might be considered Hegel's fundamental insight into the character of Modernity—vindicates itself as a perspective symmetrical to that of modern secular rationalism. In Modernity, it seems, spirit is just as possible as it is impossible.

In the contemporary world all categorical distinctions seem to have relaxed into indifference. The distinction among value spheres becomes clouded, and internally each dissolves into an incoherent flux. The perceptual world becomes a phenomenal and incomprehensible becoming; the aesthetic is equally ugly and beautiful; the moral becomes a tangle of uncaused and unintended events. The inexplicable and unforeseen become the normative standard of everyday life, a standard which cannot yield any firm judgments. The immediate experience of life becomes a tragicomedy where all sense of directionality and purpose is immediately undermined by a single certainty: that any such sense is self-deluding. All this, too, can be described as spiritless or as spirit. We can take it or leave it; Modernity is nothing if not tolerant.

In such a world it is the very groundlessness of all phenomena that in the end permits the emergence of new absolute distinctions. Happiness becomes as possible as despair; trust as actual as anxiety; plenitude as given as emptiness. Inexplicably we awake from indifference to one or the other. And the difference of happiness and unhappiness—both from each other and from indifference—remains existentially vital. Happiness and unhappiness cannot be assimilated to the normally comprehensible flow of feeling, passage of events, or train of thought. They are not only remote from the discourse of subject and object, they are irreducible to body or to soul, or to a simple interrelation of body and soul. Happiness and unhappiness disclose an unconquerable transcendence at the center of human experience. They are modes of spirit.

The persistence of such heterogeneity, terms and realities that stubbornly refuse to be assimilated to the rationalized and disenchanted world, might easily be dismissed as an insignificant residue of "unexplained" phenomena that sooner or later (and probably sooner) will fall to the irresistible self-expansion of Modernity in general and of its project of Enlightenment in particular. But just as the modern physicist found that the residue of unexplained phenomena became the focus for a new and strange view of nature, positioning the subject within the field of happiness and unhappiness initiates a quite different view of reality and vision of human possibilities. Happiness is the quantum strangeness of human existence, its inexplicable discontinuity, its radical difference, its real presence. It is the positive version, as it were, disclosed in the deathly shadow of the body and the melancholic immediacy of the soul.

The duality of spirit is revealed in the momentary appearance and disappearance of, and inexplicable oscillation between, happiness and unhappiness. If spirit had wholly dissolved into nothing, into an all-inclusive indifference, how could we ever be happy; and equally, if spirit had completely emptied itself into the everyday world and consecrated its practices, how could we be tormented by unhappiness? The determinants of happiness and unhappiness, that is to say, lie altogether outside the plane of everyday existence. Happiness and unhappiness wrench the subject away from all reason and conventionality.

Pascal already realized this and made it a central focus of his *Pensées:* "If man had never been anything but corrupt he would have no idea of either truth or bliss." And "unhappy as we are (and we should be less so if there were no element of greatness in our condition) we have an idea of happiness but we cannot attain it" (Pascal 1966, 59). We cannot help but wish to be happy, even though we have no notion of how it is constituted; "man wants to be happy, only wants to be happy, and cannot help wanting to be happy"; it is a kind of demon that betrays his spirit. And Hegel, complicating the tradition of rationalism, makes its central to the odyssey of spirit in the world. Prompted by "Unhappy Consciousness," spirit transforms itself, alienates itself into the Other, and seeks to reconcile itself with itself in a higher form, a form of happiness.

The persistence of happiness and unhappiness is the most insightful guide to the fate of spirit in the contemporary world. As spirit is absorbed into secular experience, happiness becomes identified with pleasure, and unhappiness with unpleasure. But this identification is illusory, and it is at this point that a critical analysis of the contemporary experience of life becomes possible. Pleasure is an ego relation and affirms the secular self in terms of an interior soul. Happiness, however, is anterior to both pleasure and the ego, so that the conscious pursuit of pleasure in fact becomes an obstacle to its realization. And the possibility of happiness is given not in the imagined generalization and intensification of pleasure but in the real experience of melancholy and despair. If we are afflicted by "sorrow without cause," then hope remains that we might be visited by groundless happiness.

Thus Kierkegaard or, rather, Judge William advises the melancholic to "choose despair," because melancholy is the choice of spirit over the empty conventionality of the Present Age. And through the intensification of melancholy, new transformations of spirit appear, new forms oriented ultimately toward happiness as a possibility. In this spirit is conceptualized as nothing more or less than existence.

In this perspective traditional religious categories are spiritually refreshed, and life is ordered in terms of the distinction between faith and sin. In faith immediacy is regained. There is no gap between spirit as faith and spirit as immediacy; the two flow effortlessly together. Similarly there is no effort involved in subordinating the self under ethical universals. Faith is a subjective liberation in which the self emerges in its most highly determined form.

The Kierkegaardian pseudonyms apparently present a series of personal images of spirit, in various stages of individuation and concreteness, for which faith accomplishes the realization of selfhood that the young man sought in vain. Spirit is thus invoked as an essential aspect of Modernity. There is no question here of living in a spiritless age, other than in the sense that the vast majority of people are stuck in the first sphere or, indeed, fail even to develop to that extent and exist, undisturbed, in a cocoon of bourgeois philistinism. Spirit is present as an absence, as melancholy that spreads and deepens until finally it transforms itself into the groundless happiness of faith. But this final leap of faith is so difficult that its existence even as a possibility, for most people, remains remote. Not only does it announce itself in the terrifying "teleological suspension of the ethical," it flies in the face of all logical thought and the habits of rationality that are already so well ingrained.

The pseudonyms, in fact, round on Judge William's bourgeois preoccupations with morality and reason. For them the immediacy of pleasure and of faith is a more stringent test of reality and a more certain route of self-development. This critique of bourgeois rationality is most brilliantly developed in the writings of Johannes Climacus, who defends a subjective view of faith against all pseudorational trivializations. Like Ulrich, the man without qualities, Climacus is opposed to all notions of faith as intellectual certainty; but unlike Ulrich he regards faith as the most complete form, rather than the dissolution, of the self. Faith is not to be confused with a "belief" about the nature of the world; it is something completely "subjective" in the sense of a freely chosen orientation to the entire world of experience. For Climacus, who is a gifted intellectual antiphilosopher, spirit always presents itself, in opposition to all systematic philosophy, as paradox and contradiction. It is always something decidedly offensive both to reason and to morality; it is terrifying: "Christianity is spirit; spirit is inwardness; inwardness is subjectivity; subjectivity is essentially passion, and at its maximum an infinite, personally interested interest for one's eternal happiness" (Kierkegaard 1992, 33).

For Climacus faith is the transcendence of despair rather than the resolution of doubt. Where Descartes had divided the subject against itself and opposed thinking (in the broadest sense) characterized by doubt to the self-certainty of personal existence, Climacus draws a close parallel between doubt as the uncertain road to knowledge and despair as the route to the self-confidence of faith. On the one hand, therefore, his understanding is distinctively modern; faith is, so to speak, the self-creation of the individual in his or her fullness and concreteness. On the other hand, however, he rejects the modern prejudice in favor of objective knowledge as the only fundamental (and not simply the most significant) relation between selfhood and the world it inhabits. No empirical knowledge can offer an adequate foundation for "faith"; all such knowledge is an approximation and a temporary perspective. Anticipating Nietzsche, Climacus argues that for any "objective" view "truth itself is transformed into a *desideratum,* and everything is placed in the process of becoming (*Vorden*), because the empirical object is not finished, and the existing knowing spirit is itself in the process of becoming" (Kierkegaard 1992, 189). For Climacus spirit is the self, and the self is a synthesis of body and soul which relates itself to itself. This sui generis reality does not depend upon anything other than itself for its existence.

The unfolding of the self, therefore, is unlike the growth of knowledge; the forced analogy between the two had led Hegel into the absurdity of a virtual identity of faith and knowledge. For Climacus subjectivity develops in a series of discontinuous and irrational leaps in which the spirit gathers and transforms itself. These unpredictable movements, if they are to be likened to any specific aspect of the self-relation, might more appropriately be viewed as arbitrary acts of will than as the cumulative increments in the growth of knowledge. But even this does not adequately characterize the "subjective thinker" whose periodic transformation is a phenomenon of pathos rather than of insight. Additionally, unlike the growth of knowledge, the "pathos-filled transitions" are not once-and-for-all movements but, rather, oscillations of spirit in which the individual is caught up. Climacus in this way defends a religious view of spirit from Modernity by using some of its premodern aspects as ways of describing Modernity itself. His rejection of rationalism and bourgeois respectability is forward looking and anticipates the fin-de-siècle dissolution of the ego.

Climacus is the most developed of Kierkegaard's post-Romantic pseudonyms. But, in fact, even he cannot make the "double-movement" of faith in this way. He sees clearly that faith, which is certain of itself, and self-certainty, which is groundless faith, become identical in the modern world. One cannot argue one's way to faith or have its necessity demonstrated in some way by scientific means, nor can one surrender to it as a supreme ethical value; it is ultimately wholly unlike knowledge or morality, though it must exist in relation to, and through, both. Faith (happiness) does not yield to a conscious pursuit or succumb to the infectious ease of the rational calculation of means.

Climacus, therefore, is the most unhappy of the pseudonyms, the most wracked by melancholy, and the most spiritually sensitive. Climacus and the Romantic tradition on which he still leans favor unhappiness as the test of spiritual vitality and as an indicator of spiritual awareness and sensitivity. The most for which he can hope is that the melancholy of resignation might overcome the torment of guilt. His repeated claim that "subjectivity is truth" not only fails to relieve him of the obligation of seeking objective knowledge (of objective things), it fails to liberate his self as spirit; it plunges him ever deeper into melancholic hopelessness. Indeed the programmatic "subjectivity is truth" imposes upon him an obligation to reveal within himself the given reality of spirit. Albeit that he fails to do this, he does realize that "subjectivity" is quite unlike the existential freedom of the Romantics (in this Climacus is no contemporary existentialist) but requires the decisive unfolding of a definite pregiven structure of selfhood.

Spirit is the self, the self is spirit: despair is not to have a self. Despair, then, can take the form of spiritual weakness, not to will to be the self and the dissipation of the self in innumerable projects and occasions. But it can also take the form of defiance: to will not to be the self. This might be called the ironic form of the despair, a deliberate turning of the self away from itself as spirit and a form of self-identification with unpleasure, evil, and sin. In this sense it remains closer to happiness than it does to boredom; the negative or perverse spirit is, after all, still spirit and conquers the boredom and busyness of the Present Age.

All this amounts to a sustained attack on the Present Age. But it appears contradictory. If spirit is self, then a perverse or misrelated self should be due to a perverse spirit. Kierkegaard supposes not: that there is nothing wrong with spirit in Modernity, it is only the spirit of Modernity (bourgeois philistinism in all its forms) that is the obstacle to real happiness. How can this have come about? And how can spirit reveal itself in its uncorrupted state?

That the spirit of Modernity should obstruct spirit in Modernity is, perhaps, the central theme of the pseudonymous works. The devotion to secular values, to either bourgeois values or their Romantic counterpart, and especially to their "highest" and most developed forms—reason, love, truth—represents spirit's negative synthesis. It is this paradox which uniquely describes the experience of Modernity. This might be expressed by saying that since the Renaissance the spirit of Modernity has been the search for human autonomy and self-understanding in terms of purely human attributes. To the extent that this is successful, Modernity secures itself against any possible criticism. Rather than being poised between two infinities, the human takes those infinities into itself and transforms them into the concrete reality of the secular world. But the human is always more than the immediate and particular human being. Pascal, the most gifted psychologist of spirit before the pseudonyms, anticipates this insight: "Man infinitely transcends man" (Pascal 1966, 131). And Nietzsche, the most sensitive of their descendants, agrees; the human being is "an unfinished animal." Modernity as the self-understanding and self-proclamation of humanity as autonomous is always in danger, therefore, of reducing the human to an essentially spiritless being.

But the transcendence of spirit in Modernity no more invokes a reality beyond our experience than does the wholly secularized spirit of Modernity (as commodity, value, or the sacred/profane). Using the pseudonym

SK and adopting many aspects of traditional religious language, Kierke-gaard provides, simultaneously with his aesthetic works, a series of *Up-building Discourses* (in some translations *Edifying Discourses,* recalling He-gel's demand for an active philosophy of spirit, rather than a dead philosophy of mind), in which is presented a precise and psychologically realistic account of spirit in its unclouded and nonmelancholic form. These neglected texts, which Heidegger was almost alone in recognizing as key statements about the psychology of Modernity, rather than charac-terize spirit as a striving toward the absolute, which continually retreats before its advance, describe the world of experience from the perspective of happiness possessed. The transformation wrought by spirit seizing the human individual in its completeness is assumed already to have taken place. Now everything that was difficult, strenuous, mysterious, and ex-hausting is present as an effortless grace.

The high pitch of spiritual tension, the seeking out and accentuating of the paradoxical and decisive, is suddenly relaxed; everything has changed and everything remains unaltered. This allows the *Discourses* the critical device of a distinction between the self of the pseudonyms, all ultimately aesthetic because none are born of spirit in Modernity, and the second or "true" self that does not lie anywhere beyond actuality. This second self, in fact, more completely acknowledges Modernity. The contradiction of all the pseudonyms is to attempt to realize the self in terms of an ideal that lies beyond the surface of life, while at the same time holding that there can be nothing beyond this surface. The self of the *Discourses* seeks noth-ing beyond itself, neither as knowledge, nor will, nor passion; it lives di-rectly in the world of spirit as actuality. Spirit is groundless happiness as well as tormenting melancholy. In the *Discourses* there is no working through a variety of preparatory stages to achieve happiness. Life is here pervaded by a boundless trust in its own being.

But this weightless happiness cannot be made permanent, any more than we can be wholly cured of melancholy. The *Discourses* was written si-multaneously with the pseudonymous production, and taken together they characterize the duplicity of modern experience. Subjectivity slips un-controllably between happiness and melancholy, trust and distrust in its own world.

Climacus insists that spirit is existence, and nothing else. But existence refuses to be tied down to a formula. Happiness and unhappiness succeed one another simply because they assert their right to exist "in themselves." They slip in and out of existence, coloring its every aspect, because they remain indifferent to any of its particular determinants. The almost irresistible tendency to regard circumstances as the cause of our happiness and unhappiness is an indication of the persistence of classical Modernity in its incarnation as Body, while our equally unconsidered assumption of the superiority of happiness over unhappiness as a goal indicates a similar longevity of its dynamism as Soul. A calm indifference to either marks the emergence of the postmodern, which, in denying the reality of either, is all the more surprised and embarrassed to be confronted by their periodic and unpredictable emergence from the superficiality of contemporary life.

THE RETICENCE OF
MODERN SPIRIT

One response, then, to the claim that the modern age is spiritless is to argue that all the evidence adduced in support of this claim equally supports the view that Modernity is an essentially spiritual age. As a synthesis of body and soul, which relates itself to itself as a continuous history and transforms itself in a succession of values and meanings, spirit penetrates every aspect of contemporary existence. That it appears otherwise is largely due to the persistence of premodern, inappropriate conceptions of spirit as extramundane, immaterial, and nonhuman.

What is often nowadays referred to as "postmodernity" might then be seen as something of an optical illusion. It is perfectly true that contemporary life has lost its focus on the ego; that it has become shallow, superficial, and directionless; that it no longer defines itself in terms of a metanarrative or conceives of any aspect of itself in relation to a transcendent reality which in some sense is given in the nature of things. The human world freed itself from nature and the dominance of its own past at the Renaissance; created a domain by and for its own self-development, a self-generated world which formed itself into the surface that is contemporary life. But rather than view this as the death throes of the Western spirit, it is perhaps as convincing to claim that it is simply the latest transformation of that spirit. We may have become ignorant of our past, but we are still its creatures.

The fierce rejection of metaphysics and the rooting out of all metaphysical assumptions (such as the "ego," the "self," etc.) are identified (wrongly) with the rejection of spirit. Metaphysics is not spirit, and the unmetaphysical character of contemporary life is only another token of its peculiar form of spirit, not of its spiritlessness.

The unexpected partial truth in the idea of postmodernity is found in the insistence that there is nowhere "beyond" or "above" or "within" the human subject. This, in fact, is the foundation for a self-understanding of spirit as itself: now spirit cannot appear as other than itself; that is, it becomes identical with itself as that which is essentially human.

Does this mean that the radical urge of the Renaissance—the dream of human autonomy and self-determination—an urge felt subsequently in the quest for rational self-understanding and human self-fulfillment, in the political demands for justice, for freedom, and for tolerance, has finally been realized? Is the late twentieth century witness to the successful completion of the project of Modernity? Has everything human fallen back to Earth or been sucked up from the depths and made itself real in the immediacy and concreteness of experience? Hardly. The question is evidently rhetorical and need only be put to be answered in the negative.

But we need not, in accepting an essentially self-limiting conception of Modernity, abandon ourselves to the status quo. To find a point of leverage—a fulcrum—upon which we can turn the entire experience of Modernity does not require that we leave, either metaphorically or in actuality, the surface of life, which postmodernism correctly claims to be the only life there is. We need not measure experience by an ideal standard, far less by the claims of the absolute, to discover its shortcomings. Applying a strictly practical standard, one that is bound up with the particular and limited conditions of the present, is quite sufficient to subvert every particular arrangement of the Present Age and expose every absurd claim it makes in its own defense.

Conclusion

Toward a History
of Modernity

Modernity cannot be understood simply as a period or epoch, the most recent of a series that stretches back through small transitions to the ancient past. Modernity calls into existence, as well as a new social world, new forms of knowledge and self-understanding to attest to the uniqueness of that world. Even if ill founded, the claim of radical novelty marks Modernity as unlike earlier forms of Western society. Such self-understanding, however, by its very nature conceals not only those aspects in which Modernity remains continuous with its own prehistory but, more significantly, the precise character of the transformation in which this self-conception was born. The fundamental claim of Modernity to be self-defining, therefore, is contradictory. This is no mere "theoretical" issue; the entire project of Modernity—to seize and shape the human world according to immanent principles of reason and sense—founders on its essential but irrational rejection of the past.

FORMS OF MODERNITY

The restless dynamism of modern life cannot adequately be described in terms of a single metaphor. It involves at least three different types of motion, each of which is associated with a characteristic transition from premodern society and culture.

The dynamism of Body takes the form of rectilinear motion. The inertial body is simple matter in continuous motion, the fundamental mechanism implicit in the emptying of the cosmos of substantial forms. The underlying assumption of the uniformity and endless extension of space and time was realized in a conception of nature as a realm of necessity which could be understood in terms of simple mechanical principles. These assumptions were also at the root of the conception of human dynamism as the freedom of self-movement and of reason as its guide, universal characteristics embodied as intention, purpose, and will. Body was both the elementary unit of, and general model for, the self-sustaining "system of the world." Nature, society, and individual experience were conformed to, and understood in terms of, a logical and empirical atomism. These formal characteristics of the body perspective were associated with the ending of feudal society and its aristocratic aftermath, the establishment of capitalism, the formation of the centralized modern state, the transformation of subjects into citizens, and the ascendancy of the bourgeois class; that is, with the development of modern society as a collectivity of individuals defined by the possession of universal rights.

The dynamism of Soul is characterized as a process of growth and self-development. Natural forms are viewed as the unfolding of specific morphological structures inherent in the undifferentiated states of matter from which they arise. In terms of human self-understanding, this process is grasped in the immediacy of inner experience as a unique personal narrative. The soul is interiorized as the personality of the individual, which, ideally, is realized as a process of free self-expressive action. This process of progressive individuation is threatened both by the formless infinity and freedom of interiority from which the concrete soul emerges and by the concrete actuality of the world of existing forms that confronts it. The modern soul is also associated with the development of bourgeois society. It is linked particularly with the establishment of rational capitalism and the institutionalization of the market as its foundational social mechanism which operate by according individuals the freedom to act as they choose. It is associated also with the differentiation of private from public life and the growing emphasis on the former as, ideally, a domain of freedom, including recreative and imaginative freedom.

The dynamism of Spirit can be conceptualized as an oscillatory motion, a restless movement between the profane and the sacred, want and satisfaction, tradition and reason. It is an intermittent and uncertain synthesis of body and soul. On the large scale spirit is nothing other than the historical process itself, and its conceptualization introduces irresolvable contradictions into any notion of Modernity as human autonomy. If Modernity is a creation ex nihilo, then the continuity of spirit is broken, and with it the claim of human autonomy to be human, that is, to be a historical rather than a natural or divine being. If, on the other hand, spirit conserves itself and pours itself into modern forms, then the claim of human autonomy to be autonomous is compromised, and every form of spirit remains Other. This contradiction is not resolved in the process of secularization. The Other takes on a wholly human form, as History, but remains antagonistic to every present claim to human freedom and autonomy. Marx, in a famous passage, thus expresses the central paradox of Modernity: "Men make their own history, but not of their own free will; not under circumstances they themselves have chosen, but under the given and inherited circumstances with which they are directly confronted" (Marx 1973, 143).

Modernity is a continuing project rather than a specific and completed mode of life. As well as distinguishing itself from premodern society and culture in terms of specific transformations of Body, Soul, and Spirit, Modernity itself undergoes a series of characteristic developments within and through these characteristically dynamic forms. However, though the perspectives of Body, Soul, and Spirit are associated in their dominant periods with particular phases in its development, they are not themselves, nor do they represent, sequential stages in the history of Modernity. Body and Soul cannot be grasped, here, as object and subject, nor can they be reduced to moments in the dialectical unfolding of Spirit. Body, Soul, and Spirit, rather, each provide a distinctive point of view from which the character and development of Modernity can be understood, and each represents a totality, an exclusive and exhaustive reality from which all other perspectives are, in principle, excluded.

Thus, as the perspective of Body, Modernity was established in the concept and in the practical reality of the individuated and closed body image. The point-mass was the theoretical and real atom from which every structure was composed. This conceptualization, dominant from the mid-eighteenth to the mid-nineteenth century, was seriously undermined by developments in the physical sciences and by the beginning of the twentieth century was radically overhauled in favor of field concepts of matter and force.

At the same time Modernity was conceived in the perspective of the Soul as the formation of an interior world of psychic contents: as the ego. This notion, too, in the observation of a variety of symptomatic illnesses and acts was undermined toward the end of the nineteenth century and gradually (and incompletely) replaced by new conceptions of the soul as the sensitive and radiant surface (rather than the secret interior) of the body.

And, similarly, spirit at first established its Modernity by proclaiming its autonomy from God and Nature, then rediscovered its Otherness as human history before dissolving into a postmodern, tensionless state of indifference.

Body, Soul, and Spirit are three forms of subjectivity, not divisions within a single object-subject reality; three worlds of experience from which can be constructed more or less convincing human self-images. Each in turn is subdivided and fragmented, so that we respond to reality in a number of possible ways. Each perspective is a world to itself and not a segment of an ideally united reality. Body is not subordinated to Soul, or Soul to Body. Spirit is an alternative to either, or both fused in some ideal interaction. The coexistence of these perspectives, which remains an unresolved difficulty at a theoretical level, poses few real problems beyond the occasional academic border dispute. Indeed, not only do we conduct our lives as if first one, then another, of these perspectives was exclusively valid, we allow a whole series of premodern conceptualizations of Body, Soul, and Spirit their place in the ample historicism of the present.

SOCIETY AND SUBJECTIVITY

Modernity begins with the rejection of social hierarchy and the emergence of a new universalized social space and time within which interaction can occur on the basis of simple universal criteria rather than essential qualities. This universalization is related to the generalization of a commodity form of production, a process which calls into existence a world of estranged "objects" that remain, in principle, impenetrable so far as their qualities are concerned. The world of "subjects" cannot participate directly in this world and withdraws into private and interior forms of consolation.

The problems of control that seemed to be inherent in this individualistic culture were, in fact, solved by the self-regulating principles of the market. However much the depths of the soul were shrouded in inwardness, individuals could effectively be controlled without trampling upon their new freedoms by depriving them of all means of livelihood other than work. A common principle of rationality, at least to the extent of recognizing the necessity of work, mitigated the anarchy otherwise implied in ceding to individuals the right to decide all the most fundamental and profound issues of the day. Conscience was no threat to good order because conscience was bound to dictate the necessity of survival before everything else. A new bourgeois order emerged based on notions of self-control, self-development, and self-actualization. But the "self" realized in this order, rather than objectifying authentic inwardness, was understood in a superficial and conventionalized way. The trick of bourgeois culture is the discovery that the most significant issues, socially and politically, were never the most profound and that, consequently, it was quite safe to allow people to make up their own minds or remain no-minded about such matters. The absolute liberty of the soul could thus be proclaimed as a triumph for Modernity; an absolute inner freedom became its most cherished value just because the soul was of no consequence to the practical affairs of life.

Throughout the development of Modernity, the relations of mutual estrangement between Subject and Object underwent a series of changes; the drawing apart and mutual self-closure were followed by an opening out and intermingling. This reconciliation was prompted by the demand for continuing economic growth and the self-expansion of the commodity sphere, an expansion which can be accomplished (new markets having been systematically assimilated) by the relentlessly increasing stimulation of consumer wants. The long-term development of Modernity required that private and inner life ultimately become once again visible and quasi-public. This was not because the inner world of individuals was of any concern from the point of view of legal freedom or even the maintenance of public order and public decency, but because the wishes and fantasies that had developed within the uncensored freedom of the modern soul could be exploited, and indeed had to be exploited, by the imperious self-expansion of the commodity world. The soul became important (in a superficial sense, which, after all, was its most important sense) when it was discovered that the commodity world (the world of objectified body) depends upon its needs and wishes. Indeed, wants or needs, which originate in the secret recesses of the soul, became insignificant in comparison with the more accessible and mobile wishes that characterize contemporary experience. This makes the (purely human) object world once again an intimate part of personal existence.

In this process, however, Object and Subject have merged into a new interactive reality; Objects become carriers of meaning and identity, and Subjects experience themselves and the world as living objects. The duality in which Modernity was born and through which it declared its novelty no longer describes the reality of contemporary social life. Grasping this reality requires both the forging of new concepts adapted to new forms of life and the continuous revision of older vocabularies of thought. In spite of the accretion of long superseded forms of understanding that cling to the terms, Body, Soul, and Spirit offer the genuine possibility of gaining fresh insight into the distinctive character of the present.

DOMESTICATION OF
THE BAROQUE

Viewing Modernity in terms of the transformation of Body, Soul, and Spirit—rather than as Subject-Object relations—allows for a fuller understanding of both the genuine novelties in its development and the sense in which it depended upon the past. It provides, that is to say, the possibility of a genuinely historical view of the present. First, it seeks to illuminate novel features of modern society and culture in terms of the transformation of premodern social forms, ideologies, cultures, and, most significantly, modes of feeling. And, second, it suggests a conception of Modernity as itself a process of immanent development. This gives rise, in fact, to a descriptive account of Modernity in terms of three basic "stages," each distinguished by a characteristic pattern of institutionalization, cultural dynamics, and form of self-understanding: the early modern (Baroque), classical Modernity (bourgeois), and contemporary society (postmodernity). In this perspective, furthermore, the orthodox historiography of Modernity (geographically centered on northwestern Europe and socially on the rising bourgeois class) is redefined as a transitional stage between the early modern (located in the declining aristocracies of the Mediterranean and central Europe) and an emerging postmodern world (dispersed as a globalized and populist culture), which bear greater affinities with each other than does either to the normative model.

Baroque culture can now be seen, after a long period of neglect, to have been as fundamental to the character of Modernity as was the Enlightenment from which, more generally, cultural historians have taken their point of departure. The institutionalization of self-regulatory manners and the establishment of a rational scientific means of control of nature, including human nature, now seem remote from the spectacular and voluptuous forms of life and imagination that immediately preceded them. But a contemporary disillusionment with the many aspects of the scientific worldview and its implications encourages the reinvestigation of an age rich in anticipations of cultural discoveries we thought peculiarly our own. The Baroque, that is to say, might be viewed as simultaneously both premodern and postmodern.

Developing first and most completely in Spain, the Baroque is a culture incubated outside the main lines of historical development that, since the writings of Max Weber, have provided the basic points of reference for sociological investigations of the emergence of modern society. Spain during the first half of the seventeenth century was remote from those forces which, in northern and western Europe, were bringing capitalism and its bourgeois sobriety into prominence by sweeping aside the surviving forms of feudalism. The Baroque was formed within a decaying empire; it reflected upon a society responsible for the discovery and naming of a new world, but one whose period of growth and world domination had been over for some time. Its aristocratic ruling class was no longer insulated from criticism, and the prevention of popular insurrection became the major preoccupation of the state. Indeed, "everything that belongs to the Baroque emerges from the necessities of manipulating opinion and feelings on a broad public scale" (Maravall 1986).

The growth of a rootless population, together with the marked decline in Spain's political and cultural preeminence, gave a new urgency to the control of public opinion. But, while for northern and western Europe new mechanisms of self-control were institutionalized through religious and educational reforms (a culture within which science and humanism were identified as progressive elements), Baroque culture established direct techniques of mass control.

The presence of authority was everywhere made manifest, particularly in military establishments, public buildings, and palaces. The grandeur of Baroque building was designed to intimidate; it was part of the violence that constituted the "Baroque pedagogy of the sentiments." It was, above all, a society of the spectacle: its "aesthetic of exaggeration and surprise" was "invented to evoke wonder in the public." And its most significant and characteristic cultural form was the theater. The reversible identity of theatrical and public order, of art and life, became the "major vehicle for expressing the radical Baroque conviction that the phenomenal world is illusion" (Warnke 1972).

It is just this "Baroque sensualization of experience" which links Kepler and Cervantes and distinguishes them both from Descartes. It is a world, as Piero Camporesi has revealed in a series of remarkable studies, in which no absolute distinctions exist, in which forms flow continually into one another, where outside and inside interpenetrate, where every boundary remains sensuously indefinite, and whose hidden structure is defined by the scale and proportion of the human body. The body was torn open, revealed, anatomized, tortured, illustrated, and preserved: "The open cadaver, a dualistic image of perfection and decay, became the most genuine *momento mori* of the time" (Calvi 1989).

The "nightmare of universal putrefaction" was a terrifying vision of a lifelong struggle against the forces of nature. It was a form of sensuousness associated with catastrophic instability rather than with slow, vegetative decay. And because this dizziness affected all the senses, it was more terrifying and immediate than the most apocalyptic picture of reality. Not simply a vision, the overwhelming sense of chaos was also a "sublime olfactory deliria." Wrenched from the stability (or imagined stability) of premodern social life, everything became infected with turbulence.

Yet, simultaneously and without contradiction, the Baroque world was permeated by metaphysical tensions. The "paradoxical and the phantasmagoria" were everywhere in evidence; the popular trompe l'oeil in ceiling decoration was a playing with perspective techniques that could just as easily be used to create a false as a true impression. This kind of illusionism also highlights the Baroque fascination with infinity. Gilles Deleuze has characterized the Baroque imagination at its most metaphysical, in the writing of Leibniz, as an "operative function" which "endlessly produces folds . . . pushing them to infinity" (Deleuze 1993). Matter and soul are morphologically distinct aspects of the infinitely folded "muscular" continuity of Nature.

For the Baroque, that is to say, social world, body image, and nature are "open" and open to one another rather than "closed" homological structures. The Baroque anticipates all those characteristics of the modern age which we take to be most decisively postmodern: perspectivism, sensuousness, the interpenetration of soul and body, the merging of spatial and temporal categories, the superficiality and theatricality of social life, the "feminization" of philosophy, art, and religion with all that it entails for the reorientation of the subject toward reality in terms of immediacy rather than of reflection, and, above all, the preeminence of the human body in every experience of life. The interrupted tradition of Modernity, linking the culture of the Baroque with contemporary fashion, not only contextualizes the otherwise incomprehensible fragmentation of the present, it redefines the rationality of the classical bourgeois world as a deviation from the normative pluralism characteristic of its origins.

Contemporary society, however, is not simply a resurgence of the Baroque. The Baroque festival of the body was a demonstration of the absolute superiority of the state over each of its (inherently rebellious) subjects; contemporary sensuousness, however, is possible just because it is inconsequential. To parody Max Weber, it might be said that while the Baroque masses were forced to be distracted, the modern public wants to be. The difference lies essentially in the triumph of a distinctively bourgeois principle of self-regulation, a principle which became so well established that it was viewed simply as the "natural" predisposition of the body. For the Baroque era, however, it was not yet clear that modern society would become self-regulating. The liberation from feudal forms of constraint and the consequential mobility of the populace on a hitherto unknown scale posed a genuine threat to social stability. It was only gradually that the inefficiency of Baroque techniques of constraint gave way to the institutionalization of the market and to powerful new means of social control through rational self-regulation. Once deprived of all means of self-preservation other than through the exchange of commodities, the populace could gradually be released from external forms of mass constraint and progressively integrated into modern society through the contract of work. Everyone was free to act as they willed; reason dictated that they willed to work. This fundamental, and ingeniously concealed, mode of domination rendered obsolete the more spectacular Baroque techniques of coercion and the manipulation of public opinion. Thus, whereas the public magnificence and spectacle of the Baroque era were a state policy predicated on fear and distrust of the masses, the contemporary "culture of excess" is predicated on the dynamic (and presumed beneficial) consequences of private consumption.

THE PARADOX OF MODERNITY

The whole development of Modernity, nonetheless, can be grasped as the continuous unfolding of the fundamental postulate of human self-autonomy. This demanded a radical transformation in people's orientation to the world, to each other, and to themselves. Expressed in terminology that was itself the product of this transformation, the symbolic unity of creation fell apart into the categorical opposition and dualities of Subject/Object, Self/Other, and Ego/World. In these terms Modernity was established over any alternative position, all of which, as ignorance, superstition, nostalgia, conservatism, became conceived as the illegitimate claims of the past and the authority of tradition.

From the larger perspective of Body, Soul, and Spirit, however, the postulate of human self-autonomy reveals itself as inherently self-limiting and incomplete. This is not a matter simply of adopting a premodern perspective and, in a willful and artificial manner, inverting the judgments of

Modernity. Body, Soul, and Spirit are immanent to Modernity, and the transformation in each, in a distinctive way, reveals its radical novelty. At the same time, however, reflection on each runs up against realities that cannot be assimilated to such an understanding of Modernity. It is not the illusory survivals of a premodern era but the rationally incomprehensible character of present experience that confounds the project of Modernity.

For Modernity, thus, Body becomes a simple material substance, a self-sufficient object. But every effort to grasp the body as "nothing but" materiality ends in bewildering contradiction. To experience the body—the body-in-itself—means to construct an image, which is itself part of a complex history of such images. Even if we surrender to what we take to be the immediate sensuousness of the body, we do so only through the intermediary of cultural constructs that make such an experience possible. We cannot "reach" the materiality of the body, in spite of declaring it to be the fundamental, indeed, the only, reality. Yet even as we construct such images, we are aware of our bodies as a dark presence which eludes representation. Considering the most commonplace aspects of experience—the experience of the body—raises issues that cannot be stated, far less resolved, through a discourse of Modernity established in the "self-evident" division of subject and object. The fundamental postulate of Modernity, which can be expressed in the notion of the sovereignty of experience, immediately betrays itself; the universal experience of the body is incomprehensible and undermines every effort to establish human self-understanding on the basis of empirical science and the transparency of reason.

Equally, Soul, withdrawing into the individuated interiority of the wholly modern human subject, is crystallized in every psychic activity and function. However, in thus becoming concrete, the soul continues, albeit in a new way as the search for authenticity, to be the focus of older conceptions of reality. And Spirit, illuminating itself as history and culture, far from providing modern human beings with the means to rational self-development and control of their own nature, persists enigmatically as a self-created domain of both alienation and happiness.

Bibliography

Abrams, M. B. 1971. *Natural Supernaturalism: Tradition and Revolution in Romantic Literature*. Oxford: Oxford Univ. Press.

Adkins, A. W. H. 1970. *From the Many to the One*. London: Constable.

Amiel, Henri-Frédéric. 1906. *Amiel's Journal*. Trans. Mrs. Humphry Ward. London: Macmillan.

Ariès, Philippe. 1983. *The Hour of Our Death*. Harmondsworth: Penguin.

Aristotle. 1912. *The Works of Aristotle*. Vol. 5. Ed. J. A. Smith and W. D. Ross. Oxford: Oxford Univ. Press.

Armstrong, A. H. 1986. *Classical Mediterranean Spirituality*. London: Routledge.

Auerbach, Erich. 1968. *Mimesis: The Representation of Reality in Western Literature*. Trans. Willard R. Trask. Princeton: Princeton Univ. Press.

Bakhtin, Mikhail. 1968. *Rabelais and His World*. Trans. H. Iswolsky. Cambridge: Harvard Univ. Press.

Bataille, Georges. 1989. *Theory of Religion*. Trans. Robert Hurley. New York: Zone Books.

Beard, George M. 1881. *American Nervousness: Its Causes and Consequences*. New York: G. P. Putnam.

Belting, Hans. 1994. *Likeness and Presence: A History of the Image before the Era of Art*. Trans. Edmund Jephcott. Chicago: Univ. of Chicago Press.

Benjamin, Walter. 1973. *Illuminations*. Trans. Harry Zohn. London: Fontana.

Bergson, Henri. 1935. *The Two Sources of Morality and Religion*. Trans. R. Ashley Auda and Cloudesley Brereton. London: Macmillan.

———. 1995. *Matter and Memory*. New York: Zone.

Bernheim, H. 1980. *Bernheim's New Studies in Hypnotism*. Trans. Richard S. Sander. New York: International Universities Press.

Binet, Alfred. 1977. 1st French ed. 1890, 1896. *Alterations of Personality / On Double Consciousness*. Ed. Daniel N. Robinson. Washington, D.C.: Univ. Publications of America.

Bloch, Marc. 1965. *Feudal Society*. 2 vols. Trans. L. A. Manyon. London: Routledge and Kegan Paul.

Blumenberg, Hans. 1983. *The Legitimacy of the Modern Age*. Trans. Robert M. Wallace. Cambridge and London: M.I.T. Press.

———. 1987. *Genesis of the Copernican Revolution*. Trans. Robert M. Wallace. Cambridge and London: M.I.T. Press.

Boltzmann, Ludwig. 1974. *Theoretical Physics and Philosophical Problems*. Ed. Brian McGuinness. Dordrecht and Boston: Reidel.

Bourdieu, Pierre. 1986. *Distinction*. Trans. Richard Nice. London: Routledge.

Bousquet, Jacques. 1964. *Les thèmes du rêve dans la littérature romantique*. Paris: Didier.

Braudel, Fernand. 1983. *The Wheels of Commerce*. Trans. Siân Reynolds. London: Collins.

Brewer, John, and Roy Porter, eds. 1993. *Consumption and the World of Goods*. London: Routledge.

Brown, Peter. 1988. *The Body and Society: Men, Women, and Sexual Renunciation in Early Christianity*. New York: Columbia Univ. Press.

Burckhardt, Jacob. 1990. *The Civilization of the Renaissance in Italy*. Trans. S. G. C. Middelmore. Harmondsworth: Penguin.

Burnet, John. 1929. *Essays and Addresses*. London: Chatto and Windus.

Burton, Ernest Dewitt. 1918. *Spirit, Soul, and Flesh*. Chicago: Univ. of Chicago Press.

Burton, Robert. 1932. *The Anatomy of Melancholy*. 3 vols. London: Dent.

Buytendijk, F. J. J. 1994. *Prolegomena to a Phenomenological Physiology*. Pittsburgh: Duquesne Univ. Press.

Bynum, Caroline Walker. 1987. *Holy Feast and Holy Fast: The Religious Significance of Food to Medieval Women*. Berkeley and London: Univ. of California Press.

———. 1992. *Fragmentation and Redemption: Essays on Gender and the Human in Body in Medieval Religion*. New York: Zone Books.

———. 1995. *The Resurrection of the Body in Western Christianity, 200–1336*. New York: Columbia Univ. Press.

Caillois, Roger. 1939. *L'homme et le sacré*. Paris: Presses de France.

———. 1966. "Logical and Philosophical Problems of the Dream." In *The Dream and Human Societies*, ed. G. E. von Grunebaum and Roger Caillois. Berkeley and Los Angeles: Univ. of California Press.

Camporesi, Piero. 1994. *The Anatomy of the Senses: Natural Symbols in Medieval and Early Modern Italy.* Trans. Allan Cameron. Cambridge and Oxford: Polity Press.

Cassirer, Ernst. 1953. *The Platonic Renaissance in England.* Trans. James P. Pettegrove. London: Nelson.

Castells, Manuel. 1997. *The Rise of Network Society.* Oxford: Blackwell.

Charcot, Jean-Martin. 1889. *Clinical Lectures on the Diseases of the Nervous System.* 3 vols. Trans. Thomas Savill. London: New Sydenham Society.

———. 1987. *Charcot the Clinician: The Tuesday Lessons, 1887/88.* Trans. and commentary Christopher G. Gretz. New York: Raven Books.

Claus, David B. 1981. *Towards the Soul.* New Haven and London: Yale Univ. Press.

Copenhaver, Brian P., and Charles B. Schmit, eds. 1992. *Renaissance Philosophy.* Oxford: Oxford Univ. Press.

Couliano, Ioan P. 1987. *Eros and Magic in the Renaissance.* Trans. Margaret Cook. Chicago and London: Univ. of Chicago Press.

Crombie, A. C. 1995. *Styles in Scientific Thinking.* 3 vols. Cambridge: Cambridge Univ. Press.

David-Ménard, David. 1988. *Hysteria from Freud to Lacan.* Trans. Catherine Porter. Ithaca and London: Cornell Univ. Press.

Deleuze, Gilles. 1991. *Bergsonism.* Trans. Hugh Toulman. New York: Zone.

———. 1993. *The Fold: Leibniz and the Baroque.* Trans. Tom Conley. London: Athlone Press.

Deleuze, Gilles, and Felix Guattari. 1977. *Anti-Oedipus: Capitalism and Schizophrenia.* Trans. Robert Hurley. New York: Viking Press.

Descartes, René. 1984. *The Philosophical Writings of Descartes.* Vol. 1. Ed. John Cottingham, Robert Strothoff, and Dugald Murdoch. Cambridge: Cambridge Univ. Press.

———. 1985. *The Philosophical Writings of Descartes.* Vol. 2. Ed. John Cottingham, Robert Strothoff, and Dugald Murdoch. Cambridge: Cambridge Univ. Press.

Dodds, E. R. 1951. *The Greeks and the Irrational.* Berkeley and Los Angeles: Univ. of California Press.

Donzelot, Jacques. 1980. *The Policing of Families: Welfare versus the State.* London: Hutchinson.

Dostoevsky, Fyodor. 1972. *Notes from Underground / The Double.* Trans. Jessie Coulson. Harmondsworth: Penguin.

Douglas, Mary. 1970. *Purity and Danger.* Harmondsworth: Penguin.

———. 1972. *Natural Symbols.* Harmondsworth: Penguin.

duBois, Page. 1988. *Sowing the Body: Psychoanalysis and Ancient Representations of Women.* Chicago and London: Univ. of Chicago Press.

Duby, George. 1980. *The Three Orders: Feudal Society Imagined.* Chicago: Univ. of Chicago Press.

Durkheim, Emile. 1995. *The Elementary Forms of Religious Life.* Trans. Karen E. Fields. New York: Free Press.

Edgerton, Samuel Y., Jr. 1991. *The Heritage of Giotto's Geometry.* New York: Cornell Univ. Press.

Elaide, Mircea. 1959. *The Sacred and the Profane: The Nature of Religion.* Trans. Willard R. Trask. New York: Harcourt, Brace and Company.

Elias, Norbert. 1978. *The Civilizing Process.* Vol. 1. *The History of Manners.* Trans. E. Jephcott. Oxford: Blackwell.

———. 1991. *The Society of Individuals.* Oxford: Basil Blackwell.

Ellenberger, Henri F. 1970. *The Discovery of the Unconscious.* London: Allen Lane.

Fabian, Johannes. 1983. *Time and the Other: How Anthropology Makes Its Object.* New York: Columbia Univ. Press.

Fenves, Peter. 1993. *"Chatter": Language and History in Kierkegaard.* Stanford: Stanford Univ. Press.

Ferguson, Harvie. 1992. *Religious Transformation in Western Society: The End of Happiness.* London: Routledge.

———. 1996. *The Lure of Dreams: Sigmund Freud and the Construction of Modernity.* London: Routledge.

———. 1997. "Me and My Shadows: On the Accumulation of Body-Images in Western Society." Parts 1 and 2. *Body and Society* 3 (3):1–31 and 3 (4):1–31.

Foucault, Michel. 1977. *Discipline and Punish: The Birth of the Prison.* Trans. Alan Sheridan. London: Allen Lane.

Foucault, Michel, and Ludwig Binswanger. 1993. *Dream and Existence.* Ed. Keith Hoeller. Trans. Forrest Williams and Jacob Needleman. Atlantic Highlands: Humanities Press.

Freud, Sigmund. 1953–74. *The Complete Psychological Works of Sigmund Freud.* 24 vols. Ed. and trans. James Strachey with Anna Freud, Alix Strachey, and Alan Tyson. London: Hogarth Press and the Institute of Psycho-Analysis.

Friedländer, Paul. 1958. *Plato.* 3 vols. Trans. Hans Meyerhoff. London: Routledge and Kegan Paul.

Gadamer, Hans-Georg. 1996. *The Enigma of Health.* Trans. Jason Gaiger and Nicholas Walker. Stanford: Stanford Univ. Press.

Garin, Eugenio. 1983. *Astrology in the Renaissance: The Zodiac of Life*. London: Routledge and Kegan Paul.

Gauld, Alan. 1992. *A History of Hypnotism*. Cambridge: Cambridge Univ. Press.

Gay, Peter. 1986a. *Education of the Senses*. Oxford: Oxford Univ. Press.

———. 1986b. *The Tender Passion*. Oxford: Oxford Univ. Press.

———. 1993. *The Cultivation of Hatred*. New York and London: Norton.

———. 1995. *The Naked Heart*. New York and London: Norton.

Gehlen, Arnold. 1988. *Man: His Nature and Place in the World*. Trans. Clare McMilan and Karl Pillener. New York: Columbia Univ. Press.

Gent, Lucy, and Nigel Llewellyn, eds. 1990. *Renaissance Bodies: The Human Figure in English Culture, c. 1540–1660*. London: Reaktion Books.

Gernet, Louis. 1981. *The Anthropology of Ancient Greece*. Trans. John Hamilton and Blaise Nagy. Baltimore and London: Johns Hopkins Univ. Press.

Giedion, Siegfried. 1948. *Mechanization Takes Command*. New York: Oxford Univ. Press.

Gilson, Etienne. 1936. *The Spirit of Medieval Philosophy*. London: Sheed and Ward.

Girard, René. 1965. *Deceit, Desire, and the Novel: Self and Other in Literary Structure*. Trans. Yvonne Freccero. Baltimore and London: Johns Hopkins Univ. Press.

Goldmann, Lucien. 1964. *The Hidden God*. London: Routledge.

Goldstein, Kurt. 1939. *The Organism*. New York: American Book Company.

Greenblatt, Stephen. 1980. *Renaissance Self-Fashioning: From More to Shakespeare*. Chicago and London: Univ. of Chicago Press.

Gurevich, A. J. 1985. *Categories of Medieval Culture*. Trans. G. L. Campbell. London: Routledge and Kegan Paul.

Gusdorf, Georges. 1948. *La découverte de soi*. Paris: Presses Universitaires de France.

———. 1982. *Fondemants du savoir romantique*. Paris: Payot.

———. 1983. *Du néant á dieu dans le savoir romantique*. Paris: Payot.

———. 1984. *L'homme romantique*. Paris: Payot.

———. 1985. *Le savoir romantique de la nature*. Paris: Payot.

Habermas, Jurgen. 1987. *The Philosophical Discourse of Modernity*. Trans. Frederick Lawrence. Cambridge: Polity.

Hacking, Ian. 1995. *Rewriting the Soul: Multiple Personality and the Sciences of Memory*. Princeton: Princeton Univ. Press.

Hale, John. 1994. *The Civilization of Europe in the Renaissance*. London: Fontana.

Hallyn, Fernand. 1990. *The Poetic Structure of the World: Copernicus and Kepler*. Trans. Donald M. Leslie. New York: Zone.

Haren, M. 1985. *Medieval Thought: The Western Intellectual Tradition from Antiquity to the Thirteenth Century.* London: Macmillan.

Hartley, David. 1810. *Observations on Man.* 5th ed. Bath: R. Cruttwell.

Head, Henry. 1920. *Studies in Neurology.* 2 vols. London: Henry Frowde.

———. 1926. *Aphasia: and Kindred Disorders of Speech.* Cambridge: Cambridge Univ. Press.

Hegel, G. W. F. 1977. *Phenomenology of Spirit.* Trans. A. V. Miller. Oxford: Oxford Univ. Press.

Hendry, John. 1986. *James Clerk Maxwell and the Theory of Electromagnetic Field.* Bristol and Boston: Hilger.

Heninger, S. K., Jr. 1974. *Touches of Sweet Harmony: Pythagorean Cosmology and Renaissance Poetics.* San Marino: Huntington Library.

———. 1977. *The Cosmographical Glass: Renaissance Diagrams of the Universe.* San Marino: Huntington Library.

Hennis, Wilhelm. 1988. *Max Weber: Essays in Reconstruction.* Trans. Keith Tribe. London: Allen and Unwin.

Hersey, G. L. 1976. *Pythagorean Palaces: Magic and Architecture in the Italian Renaissance.* Ithaca: Cornell Univ. Press.

Hertz, Robert. 1960. *Death and the Right Hand.* London: Cohen and West.

Holmes, Richard. 1985. *Firing Line.* London: Jonathan Cape.

Husserl, Edmund. 1989. *Ideas Pertaining to a Pure Phenomenology and to a Phenomenological Philosophy: Second Book.* Trans. Richard Rojcewick and André Schuwer. Dordrecht, Boston, and London: Kluwer.

Hynes, Samuel. 1998. *The Soldier's Tale.* London: Pimlico.

Jackson, John Hughlings. 1931. *Selected Writings of John Hughlings Jackson.* Ed. James Taylor. 2 vols. London: Hodder and Stoughton.

Janet, Pierre. 1898. *Névroses et idées fixes.* 2 vols. Paris: Alcan.

———. 1925. *Psychological Healing: A Historical and Clinical Study.* 2 vols. Trans. Eden and Cedar Paul. London: George Allen and Unwin.

———. 1965. *The Major Symptoms of Hysteria.* New York and London: Hafner.

———. 1977. 1st French ed. 1901. *The Mental State of Hystericals.* Ed. Daniel N. Robinson. Trans. Caroline Rollin Carson. Washington, D.C.: Univ. Publications of America.

Jaspers, Karl. 1963. *General Psychopathology.* Trans. J. Hoenig and Marion W. Hamilton. Manchester: Manchester Univ. Press.

Judovitz, Dahlia. 1988. *Subjectivity and Representation in Descartes: The Origins of Modernity.* Cambridge: Cambridge Univ. Press.

Kenny, Michael G. 1986. *The Passion of Ansel Bourne: Multiple Personality in American Culture.* Washington, D.C., and London: Smithsonian Institution Press.

Kern, S. 1983. *The Culture of Time and Space, 1880–1918.* Cambridge: Harvard Univ. Press.

Kierkegaard, Søren. 1978. *Two Ages.* Trans. and ed. Howard V. Hong and Edna H. Hong. Princeton: Princeton Univ. Press.

———. 1980. *The Sickness unto Death.* Trans. and ed. Howard V. Hong and Edna H. Hong. Princeton: Princeton Univ. Press.

———. 1990. *Eighteen Upbuilding Discourses.* Trans. and ed. Howard V. Hong and Edna H. Hong. Princeton: Princeton Univ. Press.

———. 1992. *Concluding Unscientific Postscript to Philosophical Fragments.* 2 vols. Trans. and ed. Howard V. Hong and Edna H. Hong. Princeton: Princeton Univ. Press.

King, John Owen, III. 1983. *The Iron of Melancholy.* Middletown: Wesleyan Univ. Press.

Kirschner, Suzanne R. 1996. *The Religious and Romantic Origins of Psychoanalysis.* Cambridge: Cambridge Univ. Press.

Kolb, Lawrence C. 1954. *The Painful Phantom.* Springfield: Charles C. Thomas.

Koyré, Alexandre. 1957. *From the Closed World to the Infinite Universe.* Baltimore and London: Johns Hopkins Univ. Press.

———. 1965. *Newtonian Studies.* London: Chapman and Hall.

———. 1978. *Galileo Studies.* Trans. John Mepham. Hassocks: Harvester.

Kristeva, Julia. 1989. *Black Sun: Depression and Melancholia.* Trans. Leon S. Roudiez. New York: Columbia Univ. Press.

———. 1991. *Strangers to Ourselves.* Trans. Leon S. Roudiez. New York: Columbia Univ. Press.

La Mettrie, Julien Offray de. 1912. 1st ed. 1747. *L'homme machine.* Ed. Aram Vartanian. Princeton: Princeton Univ. Press.

Lear, John. 1965. *Kepler's Dream.* Berkeley and Los Angeles: Univ. of California Press.

Leclerq, Jean. 1978. *The Love of Learning and the Desire for God.* London: S.P.C.K.

Le Goff, Jacques. 1980. *Time, Work, and Culture in the Middle Ages.* Chicago and London: Univ. of Chicago Press.

———. 1984. *The Birth Of Purgatory.* Trans. Arthur Goldhammer. London: Scolar Press.

Lenoir, Timothy. 1982. *The Strategy of Life.* Dordrecht, Boston, and London: D. Reidel.

Leppert, Richard. 1993. *The Sight of Sound: Music, Representation, and the History of the Body.* Berkeley and London: Univ. of California Press.

———. 1996. *Art and the Committed Eye: The Cultural Functions of Imagination.* Boulder and London: Westview Press.

Le Rider, Jacques. 1993. *Modernity and Crisis of Identity: Culture and Society in Fin-de-Siècle Vienna.* Trans. Rosemary Morris. New York: Continuum.

Lesky, Erna. 1976. *The Vienna Medical School of the 19th Century.* Trans. L. Williams and I. S. Levy. Baltimore and London: Johns Hopkins Univ. Press.

Lévinas, Emmanuel. 1961. *Totality and Infinity: An Essay on Exteriority.* Trans. A. Lingis. Pittsburgh: Univ. of Duquesne Press.

———. 1973. *The Theory of Intuition in Husserl's Phenomenology.* Trans. André Orianne. Evanston: Northwestern Univ. Press.

Lévi-Strauss, Claude. 1966. *The Savage Mind.* London: Weidenfeld and Nicolson.

Lhermitte, Jean. 1960. *L'image de notre corps.* Paris: Nouvelle Revue Critique.

Lockridge, Laurence S. 1989. *The Ethics of Romanticism.* Cambridge: Cambridge Univ. Press.

Lovejoy, Arthur O. 1960. *The Great Chain of Being.* New York: Harper.

Löwith, Karl. 1949. *Meaning in History.* Chicago and London: Univ. of Chicago Press.

———. 1964. *From Hegel to Nietzsche: The Revolution in Nineteenth-Century Thought.* Trans. David E. Green. London: Constable.

———. 1982. *Max Weber and Karl Marx.* Trans. Hans Fantel. London: Allen and Unwin.

Löwy, Michael, and Robert Sayre. 1992. *Révolte et mélancolie.* Paris: Editions Payot.

Lull, Ramon. 1970. "The Book on the Order of Chivalry." In *The History of Feudalism,* ed. David Herlihy. London: Macmillan.

McGrath, William J. 1986. *Freud's Discovery of Psychoanalysis: The Politics of Hysteria.* Ithaca and London: Cornell Univ. Press.

McNish, Robert. 1830. *The Philosophy of Sleep.* Glasgow: W. R. M'Phun.

Mann, Thomas. 1960. *The Magic Mountain.* Trans. H. T. Lowe-Porter. Harmondsworth: Penguin.

Maravall, José Antonio. 1986. *Culture of the Baroque.* Trans. Terry Cochran. Manchester: Manchester Univ. Press.

Marcel, Gabriel. 1949. *Being and Having.* Trans. Katharine Farrer. Westminster: Dacre Press.

Marx, Karl. 1973. *Surveys from Exile.* Ed. David Fernback. Harmondsworth: Penguin.

——. 1975. *Early Writings*. Ed. Lucio Colletti. Harmondsworth: Penguin.

——. 1976. *Capital*. Vol. 1. Trans. Ben Fowkes. Harmondsworth: Penguin.

Matuštík, Martinus, and Merold Westphal, eds. 1995. *Kierkegaard in Post/Modernity*. Urbana: Indiana Univ. Press.

Merleau-Ponty, Maurice. 1962. *The Phenomenology of Perception*. Trans. Colin Smith. London: Routledge and Kegan Paul.

Meyerson, Emile. 1930. *Identity and Reality*. Trans. Kate Lowenberg. London: Allen and Unwin.

Miller, Daniel. 1987. *Material Culture and Mass Consumption*. Oxford: Blackwell.

Miller, Michael B. 1981. *The Bon Marché: Bourgeois Culture and the Department Store, 1869–1920*. Princeton: Princeton Univ. Press.

Mitchell, S. Weir. 1872. *Injuries of Nerves and Their Consequences*. Philadelphia: J. B. Lippinott and Co.

Montaigne, Michel de. 1991. *The Essays of Michel de Montaigne*. Trans. and ed. with notes by M. A. Screech. London: Allen Lane, Penguin Press.

Moretti, Franco. 1987. *The Way of the World: The Bildungsroman in European Culture*. London: Verso.

Morris, David B. 1991. *The Culture of Pain*. Berkeley and Los Angeles: Univ. of California Press.

Mosse, George L. 1990. *Fallen Soldiers: Reshaping the Memory of the World Wars*. New York and Oxford: Oxford Univ. Press.

Musil, Robert. 1995. *The Man without Qualities*. 2 vols. Trans. Sophie Wilkins. New York and London: Alfred A. Knopf and Picador.

Needham, Rodney, ed. 1973. *Right and Left: Essays in Dual Symbolic Classification*. Chicago and London: Univ. of Chicago Press.

Newton, Isaac. 1931. 1st ed. 1704. *Opticks*. London: Bell.

Nietzsche, Friedrich. 1961. *Thus Spoke Zarathustra*. Trans. R. J. Hollingdale. Harmondsworth: Penguin.

——. 1967. *On the Genealogy of Morals / Ecce Homo*. Trans. Walter Kaufmann and R. J. Hollingdale. New York: Vintage.

——. 1968. *The Will to Power*. Trans. Walter Kaufmann and R. J. Hollingdale. New York: Vintage.

——. 1973. *Beyond Good and Evil*. Trans. R. J. Hollingdale. Harmondsworth: Penguin.

——. 1974. *The Gay Science*. Trans. Walter Kaufmann. New York: Vintage.

Nyhart, Lynn K. 1995. *Biology Takes Form: Animal Morphology and the German Universities, 1800–1900*. Chicago: Univ. of Chicago Press.

Onians, Richard Broxton. 1951. *The Origin of European Thought: About the Body, the Mind, the Soul, the World, Time, and Fate.* Cambridge: Cambridge Univ. Press.

Otto, Walter F. 1954. *The Homeric Gods: The Spiritual Significance of Greek Religion.* Trans. Moses Hadas. London: Thames and Hudson.

Pagden, Anthony, ed. 1993. *European Encounters with the New World.* New Haven and London: Yale Univ. Press.

Pannenberg, Wolfhart. 1985. *Anthropology in Theological Perspective.* Trans. Matthew J. O'Connell. Philadelphia: Westminster Press.

Panofsky, Erwin. 1991. *Perspective as Symbolic Form.* Trans. Christopher S. Wood. New York: Zone Books.

Pascal, Blaise. 1966. *Pensées.* Trans. A. J. Krailsheimer. Harmondsworth: Penguin.

Peursen, C. A. von. 1966. *Body, Soul, Spirit.* London: Oxford Univ. Press.

Plato. 1965. *Timaeu and Critias.* Trans. Desmond Lee. Harmondsworth: Penguin.

———. 1973. *Phaedrus and Letters VII and VIII.* Trans. Walter Hamilton. Harmondsworth: Penguin.

———. 1974. *The Republic.* Trans. Desmond Lee. Harmondsworth: Penguin.

———. 1993. *Phaedo.* Trans. David Gallop. Oxford: Oxford Univ. Press.

Prince, Morton. 1906. *The Dissociation of a Personality.* New York and London: Longman, Green and Co.

———, ed. 1910. *Psychotherapeutics: A Symposium.* London: Longman, Green and Co.

Rabibnach, Anson. 1990. *The Human Motor: Energy, Fatigue, and the Origins of Modernity.* Berkeley and Los Angeles: Univ. of California Press.

Rad, Gerhard von. 1972. *Genesis: A Commentary.* Trans. John H. Marks. London: S.C.M. Press.

Ribot, Théodule Armand. 1882. *Diseases of Memory.* New York: D. Appleton and Company.

Ricoeur, Paul. 1967. *Husserl: An Analysis of His Phenomenology.* Trans. Edward G. Ballard and Lester E. Embre. Evanston: Northwestern Univ. Press.

———. 1970. *Freud and Philosophy: An Essay in Interpretation.* Trans. Denis Savage. New Haven and London: Yale Univ. Press.

———. 1986. *Fallible Man.* Trans. Charles A. Kelbley. New York: Fordham Univ. Press.

———. 1992. *Oneself as Another.* Trans. Kathleen Blamey. Chicago: Univ. of Chicago Press.

———. 1995. "Imagination in Discourse and in Action." In *Rethinking Imagination: Culture and Creativity,* ed. Gillian Robinson and Jouhn Rundell. London: Routledge.

Rohde, Erwin. 1925. 1st ed. 1893. *Psyche: The Cult of Souls and Belief in Immortality among the Greeks.* Trans. W. B. Hillis. London: Kegan, Paul, Trench and Trubner.

Rossi, Paolo. 1970. *Philosophy, Technology, and the Arts in the Early Modern Era.* Trans. Sacha Rabinovitch, New York: Harper and Row.

Roth, Guenther, and Wolfgang Schluchter. 1979. *Max Weber's Vision of History.* Berkeley and Los Angeles: Univ. of California Press.

Rousseau, Jean-Jacques. 1953. *The Confession of Jean-Jacques Rousseau.* Trans. J. M. Cohen. Harmondsworth: Penguin.

Rummel, R. J. 1994. *Death by Government.* New Brunswick and London: Transaction Publishers.

Sacks, Oliver. 1985. *The Man Who Mistook His Wife for a Hat.* New York: Summit Books.

Sade, marquis de. 1991. *Juliette.* Trans. Austryn Wainhouse. London: Arrow.

Said, Edward T. 1978. *Orientalism.* London: Routledge and Kegan Paul.

Sartre, Jean-Paul. 1958. *Being and Nothingness.* Trans. Hazel E. Barnes. London: Routledge and Kegan Paul.

Saussure, Ferdinand de. 1966. *Course in General Linguistics.* Trans. W. Baskin. New York: McGraw Hill.

Sawday, Jonathan. 1995. *The Body Emblazoned: Dissection and the Human Body in Renaissance Culture.* London: Routledge.

Scarry, Elaine. 1985. *The Body in Pain.* New York and Oxford: Oxford Univ. Press.

Scheler, Max. 1987. *Person and Self-Value.* Trans. M. S. Fringly. Dordrecht and Lancaster: Nijhoff.

Schilder, Paul. 1953. 1st German ed. 1923. *Medical Psychology.* Trans. and ed. David Rapaport. New York: International Universities Press.

———. 1938. *Psychotherapy.* London: Kegan Paul, Trench, Trubner and Co.

———. 1942. *Mind: Perception and Thought in Their Constructive Aspects.* New York: Columbia Univ. Press.

———. 1964a. 1st ed. 1935. *The Image and Appearance of the Human Body: Studies in the Constructive Energies of the Psyche.* New York: John Wiley and Sons.

———. 1964b. *Contributions to Developmental Neuropsychiatry.* Ed. Lauretta Bender. London: Tavistock.

Schluchter, Wolfgang. 1996. *Paradoxes of Modernity: Culture and Conduct in the Theory of Max Weber.* Trans. Neil Solomon. Stanford: Stanford Univ. Press.

Schmitt, Carl. 1986. *Political Romanticism.* Trans. Guy Oakes. Cambridge: M.I.T. Press.

Schorske, Carl E. 1980. *Fin-de-Siècle Vienna: Politics and Culture.* London: Weidenfeld and Nicolson.

Sidis, Boris, and Simon P. Goodhart. 1905. *Multiple Personality.* New York: D. Appleton and Company.

Snell, Bruno. 1953. *The Discovery of the Mind: The Greek Origins of European Thought.* Cambridge: Harvard Univ. Press.

Sontag, Susan. 1978. *Illness as Metaphor.* New York: Farrar, Straus and Giroux.

Spragens, Thomas A. 1973. *The Politics of Motion: The World of Thomas Hobbes.* London: Croom Helm.

Starobinski, Jean. 1985. *Montaigne in Motion.* Trans. Arthur Goldhammer. Chicago: Chicago Univ. Press.

———. 1988. *Jean-Jacques Rousseau: Transparency and Obstruction.* Trans. Arthur Goldhammer. Chicago and London: Univ. of Chicago Press.

Stoichita, Victor I. 1995. *Visionary Experience in the Golden Age of Spanish Art.* London: Reaktion Books.

———. 1997. *A Short History of the Shadow.* London: Reaktion Books.

Storch, Alfred. 1924. *The Primitive Archaic Forms of Inner Experiences and Thought in Schizophrenia.* Trans. Clara Willard. New York and Washington, D.C.: Nervous and Mental Diseases Publishing Company.

Strasser, Stephen. 1957. *The Soul in Metaphysical and Empirical Psychology.* Pittsburgh: Duquesne Univ. Press.

———. 1977. *Phenomenology of Feeling.* Pittsburgh: Duquesne Univ. Press.

Straus, Erwin. 1963. *The Primary World of Senses: A Vindication of Sensory Experience.* Trans. Jacob Needleman. New York and London: Free Press and Collier-Macmillan.

———. 1966. *Phenomenological Psychology.* London: Tavistock.

Sulloway, Frank J. 1992. *Freud, Biologist of the Mind.* New York. Basic Books.

Thackray, Arnold. 1970. *Atoms and Powers.* Oxford: Oxford Univ. Press.

Tieck, Ludwig. 1831. *The Old Man of the Mountain.* London.

Tocqueville, Alexis de. 1968. *Democracy in America.* 2 vols. Trans. George Lawrence. London: Fontana.

Trinkaus, Charles. 1970. *In Our Image and Likeness: Humanity and Divinity in Italian Humanist Thought.* 2 vols. London: Constable.

Uexküll, J. von. 1926. *Theoretical Biology.* London: Kegan Paul and Trubner.

Vartanian, Aram. 1953. *Diderot and Descartes.* Princeton: Princeton Univ. Press.

Veith, Ilza. 1965. *Hysteria: A History of a Disease.* Chicago and London: Univ. of Chicago Press.

Vernant, Jean-Pierre. 1991. *Mortals and Immortals: Collected Essays*. Ed. Froma Zeitlin. Princeton: Princeton Univ. Press.

Vööbus, Arthur. 1958, 1960, 1988. *History of Asceticism in the Syrian Orient*. 3 vols. Louvain: Secretariat du Corpus SCO.

Warnke, Frank J. 1972. *Versions of the Baroque: European Literature in the Seventeenth Century*. New Haven and London: Yale Univ. Press.

Weber, Max. 1948. *From Max Weber: Essays in Sociology*. Ed. and trans. H. H. Gerth and C. Wright Mills. London: Routledge and Kegan Paul.

——. 1949. *The Methodology of the Social Sciences*. Trans. and ed. Edward A. Shils and Henry A. Finch. New York: Free Press.

——. 1952. *Ancient Judaism*. Trans. Hans H. Gerth and Don Martindale. New York: Free Press.

——. 1975. *Roscher and Knies: The Logical Problems of Historical Economics*. Trans. Guy Oakes. New York and London: Free Press.

——. 1976. *The Protestant Ethic and the Spirit of Capitalism*. Trans. Talcott Parsons. London: George Allen and Unwin.

Weinstein, Arnold. 1981. *Fictions of the Self, 1550–1800*. Princeton: Princeton Univ. Press.

Werner, Heinz. 1957. *Comparative Psychology of Mental Development*. New York: International Universities Press.

Westphal, Merold. 1987. *Kierkegaard's Critique of Reason and Society*. Macon: Mercer Univ. Press.

White, John. 1987. *The Birth and Rebirth of Pictorial Space*. London: Faber and Faber.

Whitebook, Joel. 1996. *Perversion and Utopia*. Cambridge and London: M.I.T. Press.

Williams, Rosalind H. 1982. *Dream Worlds: Mass Consumption in Late Nineteenth-Century France*. Berkeley and Los Angeles: Univ. of California Press.

Yack, Bernard. 1986. *The Longing for Total Revolution*. Princeton: Princeton Univ. Press.

Yates, Frances. 1964. *Giordano Bruno and the Hermetic Tradition*. London: Routledge and Kegan Paul.

Index

Alienation, 152, 153

Alterity, 14, 15

Amiel, Henri-Frédéric, 135

Anatomy, 37

Anselm, St., 44

Aphrodite, 160

Apollo, 160

Archaeology, 107, 108

Ariès, Philippe, 67

Aristotle, 85, 86

Asceticism, 155–58

Augustine, St., 95

Automaton, 42

Autonomy, 2, 4, 8, 13, 198

Azam, Etienne, 105

Bakhtin, Mikhail, 32

Baroque, 38, 73, 194–98

Becoming, 123

Bergerac, Cyrano de, 37

Bergson, Henri, 23, 51, 52, 171

Bernheim, Hippolyte, 104, 108, 112

Binet, Alfred, 106

Body, 6, 7, 17, 77; sociology of, 20–22; phenomenology of, 22–24; Newtonian, 39–41

Body image, 25, 26, 56, 57, 59, 73; ancient, 84–86; and history, 74–79; medieval, 31–33; and Modernity, 29; and neurology, 57, 58; postmodern, 49–53; and psychology, 59–65; Renaissance, 34–36; and soul, 81

Body shadow, 28, 65–67, 73

Boehme, Jacob, 97

Boredom, 146–49

Brentano, Franz, 108

Breuer, Josef, 109

Bright, Timothy, 132

Brosses, Charles de, 151

Brown, John, 98

Bruno, Giordano, 37, 87, 97, 132

Burckhardt, Jacob, 36

Burton, Robert, 37, 132, 133

Calvin, John, 156, 160

Camporesi, Piero, 196

Carnival, 32, 33, 43

Carus, Carl Gustav, 97

Cervantes, Miguel de, 11, 196

Charcot, Jean-Martin, 102, 103, 105, 108, 112, 113

Chirico, Giorgio di, 134

Civil society, 39

Coleridge, Samuel Taylor, 95, 98

Comfort, 73
Commodity, 44, 46, 150–53, 164, 165
Consciousness, 117, 118, 124
Copernican Revolution, 8, 12, 19, 36, 87, 125, 126
Copernicus, Nicholas, 35, 37
Cosmology, 8, 41

Death, 67–71
Deleuze, Gilles, 62, 197
Descartes, René, 4, 9, 15, 16, 42, 138, 139, 176, 183, 196
Desire, 96
Despair, 29, 142–50
Difference, 14–17, 174
Disenchantment, 61, 62, 155, 159–62
Dissociation, 101, 105–7, 114
Dostoevsky, Fyodor, 124
Doubt, 5, 6
Douglas, Mary, 62
Dreaming, 15–17, 117
Durkheim, Emile, 165, 166, 167, 168, 169, 170, 171, 172, 173, 174, 175, 176, 177, 178

Ego, 3, 11, 13, 53, 87, 99, 100; fragmentation of, 101–7, 126; and modern psyche, 114–21
Elias, Norbert, 22, 39, 47–49, 53, 62
Embodiment, 38; modern forms of, 39–44
Enlightenment, 2
Erasmus, of Rotterdam, 47
Escher, Maurits Cornelis, 78
Experience, 51, 53

Feeling, 129–30
Feuerbach, Ludwig, 24
Fichte, Johann Gottlieb, 95
Ficino, Marsilio, 35, 87, 97

Fludd, Robert, 35
Foucault, Michel, 22
Frank, Johann Peter, 98
Frazer, Sir James, 171, 172, 176
Freud, Sigmund, 10, 23, 51, 53, 56, 57, 74, 99, 106, 107, 108, 109, 110, 111, 112, 113, 114, 115, 116, 117, 118, 119, 120, 121, 123, 125, 126
Friedrich, Caspar David, 134

Galileo (Galilei, Galileo), 7, 40, 92
Gall, Franz Josef, 98
Gillen, Francis James, 171
Goethe, Johann Wolfgang von, 57, 82, 99
Guattari, Felix, 62
Gusdorf, Georges, 91

Harmony, 34–36
Hartley, David, 41
Head, Sir Henry, 58
Hegel, Georg Wilhelm Friedrich, 2, 141, 150, 155, 159, 181, 183
Heiberg, Johan Ludvig, 143
Heidegger, Martin, 186
Hertz, Robert, 175
Hobbes, Thomas, 41, 176
Humanism, 37
Hume, David, 100
Husserl, Edmund, 22, 23, 51, 54, 55, 56, 50, 122
Hypnotism, 104–7, 110
Hysteria, 26, 101–7; Freud's theory of, 108–14

Identity, 52
Illness, 71, 72
Image, 24–26
Individuation, 38, 44, 46, 48, 49
Inertia, 8

Interiority, 45, 88, 89

Jackson, John Hughlings, 57, 58
Janet, Pierre, 106, 113
Jaspers, Karl, 50, 62
Johnson, Ben, 132
Joyce, James, 51

Kafka, Franz, 51
Kant, Immanuel, 95, 98
Kepler, Johannes, 35, 37, 40, 97, 196
Kierkegaard, Søren, 139, 140, 141, 142,
    143, 144, 145, 146, 147, 148, 149,
    150, 151, 155, 181, 182, 183, 184, 185,
    186, 187

La Mettrie, Julien Offray de, 42
La Tourette, Gilles de, 103
Leibniz, Gottfried Wilhelm von, 197
Lermontov, Mikhail, 146
Libertine, 43, 44
Locke, John, 7, 58

McLennan, John Ferguson, 171
McNish, Robert, 105
Mach, Ernst, 126
Macrocosm, 29
Mann, Thomas, 68, 72, 131
Manners, 47
Marcel, Gabriel, 22, 23, 73
Marcuse, Herbert, 53
Marey, Etienne-Jules, 52
Marx, Karl, 20, 24, 150, 151, 152, 153,
    157, 158, 191
Maxwell, James Clerk, 50, 61
Melancholy, 130–35, 147
Memory, 93, 94, 99, 105–7
Merleau-Ponty, Maurice, 22
Metaphor, 33
Microcosm, 29, 35

Mirandolo, Piero della, 12
Modernity, 18, 19; and Body, 22; and
    body image, 29; concepts of, 1–14,
    18, 19; forms of, 189–92; paradox
    of, 89, 198, 199; and Soul, 80–82
Moebius, Paul Julius, 108
Montaigne, Michel de, 10, 11, 13, 41,
    88, 132, 133
Morgan, Sir Henry, 171
Motion, 3, 4, 11, 12
Musil, Robert, 122, 126, 127, 128, 129,
    130, 147

Nashe, Thomas, 132
Newton, Sir Isaac, 7, 39, 40, 41
New World, 2, 10
Nietzsche, Friedrich, 23, 51, 79, 122,
    123, 124, 125, 126, 154, 183, 185
Novelty, 4

Object, 3, 11, 18, 44, 46; Cartesian, 4–9
Old World, 10
Other, 3, 9

Pascal, Blaise, 45, 89, 133, 181, 185
Perspectivism, 100–101
Phantom, 64
Phenomenology, 22, 54–46, 122, 125
Plato, 33, 59, 84, 85, 86
Postmodernism, 49, 136–38
Premodern, 3
Prince, Morton, 114
Profane, the, 168, 169, 174, 178, 179
Proust, Marcel, 51, 128
Puritanism, 89–91
Pushkin, Alexander, 146

Qualities, 7

Reason, 40, 46, 81, 113

Reformation, 2, 89, 156, 160
Renaissance, 1, 2, 12, 33, 34–36, 38
Ribot, Théodule, 46
Richardson, Samuel, 43
Ricoeur, Paul, 22
Rohde, Erwin, 26
Romanticism, 57, 81, 82, 91–96; and science, 98, 99
Rousseau, Jean-Jacques, 92, 93, 94

Sacred, the, 165–70, 174, 175
Sade, marquis de, 43, 44
Sartre, Jean-Paul, 22
Schelling, Friedrich Wilhelm Josef von, 82, 98
Schilder, Paul, 50, 58, 59, 60, 61, 62, 63, 64, 75
Schiller, Friedrich Wilhelm Joseph von, 95
Schleiremacher, Friedrich, 173
Schubert, Gotthilf Friedrich von, 97
Scientific Revolution, 2
Self, 3, 9, 10; self-development, 13, 93–96; self-examination, 36–38; self-fashioning, 13, 87, 88–90; self-movement, 12, 41, 42
Sensitivity, 124–26
Shadow, 27
Simmel, Georg, 51
Smith, William Robertson, 171
Soul, 18, 80; in ancient world, 83–86; and body image, 81; in contemporary culture, 121–35; and Modernity, 87–99; in relation to Freud's writings, 107–21
Space, 41, 50
Spencer, Sir Baldwin, 171
Spirit, 18, 139; definitions of, 139–42, and commodity, 150–53; and happiness, 179–87, and Modernity, 155–65, 187, 188; in relation to value, 153–57
Stoichita, Victor, 28
Subject, 3, 4, 11, 18, 44, 46; Cartesian, 4–9
Subjectivity, 5, 14, 19, 45, 81, 192, 193
Substance, 5–7
Symbol, 30, 33

Tieck, Ludwig, 134
Tocqueville, Alexis de, 143
Totemism, 171–74
Tylor, Sir Edward, 172, 176

Unconscious, the, 51, 52, 118

Veblen, Thorstein, 51
Vesalius, Andreas, 37

War, 68–70
Weber, Max, 90, 153, 154, 155, 156, 157, 158, 159, 160, 161, 162, 163, 164, 165, 195, 197
World, 3, 11, 13

Zarathustra, 154

Page-Barbour and Richard Lectures
(in print)

Sir John Summerson
The Architecture of Victorian London

Johannes Fabian
*Moments of Freedom: Anthropology
and Popular Culture*

Ian Hacking
*Mad Travelers: Reflections on the Reality
of Transient Mental Illnesses*

Harvie Ferguson
*Modernity and Subjectivity: Body,
Soul, Spirit*